THE DRUGS-CRIME CONNECTION[1]

Other Books in this Series:

SAGE Annual Reviews of Drug and Alcohol Abuse
Volume 5

THE DRUGS-CRIME CONNECTION

JAMES A. INCIARDI, Editor

SAGE PUBLICATIONS   Beverly Hills   London

For information address:

SAGE Publications, Inc.
275 South Beverly Drive
Beverly Hills, California 90212

SAGE Publications Ltd
28 Banner Street
London EC1Y 8QE, England

Printed in the United States of America

Library of Congress Cataloging in Publication Data

Main entry under title:

The Drugs-crime connection.

    (Sage annual reviews of drug and alcohol abuse;
v. 5)
    Bibliography: p.
    Contents: Crime and drugs / Cheryl Tieman—
Research strategies in the study of crime and drugs
/ Richard Clayton—Methodological issues / Anne
E. Pottieger, Charles E. Faupel—[etc.]
    1. Drug abuse and crime—United States—Addresses,
essays, lectures. 2. Drug abuse and crime—Research
—United States—Addresses, essays, lectures.
I. Inciardi, James A. II. Series.
HV5825 D83   364.2′4   81-5328

ISBN 0-8039-1634-5   AACR2
ISBN 0-8039-1635-3 (pbk.)

FIRST PRINTING

CONTENTS

DRUG USE AND CRIMINAL BEHAVIOR
Major Research Issues

JAMES A. INCIARDI

Much has been said about the relationship between illegal drug use and criminal behavior, and the first speculations as to a possible connection between the two phenomena appeared well over a century ago. Since that time, commentary on the issue has been persistent. And too, research on the topic has been enduring. Yet an overview of the scholarly, scientific, and popular literature to date, with few exceptions, has provided only minimal useful information or conclusions. Alternatively, a variety of schools of thought, academic postulations, political rhetoric, and popular belief systems have come and gone that have served only to confuse our understanding of the issue even further.

Initially, and within the research literature, a variety of questions have been posed and repeated over the years. Is crime, for example, the result of, or perhaps some response to, a special set of life circumstances brought about by addiction to narcotic drugs? Conversely, is addiction per se some deviant tendency characteristic of individuals already prone to offense behavior? Taking these questions together, one can reduce them to the more simplistic chicken-egg inquiry: Which came first in the offender's career, crime or drugs?

From this point of departure, researchers in the fields of medicine, law, and the social sciences began to examine the sequential patterns of drug use and criminal behavior attempting to answer the basic chicken-egg question, while at the same time pondering causal linkages between the two phenomena. The findings that emerged, however, led to a series of peculiar and contradictory perspectives.[1] Some researchers found that the criminal histo-

7

ries of their sampled cases considerably preceded any evidence of drug use; thus, their conclusion was that the heroin user was indeed a criminal. Other investigators found in their data that the temporal sequence of crime and drug use was in the reverse direction. Still a third group found that portions of their samples had been criminals first, with the remainder having been drug users first.

As a perhaps logical and natural consequence of these research findings, various levels of interpretation of the data began to appear in the medical, social science, law enforcement, and popular literature. Some commentators and analysts spoke of a "criminal model of drug abuse," in which they suggested that addicts ought to be the objects of vigorous police activity, since the vast majority were members of the "dangerous and criminal classes" and their drug use was simply one of the later phases in their nefarious careers of crime and wickedness. Within the scenario, one cannot help being reminded of the now somewhat comical ravings of the late Captain Richard Pearson Hobson, an avid prohibitionist and the first celebrated hero of the Spanish-American War. Through syndicated newspaper columns and national radio broadcasts during the early decades of this century, Hobson popularized the notion that addicts were "beasts" and "monsters" who spread their behavior like medieval vampires and who were responsible for much of the nation's robberies, murders, and street crime (Epstein, 1977: 23–24).

More recently, and in what may represent one of the most prejudiced and ignorant studies in this behalf, James P. Morgan, a special agent of the Federal Bureau of Investigation and former detective in the narcotics bureau of the New York City Police Department, compiled data to demonstrate that drug addiction *was indeed* a criminal problem (Morgan, 1965). His sample included 135 narcotics users he had personally arrested during the period 1959 through 1963. Playing the roles of both arresting officer and "scientific" researcher, Morgan extensively questioned his quarries regarding their careers in crime and addiction. In terms of the validity and reliability of the answers he received from his arrestees, Morgan was confident that the information was very accurate. He stated, "I do not believe that any false answers were given to the questions." Morgan's analysis indicated that "only fifteen of those addicts studied were able to prove that they were lacking a criminal background." So logically, he concluded:

> The statistical results of this study revealed that those addicts studied become what they are, not by accident, but as a result of criminal tendencies which they had already exhibited.

Reading on in Morgan's work, and in works similar to his which addressed "criminal tendencies" in a serious vein, one cannot avoid recalling the studies of criminal anthropology at the turn of the century that focused on "atavisms," "born criminals," and inherited predispositions to crime. Aside from Morgan's problems in sample bias and interpretation, perhaps if he had been given a chance he might have resurrected the ideas of Lombroso. After all, if addicts do have criminal tendencies, maybe head size and shape is indeed a significant factor in the understanding of their behavior!

What Agent Morgan and Company were responding to in their commentaries were the clinicians and social scientists of the late 1950s and early 1960s who supported the notion of a "medical model" of drug abuse as opposed to the "criminal" view. Addiction, this latter group suggested, was a chronic and relapsing disease, and the addict, they continued, should be dealt with as any patient suffering from some physiological or medical disorder. At the same time, numerous proponents of this view sought to mitigate the criminal involvement of narcotics users by putting forth an "enslavement theory of addiction." Within this perspective, it was maintained that the monopolistic controls over the heroin black market forced the "sick" and otherwise law-abiding drug user into a life of crime in order to support his or her habit. The "solution" to the problem was simple: Legalize heroin, and the need for crime would be removed.

What might be stated here is that a number of additional issues and consequences were tied both directly and indirectly to all of the research that heretofore had emerged. *First,* the hypotheses, theories, conclusions, and other findings generated by almost the entire spectrum of research through the first six decades of the current century were of little usefulness. Much of the information was meaningless if one were to consider, in retrospect, the awesome biases and deficiencies in the very nature of the research. Data-gathering enterprises on criminal activity had usually restricted themselves to heroin users' arrest histories, and there can be little argument as to the inadequacy of official statistics as measures of the incidence and prevalence of criminal behavior. Those studies that did manage to go beyond arrest figures to probe self-reported criminal activity were invariably limited to small samples of either incarcerated heroin users or addicts placed in treatment settings. And the few efforts that did manage to locate active heroin users typically examined only their samples' drug-taking behaviors to the exclusion of their drug-seeking behaviors.

Second, despite the work of the proponents of the "medical model" of drug abuse combined with the presence of some accurate data on heroin users' lifestyles, a complex mythology targeting drug users had developed that served to denegrate their image totally. Protagonists of the "criminal model" and other moral entrepreneurs had been fully successful in communicating their ideas.[2] By the 1940s, a body of literature had begun to develop that stereotyped drug users as sex-crazed maniacs, degenerate street criminals (some as members of a professional criminal subculture), and members of the "living dead." Narcotics reportedly ravaged the human body; they destroyed morality; addicts were sexually violent and criminally aggressive; drug users in general were weak and ineffective members of society; addiction was contagious, since users had a mania for perpetuating the social anathema of drug-taking; and finally, once addicted, the user entered into a lifetime of slavery to drugs.

Without question, segments of these mythical images had some basis in fact. Many addicts, if not most, did indeed commit crimes; many, while addicted to narcotics were ineffective members of society; and the cycle of addiction-abstinence-relapse could suggest the idea, "once a junkie, always a junkie." But the stereotypes had been uniformly applied to all drug users. Furthermore, since studies had typically ignored intensive investigation of the types and magnitude of crimes engaged in by users, prognostications descriptive of their aggressive and violent tendencies ought to have been viewed as fabrications.

With the onset of the 1970s and the work of a variety of enlightened researchers—combined with the efforts of the National Institute on Drug Abuse (NIDA), the National Institute of Justice (NIJ), and the near-defunct Law Enforcement Assistance Administration (LEAA)—the generation of accurate data on the nature and extent of drug-related crime, the criminal involvement of narcotics users, and the causal linkages between drug use and criminality has taken on a forward movement.

Within this perspective and direction, the opening essay, "Federal Drugs-Crime Research: Setting the Agenda" by Richard R. Clayton of the University of Kentucky, examines the movement of the federal drug bureaucracy in stimulating drugs-crime research. Clayton's chapter is concerned with the *process* of constructing the research agenda at the federal level that addresses the crime-drug linkage. It has three different but interrelated goals: to describe the key events, actors, and documents that have emerged since early 1975; to analyze the many factors that have made the construction of such an agenda difficult to achieve; and to synthesize what has been learned from this half-decade of fitful starts and stops. Professor Clayton's comments are especially important here when one considers that the majority of the essays appearing in this volume are an outgrowth of the federal research agenda.

Focusing directly on the criminal activities of heroin users, "The Criminality of Heroin Addicts: When Addicted and When Off Opiates" by John C. Ball, Lawrence Rosen, John A. Flueck, and David N. Nurco advances the thesis that daily heroin use potentiates criminal behavior among street addicts. This study of 243 male opiate addicts has two broad objectives: (1) to ascertain the frequency and types of offenses committed by addicts during an eleven-year period while at risk, or "on the street"; (2) to compare criminality during addiction periods with criminality during periods off regular opiates.

It was found that these 243 addicts committed more than 473,738 offenses during their years at risk. The extent of their criminality was measured by the number of "crime-days" accumulated. A crime-day is a 24-hour period during which one or more crimes are committed (not including drug use or drug possession). The mean number of crime-days per year at risk per addict was 178.

With respect to criminal careers, it was found that 156 of the addicts were primarily engaged in theft, 45 were drug dealers, and 36 were involved in assorted other crimes. For each of these groups, the extent of criminality was markedly affected by addiction status. Subjects' average crime-days per year at risk when addicted was 248.0; when off regular opiates, it was 40.8. Thus, there was a six-fold increase in their frequency of crime when addicted.

The findings of Drs. Ball, Rosen, Flueck, and Nurco have considerable significance for both research and policy implications, especially when one compares their data with those of other research in alternative geographical locations.[3]

Dr. Paul J. Goldstein of Narcotics and Drug Research, Inc., in New York City provides a view of a little-known aspect of drug users' support mechanisms. In his essay, "Getting Over: Economic Alternatives to Predatory Crime Among Street Drug Users," his ethnographic research reports the wide variety of ways that street opiate users make a living and manage to use drugs. A storefront field research station was opened in an area of high drug activity and staffed with both social scientists and indigenous field workers. Opiate users reported to the storefront on a daily basis and were debriefed on their previous day's activities. Field staff also spent time with subjects on the streets. Data collected from fifty-one subjects, covering 1883 person-days, are reported.

Subjects often recounted their economic successes by using the term *getting over*. The import of this phrase blurs many of the traditional distinctions that social scientists tend to make when discussing income-generating activities, such as legal versus illegal income. Predatory crime, while the

major single source of cash income, is only one of the ways in which street
opiate users are able to get over. Among the alternatives to predatory crime
that are discussed are nonpredatory crime, legitimate employment, public
support, contributions from friends and/or family and miscellaneous hustling. Within the category of nonpredatory crime, working within the drug
business constituted the predominant activity. A variety of roles are described in this regard, including *dealers, holders, touts, cop men, resource
providers* and *testers*.

The street opiate users studied here tended to engage in opiate use with
relatively little cash income. They were frequently given rooms, meals,
cash, alcohol, and drugs by friends or relatives. Substantial proportions of
heroin and cocaine consumed by subjects were obtained with no cash outlay.
The bartering of services, especially in the drug business, is shown to be an
important means for obtaining drugs. All of these factors tended to reduce
the likelihood that subjects would engage in income-generating predatory
crime.

While much of the work on drugs and crime has focused on the male user,
Susan K. Datesman of Arizona State University targets women addicts. In
her "Women, Crime and Drugs," Professor Datesman reviews the literature
on women and drugs, explains the reasons female users have been only
minimally studied, and offers current data on samples of women engaged in
drug use and crime. In her conclusions she points to how little we know
about these phenomena as they relate to women, and suggests the important
directions that future research must take.

On the topic of violence, "Drugs and Violence" by Duane C. McBride of
the University of Miami School of Medicine examines the relationship
between type of crime committed and type of drug used in a population of
incarcerated users. Dr. McBride concludes that the current literature implies
that drug abuse is *not* related to violent behavior. However, he suggests, an
examination of the role of violence in the daily lives of drug abusers and new
evidence of a relationship between the use of narcotics and violent crime
imply that, increasingly, violence is associated with drug abuse and that the
role of violence in drug abusing groups deserves considerably more study.

"Criminal involvements of Minority Group Addicts" by Carl D. Chambers, Sara W. Dean, and Michael F. Pletcher, all from the Consortium for
Health Education in Appalachia, Ohio, presents information on the relationship between drug taking and criminal behavior for two minority groups:
blacks and Mexican-Americans. A historical perspective is presented, based
on analyses conducted on voluntary and prisoner admissions to the former

Public Health Service hospitals at Lexington, Kentucky, and Fort Worth, Texas. A contemporary perspective is also presented, based on analyses conducted with active addicts and incarcerated addict criminals in Washington, Detroit, San Antonio, and Los Angeles. Where possible, comparisons between males and females, between "hard" drug users and "soft" drug users, and between the minority populations and the white population are presented. Finally, changes in the criminal behavior of drug users from the historical period to the contemporary period are identified and presented.

In an alternative area of inquiry, while drug abuse and crime tend to have an affinity for one another, the complicated interplay of contributing factors and intervening social conditions makes nearly any explanation of how they are related seem "reasonable," albeit "partial." But a single drug, heroin, brings them together in a rush of pharmacology and economics. And economics, which is given so little utility for understanding either of these deviant behaviors, often dominates as an explanation of their association. On this point, Fred Goldman of Columbia University argues that if the relationship between heroin use and crime is "obvious," for scientist and citizen alike, the explanation rests with three principal variables: the cost of heroin, its addictive properties, and the earnings potential of those who consume it. The logic, he suggests, is simple. Heroin is very expensive and its regular and frequent use creates tolerance and dependence in the user. Since there are few legitimate opportunities for heroin users to meet the exorbitant costs of a "habit," the users "must inevitably" quit using the drug or turn to crime for its support. For many users, the fear or pain of withdrawal, or the sheer delight of the drug, a craving, preclude opting out. Hence, the "inevitability hypothesis." Yet, he continues, an analysis of the three principal variables suggests that the conventional view that drug abuse leads to crime is a tenuous one, where it solely relies on a pharmaeconomic determinism of heroin consumption. Dr. Goldman maintains that the likelihood of the relationship cannot be ruled out, however, for heroin or any other drug. There may very well be a systematic relationship between a propensity to consume and a propensity to earn, and a role for pharmacology, albeit one that is less decisive.

In the area of treatment, Charles E. Faupel of the University of Delaware maintains that treatment for opiate addiction in the United States has been characterized by a great deal of experimentation and inconclusive results. In his chapter, "Drug Treatment and Criminality: Methodological and Theoretical Considerations," he suggests that the goal of treatment was simply "withdrawal," with the primary debate among medical men being whether withdrawal should be effected gradually or abruptly. The social and psychological dynamics of addiction were soon realized, which spawned a number of treatment "modalities"—simple detoxification, methadone maintenance, outpatient drug-free treatment, and the therapeutic community being the major ones.

Yet Mr. Faupel argues that the effectiveness of treatment in reducing criminal behavior is still open to debate. Unquestionably, treatment efforts have experienced some success, but the precise nature and extent of this success is still uncertain due to methodological shortcomngs in the studies evaluating treatment effectiveness. After examining some 40 studies, he observes three broad trends in the literature: (1) a lopsided focus on the effectiveness of methadone maintenance; (2) an overreliance on official statistics as indicators of criminal behavior, as well as a number of other methodological shortcomings; and (3) a lack of theoretical accountability for how and why treatment is (or should be) effective. Studies addressing the effectiveness of methadone treatment and therapeutic communities are discussed as representative of the kinds of problems inherent in the evaluation of treatment outcome. Finally, a framework is briefly proposed for a theoretical model that might account for the effectiveness of therapeutic communities in terms of processes of "dissociation" (from an addict/criminal lifestyle) and "association" (with a conventional lifestyle).

One result of the extensive American experimentation with treatment modalities has been a new source of accessible subjects for drugs/crime research. Today, treatment samples are almost as common as samples of incarcerated offenders. But in her chapter entitled "Sample Bias in Drugs/Crime Research: An Empirical Study," Anne E. Pottieger of the University of Delaware notes the limitations of studies based on either type of "captive sample." After pointing out the serious difficulties in the sometimes-posited argument that captive samples *are* representative of all drug- and crime-involved persons, Dr. Pottieger argues that part of the problem in understanding captive sample biases is that we are unable to identify, by logic alone, just what those biases are. Problems of measurement comparability and the need for multiple controls make the extant drugs/crime literature unsuitable for such an analysis. Most of Dr. Pottieger's essay is therefore devoted to a direct empirical comparison of drugs/crime data from captive and on-the-street samples. Six subsamples of male heroin users aged 22–32 were selected from a recent interview study, yielding comparisons of white active and treatment samples, black active and treatment samples, and Mexican-American active and jail samples. The results suggest that the most consistent area of difference between active and captive samples is that of *relationship* between drug use and crime, possibly as a consequence of differences between those samples in patterns of drug use—differences which appear to be just as prominent in the active-jail comparison as in the active-treatment comparisons. Dr. Pottieger concludes her analysis with a discussion of the utility of, and analytic possibilities for, more specific delineation of active-captive sample differences in future research.

As an epilogue to the perspectives, findings, and conclusions offered throughout this volume, Cheryl R. Tieman of Auburn University provides a unifying perspective through an intensive review of what has come to pass through several generations of drugs-crime research. In her essay, "From Victims to Criminals to Victims: A Review of the Issues," she notes that in the 1800s addicts were patients legally receiving prescriptions or were legally buying "medicines" containing addictive substances. Their addiction was largely viewed as unfortunate or deplorable, but not as criminal. These victims were rescued by legislative action, the Harrison Act, which sought to control the distribution of addictive substances. But subsequent interpretations of this law curtailed the association of addicts with physicians, while the association of addicts with crime and criminals grew, not only in the minds of people, but in reality as well, as a practical and profitable way to continue drug use. Failure to control these substances or their users, she argues, has led to a new link justified by the newly identified victim of addiction: society.

The data and perspectives offered in this volume, clearly, do not provide all of the answers. Nor do they represent the full spectrum of drugs-crime research that is now ongoing. But they nevertheless contribute in three of the most significant areas of inquiry. *First,* they reflect a higher level of thinking in perspective and method; *second,* they offer new data on which other research can solidly rely; and *third,* they suggest in this much-belabored area of research that we are now, at last, beginning to ask the *right* questions.

NOTES

1. A number of the drugs/crime studies undertaken since the beginning of the twentieth century are referenced and discussed in various essays in this volume. In addition, for annotated bibliographies and analyses of many of these research efforts, see Research Triangle Institute (1976), Austin and Lettieri (1976), Greenberg and Adler (1974), and Inciardi (1974b).

2. For a discussion of the drug myths and stereotypes, the processes through which they emerged, and examples of the literature in which they appeared, see Inciardi (1974a), Anslinger and Cooper (1937), Anslinger and Tompkins (1953), Lindesmith (1940), Michelson (1940), and Eldridge (1962).

3. See, for example, Inciardi (1979).

REFERENCES

ANSLINGER, H. J. and C. R. COOPER (1937) "Marijuana: assassin of youth." American Magazine 74 (July): 19, 150.

ANSLINGER, H. J. and W. F. TOMPKINS (1953) The Traffic in Narcotics. New York: Funk & Wagnalls.

AUSTIN, G. A. and D. J. LETTIERI (1976) Drugs and Crime: The Relationship of Drug Use and Concomitant Criminal Behavior. Washington DC: Government Printing Office.

ELDRIDGE, W. B. (1962) Narcotics and the Law. Chicago: American Bar Foundation.

EPSTEIN, E. J. (1977) Agency of Fear: Opiates and Political Power in America. New York: G. P. Putnam.

GREENBERG, S. W. and F. ADLER (1974) "Crime and addiction: an empirical analysis of the literature, 1920–1973." Contemporary Drug Problems 3: 221–270.

INCIARDI, J. A. (1979) "Heroin use and street crime." Crime and Delinquency (July): 335–346.

———— (1974a) "Drugs, drug-taking and drug-seeking: notations on the dynamics of myth, change and reality," pp. 230–222 in J. A. Inciardi and C. D. Chambers (eds.) Drugs and the Criminal Justice System. Beverly Hills, CA: Sage.

———— (1974b) "The villification of euphoria: some perspectives on an elusive issue." Addictive Diseases 1: 241–267.

LINDESMITH, A. R. (1940) "'Dope Fiend' Mythology." Journal of Criminal Law and Criminology 31 (July/August): 199–208.

MICHELSON, T. (1940) "Lindesmith's mythology." Journal of Criminal Law and Criminology 31 (November/December): 375–400.

MORGAN, J. P., Jr. (1965) Drug Addiction: Criminal or Medical Problem. Police (July/August): 6–9.

Research Triangle Institute (1976) Drug Use and Crime: Report of the Panel on Drug Use and Criminal Behavior. Springfield, VA: National Technical Information Service.

1

FEDERAL DRUGS-CRIME RESEARCH
Setting the Agenda

RICHARD R. CLAYTON

This essay is concerned with the *process* of constructing a research agenda at the federal level that addresses the crime-drug nexus. It has three different but interrelated goals. The first goal is historical: to describe the key events, actors, and documents that have emerged since early 1975 in the quest for a federal crime-drugs research agenda. The second goal is analytical: to examine the many factors that have made the construction of such an agenda difficult to achieve. The third goal is critically to synthesize what has been learned from this half-decade of fitful starts and stops in setting a crime-drugs agenda so that it will be easier in the future to set research agendas at the federal level.

This essay is primarily a historical case study covering the period from early 1975 to mid-1980. It will focus largely on two sets of documents, both of which emerged from the Research Triangle Institute (RTI). The first set of documents was submitted to the National Institute on Drug Abuse (NIDA) by RTI as its Final Report of the PANEL on drug use and criminal behavior. Included are two volumes, an Executive Summary (1976) and an Appendix (1976b), containing a number of commissioned papers. The second set of documents were submitted as reports to the National Institute of Law Enforcement and Criminal Justice (NILECJ) and includes a critical review of the PANEL Report (Williams, 1979a) and a Final Report by Williams (1979b) entitled *Exploring the Drug Use and Criminal Behavior Nexus: A Research Agenda and Selected Research Designs*.

A secondary methodology employed in the preparation of this essay is participant observation. From June 1977 through June 1978 I was a Visiting Scientist in the Psychosocial Branch, Division of Research, at NIDA. My assigned tasks were (1) to assist in deciding what should be done with the PANEL Report; (2) to coordinate extant NIDA research efforts in the crime-drug area and stimulate new research to deal with the salient issues; and (3) to serve as NIDA's liaison with other federal agencies involved in crime-drug research, principally NILECJ.

It should be noted at the outset of this essay that I am an academician. Except for the previously mentioned assignment at NIDA, my entire professional career has been spent in the college and university setting as a teacher and a researcher.

WHAT IS A RESEARCH AGENDA?

Before we examine the process of constructing a crime-drugs research agenda at the federal level, it might be useful to discuss what a research agenda should contain. In my opinion, the following are minimum ingredients:

- a thorough, objective, and critical review of extant studies dealing with the subject
- an identification of what is known about the subject and areas/topics that need further research attention
- an assessment of the theoretical perspectives and methodological techniques that are most likely to be useful in filling in the gaps in our knowledge base
- a critical examination of the concepts and variables central to understanding the subject and a review of how they have been operationalized
- an identification of extant data sets that could be expeditiously analyzed to address the most important research questions
- a prioritized listing of the specific studies needed if we are to understand fully the relationship/subject of concern (i.e., the crime-drug nexus)

While all of the items listed above are important in developing a research agenda, the last item, "a prioritized listing of the specific studies needed" is by far the most important. After all, that's what an agenda is. It is a detailed listing of what should occur next—in order. The first five items listed above merely constitute the foundation on which a coherent and relevant research agenda can be built.

TWO "FACTS" OF BUREAUCRATIC LIFE

If we are to understand the "process" of setting a crime-drugs research agenda at the federal level it is important to note two rather obvious "facts of bureaucratic life." First, every agency has a unique history and a mandate that is always emergent (i.e., it can be amended readily by congressional oversight committees). Second, the degree to which agency staff can hand-craft a research program to coincide with its perception of priorities is determined by how flexible or rigid are the rules and procedures governing research that are imposed on or adopted by the agency. Awareness of these facts makes it relatively easy to understand how and why NIDA and NILECJ have proceeded in somewhat different ways to develop a crime-drugs agenda. These "facts of life" will be referred to later as we analyze the historical process.

WHY WAS A CRIME-DRUGS RESEARCH AGENDA NEEDED? THE CONTEXT.

The perceived need for a crime-drugs research agenda is tied directly to the two facts of bureaucratic life referred to earlier, and is anchored in the political process by which policies dealing with various social problems are formulated.

Let us first examine the history of the National Institute on Drug Abuse (NIDA). It was created in early 1975 as a way to transfer the federal drug abuse coordinating functions of the Special Action Office for Drug Abuse Prevention (SAODAP) out of the Executive Office of the White House and into the Department of Health, Education, and Welfare. Personnel from SAODAP were fused with personnel from the Center for Drug Abuse within the National Institute of Mental Health (NIMH) to form NIDA. For a six-month period SAODAP and NIDA coexisted to ease the transfer.

It is important to remember the sociocultural and political milieu that precipitated the creation of SAODAP by Executive Order in June 1971, followed by its legal and fiscal mandate from Congress in 1972.

At the time the United States was embroiled in the Vietnam war and there was more than a little protest against it at home. The epidemic of marijuana use that began around 1965 was followed by a heroin epidemic covering the 1968–1972 period (see O'Donnell et al., 1976; DuPont and Greene, 1973). This heroin epidemic was particularly bothersome to the Nixon administration for at least two reasons: (1) there was concern that an increasing level of heroin use at home was linked directly to Vietnam, and (2) an increasing number of heroin addicts, with their presumed reliance on crime to support their habits, was antithetical to the administration's stated goal of reducing crime in the streets.

Thus, SAODAP was given unprecedented latitude in coordinating all federal drug abuse programming and the wherewithal to establish a national treatment system post haste. In an election year it was wise from a political standpoint to be fighting heroin addicts and their criminality while implementing a rehabilitative treatment system to help those who might have become addicted in Vietnam.

By the time SAODAP was being phased out and NIDA was being phased in as part of the Alcohol, Drug Abuse, and Mental Health Administration (ADAMHA), the fears about massive numbers of servicemen returning from Vietnam as opiate addicts had somewhat subsided.

As a new agency, it was important for NIDA to hit the pavement running in order to retain as much of SAODAP's momentum as possible. At SAODAP it was possible to fund new research projects with a minimum of review effort. At NIDA, it was necessary to subject proposals for new research to a decidedly more rigorous and more closely scrutinized review process, since NIDA was subject to PHS guidelines.

These historical-situational forces and the more rigorous bureaucratic procedures for grant review, plus Dr. DuPont's long-standing interest in the crime-drug relationship, made this subject area a "natural" for a special focus at NIDA.

In the section that follows I will discuss in detail the process that NIDA instituted to obtain a crime-drugs research agenda. The perception that such an agenda was needed was based on a need to finesse the difficult grant review process by targeting this subject area for special attention. Later in this essay I will review the precipitating conditions that led NILECJ into the crime-drugs agenda-setting process.

NIDA'S DRUG-CRIME PANEL AND
ITS REPORT

In early 1975 NIDA convened a one-day workshop attended by a number of persons with expertise and research experience in the crime-drugs area.

On the basis of their advice, a decision was made to organize a panel of experts "to examine, review, and analyze available data; to determine what conclusions could be drawn about the state-of-the-art; and to recommend research approaches" (Research Triangle Institute [RTI], 1976a: Preface). Dr. Robert Shellow of Carnegie-Mellon University was hired as a Visiting Scientist by NIDA to coordinate the Drug-Crime PANEL and to supervise the contract awarded to RTI for technical and administrative functions.

NIDA thus used a tried and true bureaucratic approach. They got a workshop group of experts to recommend the formation of a PANEL of experts. Then experts, some of whom already had data relevant to the drug-crime relationship, would analyze their data and present the findings to the entire PANEL. The PANEL would then reach a consensus about what was known, what was not known, and what should be done to fill in the gaps in our knowledge about the drug-crime relationship (i.e., they would create an agenda for the Institute to follow in its research program).

The credentials of the PANEL members were impeccable. They represented the gamut of academic disciplines and areas of expertise: conceptual, methodological, and substantive. There was a broad range of policy-making experience among the federal agency representatives to balance the research experience of the academicians. In addition, a number of the experts from academia had served in government agencies (i.e., John Ball had been research director at SAODAP, Mark Moore had been an administrative assistant to the director of the Drug Enforcement Administration, and James Inciardi had worked for the New York State Addiction Control Commission).

Beginning in October of 1975 the PANEL held five workshops over a period of 10 months. Three subgroups were designated: one focused on the general drug-crime relationship, the second examined demand-reduction issues (i.e., treatment effects), and the third directed its attention to supply-reduction issues. In addition, the Resource Group Members proceeded to analyze their own data sets concerning the drug-crime relationship.

A total draft of the PANEL Report was submitted to NIDA in September of 1976. The first volume (RTI, 1976a) was an executive summary and contained five chapters: (1) Introduction, Summaries, and Recommendations; (2) Concepts and Measures of Drug Use, Crime, and Criminal Behavior; (3) The Relationship Between Drug Use and Criminal Behavior; (4) Impact of Demand-Reduction on Crime and Criminal Behavior; and (5) The Drug User and Market Behavior. The second volume, the Appendix (RTI, 1976b), contained 4 conceptual papers, 3 state-of-the-art papers, 7 data-analysis papers, and 8 issues papers.

Ultimately a decision was made *not* to publish the PANEL Report as a NIDA document. Thus, it was released through the auspices of the National Technical Information Services (NTIS), a publishing arm of the federal government. The NIDA decision not to publish has generated a fair share of controversy, speculation, and accusations. In the next section I will analyze some of the factors that led to this decision and will attempt to relate these factors to the crime-drug agenda-setting process at the federal level.

WHY THE PANEL REPORT IS NOT A NIDA DOCUMENT: PUBLISHED INTERPRETATIONS

Only two interpretations of the rationale behind the decision not to pub-lish the PANEL Report as a NIDA document have ever appeared in print. In a report prepared for NILECJ, Jay Williams (1979b: 1) of RTI offers this interpretation:

> In "telling it like it is," the report made itself vulnerable to the widest spectrum of debate and disagreement that the controversial topic of drugs and crime could entertain. While the report offered no final resolution to the issue, it highlighted many of the pitfalls and shortcomings of past research and sug-gested some improved approaches for future research efforts.

Weissman's (1979: 2) interpretation was more perjorative and critical in tone.

> Numerous contemporary studies have demonstrated direct statistical correla-tions between narcotics use and criminality. From these data *policy makers have drawn an inference of causality.* Now, however, on the advice of a group of distinguished scientists this conclusion is being opened to renewed exami-nation.

> Accordingly, it is not difficult to appreciate the controversy evoked by the critical *Drug Use and Crime* report. *Fundamental assumptions of American drug control policy were questioned.* Social scientists employing their profes-sional jargon of sampling, measurement and causality, have introduced uncer-tainty into what had previously been a politically sensitive but stable area of public policy [italics added].

These two interpretations imply the same things with a differing level of specificity. In my opinion, the following claims and assumptions are being made by Weissman:

● Policy makers are convinced that drug use and crime are causally connected and thus are prone to make inferences about causality from correlational data.

The policy makers at NIDA were upset that the PANEL Report called into question the existence of a causal drug-crime relationship. Therefore, *they,* the policy makers, decided not to publish the PANEL Report under NIDA auspices.

• American drug control policy is based on the assumptions that a two-pronged simultaneous attack on drug abuse via supply-reduction and demand-reduction strategies will affect drug use, crime, and the drug-crime connection. The policy makers at NIDA were upset that the efficacy of this policy was not affirmed in the Report. Therefore, *they,* the policy makers, decided not to publish the PANEL Report as a NIDA document.

THE ISSUE CAUSALITY: DIFFERING INTERPRETATIONS

In my opinion Weissman has perceived correctly that officials at NIDA were less than happy with how the issue of causality was treated in the PANEL Report. To reiterate, he implied their reaction was based on a prior assumption that drug use causes crime, an assumption he claims was seriously challenged by the Report.

I think Weissman's speculation is incorrect. There are other feasible interpretations. First, I think the officials at NIDA were of the opinion that the key issue in this whole area of research *is* causality. In fact, the PANEL was established and mandated to deal specifically with the causal issue. In Chapter 1 of the Executive Summary volume (RTI, 1976a: 11–14), the three general questions toward which the PANEL was to direct its efforts were stated. They were more clearly detailed in Chapter 3.

(1) What proportion of criminals have ever used drugs? What proportion of drug users have committed crimes?
(2) Does involvement in criminal behavior precede drug use? Does drug use precede criminal behavior? Do both criminal behavior and drug use initially occur within a restricted time span?
(3) Do criminals intensify their involvement in income-generating crimes after the onset of regular use of addictive or expensive drugs? Do changes in income-generating criminal behavior accompany changes in the drug habit cost or variations in use patterns?
(4) Are any other factors associated with criminal behavior and drug use? What are the relative impacts of particular patterns of drug use on the patterns of criminal behavior in comparison with the impacts of other variables?

Question 1 deals with statistical association, question 2 deals with temporal order, question 3 deals with interactions over time among the key variables, and question 4 is concerned with testing to see whether the crime-drug relationship is spurious. These constitute the probabilistic criteria of causality widely accepted in the social sciences (see Hirschi and Selvin, 1967) and exemplified best in the health field by the Surgeon General's report on smoking and health.

The officials at NIDA recognized that *all* of these criteria must be met to infer causality. I think they were upset that the PANEL was either unable or unwilling to take a stand on whether the crime-drug relationship is causal. In my opinion the PANEL waffled on the central issue they were to address.

A second interpretation of the NIDA reaction to the causality issue is that the PANEL adopted an ivory tower approach. The heavy reliance on scientific jargon was not balanced by the "in the pits" clinical experience of many NIDA officials. A remark I heard over and over again in my tenure at NIDA was, "If all of the PANEL members had spent a week at the Narcotic Treatment Administration interviewing real addicts about the drug-crime relationship, they would have taken an unambiguous stand on the issue of causality."

THE ISSUE OF DRUG CONTROL POLICIES

The second reason offered by Weissman to explain why NIDA chose not to publish the PANEL Report is that it questioned the basic assumptions on which American drug-control policies are based. The policies to which he refers are those of supply reduction and demand reduction that are articulated in the Federal Strategy Report. Let's examine the assertion vis-à-vis demand reduction.

The underlying assumption for the demand-reduction strategy is: Addicts enrolled in treatment will reduce their drug use and, concomitantly, their involvement in criminality. Remember the issue being discussed here is whether NIDA chose not to publish the PANEL Report because it questioned basic drug-control policies. In Chapter 4 of the Executive Summary volume there is a general literature review that begins with a quotation from the Marihuana Commission (1973: 176–177): "We have not found sufficiently responsible research to conclude that any of the treatment modalities, regardless of type, actually reduces crime." This is followed by a review of a number of studies, leading to this statement: "From these diverse studies it can probably be concluded that involvement with the criminal justice system and, possibly, involvement with criminal behavior itself is suppressed (not eliminated) while individuals are in treatment." Findings from the national follow-up study (Demaree and Neman, 1976) suggest that criminal behavior increases after the individual leaves drug treatment and *may* revert to pre-treatment levels (RTI, 1976a: 83–84).

This conclusion does not lend support to the demand-reduction strategy of drug control. In fact, many of the specific findings cited in this chapter do question the viability of the policy. While Weissman assumed the Report was not published by NIDA because of its criticisms of the effectiveness of treatment, there is an alternative explanation.

First, the officials at NIDA questioned why such a "negative" stance was taken in Chapter 4 when the paper by Nash, commissioned for the Appendix volume, and more comprehensive in the literature it reviewed than Chapter 4, came to a different conclusion:

> There have been a number of reviews of the literature and methodological critiques of the literature. Most have concluded that there is no proof that drug abuse treatment has an impact on criminality. Despite problems caused by methodological shortcomings and noncomparable data, we feel that the *weight of the evidence* from the 12 major studies reviewed in this paper clearly indicates that drug abuse treatment does reduce criminality.

The so-called policy makers at NIDA were understandably reluctant to publish a document in which an extremely negative Executive Summary statement on the efficacy of treatment effectiveness differed drastically from a conclusion reached in a comprehensive review paper on the subject commissioned by the PANEL.

A second example of this kind of contradiction is found in the following statement from Chapter 4 (1976a: 83): "Evidence from a national sample of methadone clients 5 to 6 years after leaving treatment did show that some clients were heavily involved in crime after leaving treatment. One-fifth claimed that *most* of their income was coming from illegal sources [italics added]."

The national study referred to is of the DARP follow-up sample and is from a paper by Demaree and Neman commissioned for the Appendix volume. If true, the statement is suspect because it fails to note that 80 percent of these addicts did *not* receive "most" of their income from illegal sources. The fact is, the statement is not true. Demaree and Neman observed that only 20 percent of their follow-up sample received "at least some" of their income from illegal activities, five years after admission to treatment.

These two examples of the Executive Summary statement—on the efficacy of the demand-reduction strategy/policy differing markedly from conclusions reached in the papers commissioned by the PANEL to serve as a basis for its conclusions, plus the strident tone of the chapter on demand reduction—were instrumental in the NIDA decision not to publish the PANEL Report. It is no doubt true that the policy makers at NIDA did not like the results as they were portrayed in Chapter 4. They did have a vested interest in showing that treatment works. However, in my opinion, these same officials were willing to accept conclusions that were based on a solid review of the literature. What they reviewed in Chapter 4 made them some-what suspicious of the possible ideological biases of the authors of that part of the PANEL Report. What they wanted was a solid review and a prioritized list of research questions in need of answers. They received neither of these expected deliverables.

HERETOFORE UNPUBLISHED REASONS WHY THE PANEL REPORT WAS NOT PUBLISHED BY NIDA

In earlier sections of this chapter I have discussed "published" interpreta-tions of the decision not to publish the PANEL Report as a NIDA monograph and have offered alternative interpretations. It is important to note that the Report *was not suppressed*. It was published under the auspices of the NTIS.

Two routine types of activities played an important part in the decision-making. First, Drs. DuPont and Pollin at NIDA asked Dr. John O'Donnell at the University of Kentucky to review both draft volumes of the PANEL Report. His recommendation was that NIDA should *not* publish either volume in their forms as of September 1976 because of numerous inconsis-tencies and his feeling that there was a great deal of unevenness in the quality of the papers in the Appendix. Second, personnel in the Psychosocial Branch conducted a straw poll among ten of the PANEL members, some of whom were from other federal agencies and others of whom were from academic settings. A reasonable cross-section of the academic disciplines was represented. Listed below are some of the options mentioned and the responses. Each person could endorse one or more of the options.

(a) No one endorsed the statement: The Report is excellent, publish it as is.
(b) No one agreed with the statement: The Report represents the consensus of the PANEL.
(c) One person endorsed without reservation a statement that the Report con-tained a few inaccuracies that might be corrected, and two persons endorsed this statement with some reservations.
(d) Five persons strongly endorsed the statement that the Report contained errors that must be corrected and that it seriously misinterpreted or misrepresented

some of the data, while three persons endorsed this statement with reservations.

(e) Five of the ten persons contacted expressed the opinion that the Report primarily reflected the views of the PANEL Chair and did not represent panel consensus.

Among the various options recommended to NIDA to salvage the work of the PANEL were:

(a) Reconvene the PANEL to edit and rewrite the Report. Three persons recommended that this be done by a subgroup, and there was consensus on who should be included in the subgroup. One person recommended the full group be reconvened for this task.

(b) Reconvene a subgroup to prioritize research recommendations only. Six of those polled endorsed this option, and there was general agreement on the composition of the subgroup. One person recommended using only the federal agency members, while another suggested the priorities be split into NIDA priorities and interagency priorities.

(c) Two members of the group that were contacted in the straw poll recommended that NIDA draft some RFP's and proceed along a contract route.

(d) Another option considered was to produce a different report with a new title and a new slant with no minority report. However, efforts would be made to overemphasize the materials from the original report, particularly the Appendix.

In the long run none of these options was exercised, and the PANEL Report was published via NTIS. The important point to remember here is that NIDA did not unilaterally reject the Report. Instead, it sought the advice of a scholar with impeccable credentials and polled the opinions of a cross-section of the PANEL members. The advice received was consistent: Do *not* publish the PANEL Report as a NIDA document, because it has numerous soft spots.

There is one other reason the PANEL Report was not published as a NIDA document. This reason involves two political-bureaucratic "rules" in the process of setting research agendas at the federal level, especially when the subject is a potentially volatile one like the crime-drug relationship. The rules are: (1) There are established bureaucratic procedures for releasing information, particularly to Congress; (2) one always goes through channels before releasing information that might put the agency in a "bad" light.

The Visiting Scientist who was chairman of the PANEL broke both of those rules. On 5 August 1976 he appeared at a meeting of the U.S. Senate Subcommittee of the Judiciary and read a statement later published as "Drug Abuse and Crime: Fact or Fancy?" (see Shellow, 1976). This statement reviewed Shellow's perceptions of the PANEL's progress, selected major findings, and offered a few suggestions as to what should be done to further understand the crime-drug relationship. Shellow had not cleared his statement with the appropriate NIDA officials. As a matter of coincidence, Dr. DuPont was scheduled to testify before the same committee on the same day. Needless to say, this turn of events placed Dr. DuPont and the Agency in a less than favorable light with the Subcommittee. To add fuel to the fire, Dr. Shellow reiterated many of the observations made in his congressional testimony in an interview granted to the Boston *Globe*.

Simply put, Dr. Shellow violated some important bureaucratic rules that lend structure and predictability to agency life in Washington. His statement to Congress and his interview in the *Globe* "politicized" the work of the "scientists" on the PANEL. While such actions may have neutralized NIDA's option not to release the PANEL Report at all, it probably strengthened the resolve at NIDA not to release the Report as a NIDA document.

There is one final reason why NIDA did not want to publish the PANEL Report: It did not contain the expected deliverable, a prioritized research agenda. Williams (1979a) notes:

> The research hypotheses, questions, issues, strategies, and admonitions are scattered throughout the report with the only basis of organization for a research agenda being their presentation within the broad categories of concern in the drug/crime area. . . .

> The first chapter of the report serves as a kind of executive summary which brings much of the suggested research material together but only in proximity, not in order. The reader must work fairly hard to put the pieces together—all of the pieces are there but they need to be found. Due to this organizational problem, what might have emerged as a research agenda (with priorities setting out which research issues should be addressed) could be seen as a series of disconnected research suggestions whose only common ground is that they deal with the drug/crime issue in some way.

What Williams does not report is that the PANEL did not explicitly address the topic of developing a "prioritized research agenda" until the last afternoon of its last meeting day. Thus, for whatever reasons, the primary deliverable expected from the PANEL by the NIDA brass was not even built into the deliberative process.

Therefore, the following constitute the primary reasons the PANEL Report on drug use and crime was not published under NIDA auspices.

(1) The Report skirted and essentially scorned what NIDA officials believed was *the* key issue in the crime/drug area—causality.

(2) The pristine-pure and extremely conservative perspective from which the PANEL approached the issue of causality appeared to NIDA officials to be (a) insulated from the day-to-day reality of life on the street, and (b) counter to the thousands of clinical interviews NIDA officials had conducted with addicts.

(3) There are several important discrepancies between the Executive Summary chapter and the findings/conclusions of papers especially commissioned for the Appendix volume. These discrepancies deal with the key policy and relevant issue of the effects of treatment on both drug use and criminal behavior.

(4) A senior scholar in the drug field reviewed the PANEL's draft report and recommended it not be published because of inconsistencies and unevenness in the quality of papers in the Appendix.

(5) Ten PANEL members chosen to be representative of the entire group were polled regarding how NIDA should deal with the Report. They were unanimous in saying the Report did not represent consensus and in rejecting the idea that the Report was excellent and should be published in the form in which it was submitted.

(6) The work of the PANEL was politicized by the Chairman in unauthorized statements made to a Senate committee and in interviews granted to the press.

(7) A key deliverable expected from the PANEL was a prioritized research agenda in the crime-drugs area. The Report did not contain such an agenda.

WHY THE PROBLEMS WITH THE DRUG-CRIME PANEL? A LESSON IN SETTING RESEARCH AGENDAS

After one year of concentrated attention, approximately one-fourth of a million dollars, and the input of leading scholars and federal officials with expertise and interest in the crime-drug relationship, why did NIDA officials not receive what they wanted and expected—a prioritized crime-drugs research agenda? There are obviously many answers to this question. In retrospect, however, the following seem especially relevant to the "process" of building research agendas at the federal level.

(1) NIDA was a relatively new federal agency and its expectations for the PANEL were perhaps naive—naive in the sense that academics from differing disciplinary backgrounds are seldom able to repress a commitment to their unique perspectives in order to foster a commitment to a unified social science perspective; naive, too, in expecting that academic social scientists solve puzzles by putting the pieces together in creative synthesis. Instead, the usual approach is toward breaking the issue into smaller and smaller parts.

(2) In its efforts to be inclusive from a disciplinary perspective, NIDA allowed the PANEL to become far too large to be effective as a unit. It is not at all surprising that the Report does not represent a consensus among the PANEL members.

(3) NIDA made a serious tactical error in hiring a visiting scientist to supervise and direct this important activity. In the first place, the roles and duties of a visiting scientist are ill defined. Second, the visiting scientist did not have sufficient time to become part of the administrative structure in the agency. Thus, he was not tuned in to the needs and expectations of those responsible for directing and defending the agency's actions. Third, as an outsider he was not bureaucratically accountable for any snafus emergent from the PANEL's work. These three factors created in the end an extremely sticky mess, one that could have been avoided.

(4) On-board staff members at NIDA did not sufficiently monitor the progress and process of the PANEL's work and deliberations. On-site monitoring throughout that year could have resulted in needed clarifications of the PANEL's mandate, a greater emphasis on efforts to deal with the salient issue of causality, and a sharper and more intensive focus on development of a prioritized research agenda.

TRANSITIONAL PERIOD: FROM NIDA TO NILECJ

In late 1976 Congress amended the Crime Control Act of 1976 (P.L. 94-503), the enabling legislation for the Law Enforcement Assistance Administration, and assigned the following task to NILECJ:

> The Institute shall, in conjunction with the National Institute on Drug Abuse, make studies and undertake programs of research to determine the relationship between drug abuse and crime and to evaluate the success of the various types of drug treatment programs in reducing crime.

At about the same time NIDA was receiving O'Donnell's review and critique of the Report and conducting its straw poll of 10 of the members of the PANEL.

After about a five-month hiatus, I joined NIDA in June 1977 as a Visiting Scientist ostensibly to (1) pick up the pieces to the crime-drug initiative, (2) see what could and should be salvaged from the efforts of the PANEL, (3) start new research initiatives in the crime-drug area, and (4) serve as NIDA's liaison with NILECJ.

In early 1978 NILECJ issued an RFP asking for the grantee to (1) review and critique the PANEL Report and the extant literature, (2) devise a crime-drug research agenda, and (3) recommend and pretest specific research approaches to the issues identified in the agenda.

I served on the committee that reviewed the various proposals submitted in response to the RFP. While there were several good proposals, it was clear to the entire committee that the proposal from RTI was the best and offered the best potential for return on the investment.

I was particularly struck by the difference between the review process at NIDA and at NILECJ. At NIDA "grant" proposals were received on any and all subjects and assigned to an Initial Review Group (IRG). At least two members of the IRG, scientists appointed from outside the government, reviewed and critiqued the proposals and led a discussion of the proposed study for the entire IRG (between 10 and 15 scientists). After appropriate motions and voice/hand votes, every member was allowed privately and independently, to assign a priority score ranging from 1 to 5. The lower the mean score, the better the chance the study would be funded. NIDA staff were not allowed to indicate their evaluation of the proposed study or its salience for the program of research deemed top priority by the Institute staff. After passing through the "peer" review process, the proposed studies had to be reviewed by NIDA's National Advisory Council. This process was required for all grant proposals, no matter how large or small, regardless of the subject matter.

The review committee for the NILECJ grant awarded to RTI consisted of one NIDA representative, one Drug Enforcement Administration representative, and four staff members at NILECJ. While the review was conducted in a serious and professional manner, this was clearly not a review by peers.

Herein is a basic and very significant distinction between two federal agencies that is relevant to setting research agendas. In one case the agency (NIDA) is severely constrained by peer review requirements from imposing its priorities, however derived, on the research it funds. In the other case the agency (NILECJ) is not in the least required to solicit outside-the-government advice before committing its research dollars to justify research priorities and implement a research program it has developed (possibly in an intellectual vacuum).

In a sense the peer review process provides for NIDA the empirical equivalent of a prioritized research agenda in the crime-drug area. Attempts to develop research projects to satisfy the items on that invisible crime-drug agenda must compete in the scientific marketplace against other proposed projects likewise designed to satisfy items on other invisible agendas. Assuming most if not all of the IRG members use the same criteria of technical and scientific merit, the projects funded will constitute the best research possible. Stated differently, NIDA may not need a crime-drugs agenda. Given the extent to which its staff are constrained from interfering with the peer review process, attempts to establish a prioritized research agenda might be an exercise in futility.

On the other hand, NILECJ does not have institutionalized peer review procedures through which it can assess the scientific feasibility and viability of its research priorities and programs. This lack of ritualized input from the scientific community may explain why NILECJ has gone the route of allocating large amounts of research dollars to centers that focus attention on a particular topic. For example, at the present time there is a center, located at the Hoover Institution at Stanford University, that focuses its efforts on the economics of criminal behavior and the criminal justice system, and a center at Vera Institute of Justice examining the relationship of employment and crime. In a sense, NILECJ needed a crime-drug agenda worse than NIDA because of these differences in the grant review process.

RTI REPORT TO NILECJ: A RESEARCH AGENDA?

Subsequent to a critique of the Drug-Crime PANEL Report (Williams, 1979a) and a review and critique of the extant literature (Gandossy, 1979a, 1979b), RTI submitted to NILECJ a final grant report entitled *Exploring the Drug Use and Criminal Behavior Nexus: A Research Agenda and Selected Research Designs* (Williams, 1979b).

Using the advisory panel approach and a ranking procedure, RTI decided to focus on four major issues: economic, life cycle, patterns of drug use, and treatment. Upon a recommendation from NILECJ, the focus was reduced to the issues of life cycle and patterns of use since the Hoover Institution was already dealing with economic issues for NILECJ, and NIDA was dealing with treatment issues.

In the RTI final report, Williams (1979b: 26–33) identified and discussed the ideal research study as a prospective longitudinal panel design employing a random sample. Then (1979: 33) he outlined several disadvantages of such a study: (a) cost, (b) complexity of administration (that is, quality control of the data), (c) maintenance of subjects and research staff, and (d) length of time to complete. Earlier, Williams (1979b: Ch. 7) identified two other flies in the ideal design ointment: (1) The rarity of drug use in the general population, particularly use of opiates, would require a large baseline sample in order to obtain credible data on onset events; and (2) "much basic information about the dynamics of drug use and criminal behavior is currently lacking so that designing an adequate longitudinal survey instrument would be difficult."

In my opinion all of the arguments against the "ideal research study" listed above are specious. The next section will review the three fall-back research designs presented by RTI to NILECJ in its final report (Williams, 1979b). They would be deployed sequentially and are interdependent according to the report.

The first design, ETHNOGRAPHIC, would locate two ethnographers in each of three SMSAs. They would be responsible for (1) fully describing the process of the drug-crime nexus, (2) gathering information that would contribute to knowledge about drug-crime onset behavior and temporal sequences, (3) identifying critical variables that might explain the crime-drug connection, and (4) estimating the incidence and prevalence of the problem.

The second design, the CROSS-SECTIONAL SURVEY, would be conducted in one of the three SMSAs studied by the ethnographers. The researcher would choose a sample by stratifying schools on the likelihood the students would be involved in drug use or crime or both, and then sample classrooms. School dropouts would also be sampled. Most respondents would complete a self-administered questionnaire; some would be interviewed. Four groups would be created: drug use (no criminal behavior), criminal behavior (no drug use), drug use and criminal behavior, and neither behavior.

The third design, the PANEL study, would logically build on the ethnographic and cross-sectional survey designs. Over a period of three years the same subjects would be interviewed every six months to study the intersection of drug-using and criminal behavior.

Williams's (1979b: 73) concluding remarks are instructive: "The study of the relationships between drug use and criminal behavior is fraught with difficulties. The approach presented here to explore life cycle and patterns of behavior issues is an ambitious undertaking but one which is designed not to produce "more of the same" research. Whether research in this difficult area is totally viable will depend to a great extent on the true magnitude and complexity of the problem. This proposed research agenda is designed to successfully explore the parameters of the problem and more specifically to unravel the complexities of the relationships between drug use and criminal behavior."

The three designs presented by RTI to NILECJ might be useful for addressing the temporal sequencing and onset issues. Notice I use the word *might*. In my opinion, they would be of only marginal utility in addressing the broader issues of the crime-drug nexus or the specific issues RTI was mandated to address: issues of life cycle and patterns of use. Listed below are the reasons for this opinion:

(1) The three designs focus exclusively on young adolescents. Thus, only one segment of the life cycle is covered. This would seriously reduce the likeli-

hood of studying various patterns of use and their relationship to crime over the life cycle.

(2) The samples envisioned would be relatively small in addition to being young. This would mean small n's for opiate use, particularly heroin.

(3) Williams says that "much basic information about the dynamics of drug use and criminal behavior is currently lacking." In my opinion, this statement is misleading and perhaps even false. It ignores the vast amount of knowledge about those dynamics that is contained in the Appendix volume of the PANEL Report. The statement does not reflect the light shed on the dynamic interplay between drug use and crime found in the recent and already classic studies by Nurco and DuPont (1977), Ball et al. (1979), McGlothlin et al. (1977, 1978), and Inciardi (1979).

(4) In proposing the three designs to NILECJ, little or no attention was given to extant longitudinal studies that contain data relevant to the crime-drug nexus; prospective longitudinal studies conducted in spite of the disadvantages and obstacles identified by Williams are discussed earlier in this chapter. The studies to which I refer are: (a) Boyle and Brunswick's (1980) study of a panel of youth from Harlem; (b) the Kellam et al. (1980) longitudinal study of youth and their families from the Woodlawn neighborhood of Chicago; (c) Smith and Fogg's (1978) longitudinal study of a very large sample of youth from the Boston area; (d) the national panel study of a sample of over 2000 tenth-graders grown into young adulthood (see Bachman et al., 1979); and (e) Kaplan's (1975) longitudinal panel study of over 9000 youths in Houston. Kaplan's study is particularly important because it is explicitly designed to test causal models of deviance, including both drug use and delinquency crime. These constitute only a few of the studies that could have been cited; studies that have already employed the elusive "ideal research design" are considered too costly and problematic for RTI to endorse up front.

(5) A research agenda is, by definition, forward-looking. It is curious that little was said in the final report to NILECJ about TOPS (Treatment Outcome Prospective Study) and the Supported Work study, since both studies have received funds from LEAA and NIDA. Both of these studies contain extensive data on the crime-drug relationship, primarily for individuals in young adulthood. However, there is a subsample of unemployed minority youth in the Supported Work study. Both studies are prospective, longitudinal, and have large samples. The agenda and respective designs proposed by RTI ignored these valuable resources. Also ignored was the ongoing ethnographic study of the drugs and crime relationship being conducted in Manhattan by Bruce Johnson and Ed Preble—a study jointly funded by NIDA and NILECJ.

THE NILECJ ALCOHOL, DRUGS, AND CRIME CENTER

Given the limitations of the designs proposed by RTI to NILECJ, one might have expected a less than jubilant response. Instead, the three designs presented by RTI were used as the core (i.e., the centerfold) of an NILECJ solicitation of proposals for the purpose of establishing a center to study the relationship of alcohol, drugs, and crime. In July 1980 such a center grant was awarded to a group of collaborating investigators under the general leadership of Dr. Bruce Johnson of the New York State Division of Substance Abuse Services.

The grant is essentially for five years. During the first two years the Alcohol, Drugs, and Crime Center personnel will (1) develop testable propositions by analyzing existing theories and the empirical literature, and (2) conduct secondary analyses to aid in generating hypotheses and identifying youth at a high risk of becoming involved with alcohol, drugs, and/or crime. They will focus attention on personal crime, destructive property crime, acquisitive property crime, and drug selling and distribution. A third type of activity scheduled for the first two years will be (3) ethnographic studies among youth 10–18 years old, with attention directed toward "patterns" of drug use and crime. The fourth focus will be on (3) instrument development and pilot testing, with oversampling of high-risk youth.

During the third year the Center will conduct a cross-sectional survey of 3300 subjects 10–18 years old from two communities, including 300 school dropouts. During years 3, 4, and 5, one thousand youth will be reinterviewed five times, with high-risk youth again oversampled.

It is obvious that the persons involved in this new interdisciplinary research center gave NILECJ exactly what is asked for: a plan to implement the three designs (i.e., a research agenda) contained in RTI's final report (see Williams, 1979b).

CONCLUSIONS:
THE PAST, PRESENT, AND FUTURE

In the 1975–1980 half-decade there has been an intensive effort at the federal level to understand what is known about the crime-drug nexus, to identify soft spots in the knowledge base, and to structure research in the next half-decade or more via a federal crime-drugs research agenda. In this concluding section I want to address two questions: (1) What has been accomplished to date? (2) What can be expected in the next five or so years?

ACCOMPLISHMENTS TO DATE

In many ways there has been a great deal accomplished, much of it through the auspices of RTI: (1) In the Executive Summary volume of the PANEL Report (1976a) there are literally hundreds of pertinent and clearly stated research questions that deserve further attention by the research and federal policy communities. (2) The Appendix volume contains in one place a number of excellent papers that are saturated with clues about the crime-drug mystery. (3) The literature reviews completed by RTI for NILECJ are insightful and thorough, and provide an up-to-date compilation of findings from the extant crime-drugs literature. (4) The RTI Report to NILECJ contains a "research agenda" dealing primarily with the question of the temporal sequencing and interplay of drug-using and criminal episodes among youth. (5) NILECJ has established a center in New York City to implement over the next five years the research designs proposed by RTI.

Supplementary to but independent of these accomplishments, a number of important papers have been published dealing with the crime-drug relationship (e.g., the Ball et al. paper on crime-days, 1979; the study of the California Civil Addict Program by McGlothlin et al., 1977, and the subsequent review article by the same authors, 1978; Inciardi's 1979 article on heroin use and street crime; and the study by James et al., 1979, dealing with the crime-drug relationship among female prostitutes). In addition, there are a number of studies still in the field that should expand considerably our knowledge of the crime-drug relationship (to mention just a few, Johnson and Preble's ethnographic study of the microeconomics of street-level opiate users and nonopiate street criminals; Inciardi's continuing study of heroin use and street crime with large samples; Maddux and Desmond's longitudinal study of heroin addicts in San Antonio, many of whom are now in their forties; the further development and refinement of the crime-days concept by Ball et al., using the longitudinal data of Nurco; and McCoy and McBride's ecological study of the distribution of crime and drug abuse in Miami).

LOOKING TO THE FUTURE

Continuing analysis of data from studies like those mentioned directly above, plus the results likely from the studies to be performed by the Alcohol, Drugs, and Crime Center, make for a promising future in the crime-drugs area. In addition, we can anticipate extensive analyses of the TOPS and Supported Work data between 1980 and 1985 dealing with the crime-drugs connection.

With all of the effort expended during the last five years (1975–1980) directed explicitly toward the development of a crime-drugs research agenda at the federal level, one would expect the existence of a "master plan," a prioritized listing of studies to be conducted that will fill in the gaps of our knowledge base. Nevertheless, that agenda still does not exist in any kind of formalized document.

Those involved in the new NILECJ Alcohol, Drugs, and Crime Center will now spend two or more years searching for testable propositions, developing instruments predictive of drug use and criminal involvement, and deploying pilot studies.

In my opinion, it is naive to think that competing bureaucratic structures could or would collaborate fully to design and implement a research agenda at the federal level. Differing intraorganizational mechanisms for fielding research studies make such cooperation difficult if not close to impossible. In my opinion, any formalized crime-drugs research agenda at the federal level must consist of a post-hoc summary of what has been accomplished and what is known. On that score, the efforts expended from 1975 to 1980 have been successful.

I believe the primary task for the future in this area is not to develop a master plan, but rather to foster interagency collaboration in funding studies dealing with salient crime-drugs issues and in synthesizing findings from relatively independent research efforts.

REFERENCES

BACHMAN, J. G., L. D. JOHNSTON, and P. M. O'MALLEY (1979) "Delinquent behavior linked to educational attainment and post-high school experiences," pp. 1–43 in L. Otten (ed.) Colloquium on the Correlates of Crime and the Determinants of Criminal Behavior. McLean, VA: Mitre Corporation.

BALL, J. C., L. ROSEN, E. G. FRIEDMAN, and D. N. NURCO (1979) "The impact of heroin addiction upon criminality," pp. 163–169 in Problems of Drug Dependence 1979. Rockville, MD: National Institute on Drug Abuse.

BOYLE, J. M. and A. F. BRUNSWICK (1980) "What happened in Harlem? Analysis of a decline in heroin use among a generation unit of urban black youth." Journal of Drug Issues 10: 109–130.

DEMAREE, R. G. and J. F. NEMAN (1976) "Criminality indicators before, during, and after treatment for drug abuse: DARP research findings," In Research Triangle Institute, Appendix to Drug Use and Crime: Report of the Panel on Drug Use and Criminal Behavior. Research Triangle Park, NC: Research Triangle Institute.

DuPONT, R. L. and M. GREENE (1973) "The dynamics of a heroin epidemic." Science 181: 716–722.

GANDOSSY, R. (1979a) A Post-1975 Literature Review: A Survey and Analysis of the Extant Crime/Drug Literature. Research Triangle Park, NC: Research Triangle Institute.

——— (1979b) A Survey and Analysis of the Extant Crime/Drug Literature: Methodological Issues, Patterns of Drug Use and Criminal Behavior, Life Cycles, Economic Issues, and Drug Treatment. Research Triangle Park, NC: Research Triangle Institute.

HIRSCHI, T. and H. C. SELVIN (1967) Delinquency Research. New York: Free Press.

INCIARDI, J. A. (1979) "Heroin use and street crime." Crime and Delinquency 25: 335–346.

JAMES, J. et al. (1979) "The relationship between female criminality and drug use." International Journal of the Addictions 14: 215–229.

KAPLAN, H. B. (1975) Self-Attitudes and Deviant Behavior. Santa Monica, CA: Goodyear.

KELLAM, S. G., M. E. ENSMINGER, and M. D. SIMON (1980) "Mental health in first grade and teenage drug, alcohol and cigarette use." Journal of Drug and Alcohol Dependence (May): 273–304.

McGLOTHLIN, W. H., M. D. ANGLIN, and B. D. WILSON (1978) "Narcotic addiction and crime." Criminology 16: 293–315.

——— (1977) An Evaluation of the California Civil Addict Program. Rockville, MD: National Institute on Drug Abuse.

NASH, G. (1976a) "An analysis of twelve studies of the impact of drug abuse treatment upon criminality." Research Triangle Institute, Appendix to Drug Use and Crime: Report of the Panel on Drug Use and Criminal Behavior. Research Triangle Park, NC: Research Triangle Institute.

NURCO, D. N. and R. L. DuPONT (1977) "A preliminary report on crime and addiction within a communitywide population of narcotic addicts." Drug and Alcohol Dependence 2: 109–121.

O'DONNELL, J. A., H. L. VOSS, R. R. CLAYTON, G. T. SLATIN, and R. G. W. ROOM (1976) Young Men and Drugs: A Nationwide Survey. Rockville, MD: National Institute on Drug Abuse.

Research Triangle Institute [RTI] (1976a) Drug Use and Crime: Report of the Panel on Drug Use and Criminal Behavior. Research Triangle Park, NC: Author.

——— (1976b) Appendix to Drug Use and Crime: Report of the Panel on Drug Use and Criminal Behavior. Research Triangle Park, NC: Author.

SHELLOW, R. (1976) "Drug abuse and crime: fact or fancy?" Contemporary Drug Problems 5: 131–147.

SMITH, G. M. and C. P. FOGG (1978) "Psychological predictors of early use, late use, and nonuse of marijuana among teenage students," pp. 101–113. D. B. Kandel (ed.) Longitudinal Research on Drug Use: Empirical Findings and Methodological Issues. Washington, DC: Hemisphere.

——— (1975) "Teenage drug use: a search for causes and consequences," pp. 279–282 in D. J. Lettier (ed.) Predicting Adolescent Drug Use. Rockville, MD: National Institute on Drug Abuse.

WEISSMAN, J. C. (1979) Understanding the Drugs and Crime Connection: A Systematic Examination of Drugs and Crime Relationships. Madison, WI: STASH.

WILLIAMS, J. R. (1979a) A Critical Review of Drug Use and Crime: Report of the Panel on Drug Use and Criminal Behavior. Research Triangle Park, NC: Research Triangle Institute.

——— (1979b) Exploring the Drug Use and Criminal Behavior Nexus: A Research Agenda and Selected Research Designs. Research Triangle Park, NC: Research Triangle Institute.

2

THE CRIMINALITY OF HEROIN ADDICTS
When Addicted and When Off Opiates

JOHN C. BALL, LAWRENCE ROSEN,
JOHN A. FLUECK, and DAVID N. NURCO

INTRODUCTION

There is rather general agreement among criminologists that an increase in criminality commonly occurs following the onset of heroin addiction in the United States (Chein et al., 1964; O'Donnell, 1966, 1969; Ball and Snarr, 1969; Nash, 1973; Weissman et al., 1974; McGlothlin et al., 1978). Despite this overall consensus, however, the dynamics of the relationship between opiate addiction and crime continue to be a matter of controversy. Among the questions that remain unresolved, three seem especially crucial: (1) What is the temporal sequence of events regarding the onset of heroin addiction and the commencement of criminal behavior? (2) What are the types and frequencies of crimes committed by heroin addicts? (3) What impact do post-onset periods of abstinence or subsequent periods of addiction have on criminality?

AUTHORS' NOTE: The data collection for this project was supported, in part, by NIDA Research Grant ROI DA 01375, Principal Investigator, David N. Nurco.

Although answers to these questions will not solve the social problem of heroin addiction in the United States, which currently involves 550,000 individuals (Strategy Council on Drug Abuse, 1979), the answers could provide a means of unraveling one difficult aspect of the problem—that involving criminal behavior. An answer to the first of these three questions is derived from a critical review of pertinent scientific reports. Answers to the second and third questions are provided by an analysis of the present research findings.

THE ISSUE OF SEQUENCE REVIEWED

The issue of the temporal sequence of drug abuse and criminal behavior has been a topic of scientific concern for over fifty years. The reason for this interest has been primarily etiological—to determine which of these factors was the determining (or causal) one.

Most of the early investigators found little criminality before the onset of opiate addiction (Kolb, 1925; Terry and Pellens, 1928; Pescor, 1943). Later studies, however, have shown a high probability of criminality preceding heroin addiction (Robins and Murphy, 1967; Jacoby et al., 1973; Chambers, 1974). Thus, Jacoby reports that 71 percent of heroin users in Philadelphia had a delinquency record prior to onset of their opiate use, compared to 35 percent of all boys in the same citywide age cohort who also had such records.

This difference in the sequence of events between the early and later studies suggests that there is no invariant relationship between heroin addiction and crime. Instead, it seems that the relationship is contingent upon the particular historical period and population of heroin addicts selected. Thus, if heroin is being introduced into a noncriminal or low-criminal population (e.g., medical professionals or middle-class adults) it would be highly unlikely to find criminality preceding heroin use. Conversely, higher levels of preexisting criminality among heroin addicts would be expected within a population with a high endemic crime rate (e.g., youthful lower-class males in metropolitan slums). Support for this demographic and historical interpretation of the sequence issue is found in numerous studies of addict populations in which the sequence of onset of opiate use and the commencement of criminality differ (see Ball and Chambers, 1970).

It seems reasonable to conclude, therefore, that the issue of the sequence of unique events (first heroin use or a first act of delinquency) may be less significant than determining the continuing influences that sustain criminality and opiate addiction over a period of years or decades. This contention is supported by the fact that an initial onset experience of substance use (opiates, marijuana, alcohol, tobacco, and so on) often does not lead to continued use and dependence, and, furthermore, that most citizens engage in one or more acts of delinquency during adolescence without becoming enmeshed in a criminal lifestyle.

FURTHER CONCEPTUAL IMPEDIMENTS TO CRIME-DRUG RESEARCH

Before turning to consider the frequency and type of crimes committed by addicts and the impact of heroin addiction on these crime rates, it is pertinent to comment upon several conceptual and methodological problems confronting researchers in this area.

Although there has in recent years been a notable increase in criminological research pertaining to heroin addiction that has produced a significant knowledge base, there are still unresolved conceptual problems that tend to obscure the fundamental scientific issues and, therefore, hamper the formulation of testable hypotheses and relevant research on this topic. Among the more pressing conceptual problems, four seem most apparent: (1) inappropriate use of a unitary factor causal model, (2) failure to distinguish between onset of deviance and its continuance as separate issues, (3) lack of cross-cultural and historical perspective, and (4) general neglect of abstinence periods in studying this relationship. Each of these conceptual issues will be discussed.

A pervasive conceptual problem that has seriously impeded the advancement of research with regard to the crime-drug relationship is use of a unitary causal model, which posits that there is a single causal factor that will explain this relationship. Commonly, the researcher holds that heroin use "leads to" crime; or that crime "leads to" heroin use; or that both drug addiction and crime are caused by a single third factor. The belief that there is a single causal factor to explain both crime and drug abuse appears to be a misapplication of the infectious disease model that seeks to identify a specific causal agent. But the concept of a single, invariant causal agent is an inappropriate, and hence, fallacious, explanation for most human behavior. It is no longer meaningful to talk of *the* cause of crime, or *the* cause of drug use. There are various reasons why individuals engage in crime or become drug addicts.

A second conceptual problem involves the failure to distinguish between the onset of heroin use and the reasons for continuation of use over the years. These two phenomena are quite different. Thus, the circumstances and influences that contribute to first use of heroin are quite different from those that support long-term addiction to heroin. So it is with criminal behavior: A first illegal act is quite different from a criminal career.

A third conceptual problem has far-reaching implications, although it involves rather straightforward findings from cross-cultural and historical research. This involves the fact that crime and opiate use exist independently of one another. Consequently, it is apparent that heroin use does not always promote criminal behavior, nor does crime always promote drug use. Rather, a cross-cultural and historical perspective substantiates the proposition that there may, or may not be, a relationship between opiate use and crime within a specified population and culture (Ball, 1977).

A last conceptual point is that periods of abstinence from opiate addiction have been largely ignored in research,[1] although the contrast between periods of addiction and abstinence (or lesser use) with respect to criminal behavior could significantly further our knowledge of this relationship. This omission may be due to a lingering notion that heroin addicts are seldom if ever off drugs, except when incarcerated (which is untrue); or it may be that this research neglect is due to the difficulty of obtaining detailed data pertaining to periods of abstinence and addiction.

By way of recapitulation, it may be said that various conceptual problems have tended to hinder the formulation of specific research questions that could be investigated and resolved. The emphasis on searching for universal relationships and developing grandiose causal theories has impeded middle-range theories based on verifiable empirical generalizations.

MEASUREMENT ISSUES IN CRIME-DRUG RESEARCH

By and large, the most striking methodological weakness in contemporary research pertaining to the crime-heroin relationship is the lack of adequate measures of criminality. The measurement problems are easy to identify, but difficult to resolve.

Two measurement issues are of particular significance in the present context. First, it has been recognized that official records of crime are an inadequate measure of actual criminal behavior within most offender populations. This tends to be especially the case among persistent offenders. Thus, recent studies have reported that less than 1 percent of property offenses committed by drug abusers results in arrest (Inciardi and Chambers, 1972; McGloghlin et al., 1978). In addition to grossly underestimating the amount of crimes committed by opiate addicts, official records may also fail to provide a representative sample of the types of crimes committed.[2]

Second, there is need for a measure of criminality that will enable analysis of actual crime rates over an offender's career or lifetime. Thus, we would like to be able to measure criminal behavior on a yearly basis in order to surmount the middle-class bias of regarding crime as a unique or infrequent event. If addicts are committing hundreds of crimes a year per subject (as is the case in this study), it is not only inaccurate to depict this as reflected by one or two arrests, but it is a gross distortion of a social reality. The research need, then, is to obtain a valid and meaningful measure of criminal behavior that will facilitate the computation of yearly rates.

In stating that there are special measurement needs in studying populations who are heavily involved in criminal behavior, it is pertinent to note that most criminological research and most studies pertaining to drug users are concerned with a few officially recorded crimes or a few minor acts of delinquency.[3] As a consequence of this dominant focus on populations with a low frequency of criminality, measurement problems encountered when studying populations with a high frequency of criminal events (e.g., 200 or more crimes per year) have been neglected. For example, high monthly or yearly offense rates may prove difficult to interpret and use in comparative analysis because of the confounding effect of these few high values on sample statistics. Thus, if a few individuals commit a thousand or more offenses per year, this fact can easily distort other sample statistics unless appropriate measures are employed. Indeed, it was precisely this problem that prompted the formulation of our crime-day measure, which will be discussed below.

STATEMENT AND DEVELOPMENT OF THE RESEARCH PROBLEM

As noted previously, this study was planned to provide answers to two rather specific research questions: What are the types and frequencies of crimes committed by heroin addicts? What impact do post-onset periods of abstinence or subsequent periods of addiction have on criminality?

In pursuing answers to these seemingly straightforward research questions, we soon found ourselves involved in reviewing hundreds of interview schedules, devising new coding procedures, and otherwise becoming enmeshed in the complexities of criminological data analysis. Among the problems we encounted were the following:

(1) How should we handle multiple offenses committed on the same day? (If we count each act of theft—as in department store "boosting"—as a separate event, the large numbers obtained will not provide a meaningful basis for comparison.)

(2) How can we, or should we, differentiate among various types of felony offenses? (That is, given the extent of criminality in this sample, how can we classify their offenses in a meaningful way?)

(3) How can drug offenses, "drug-related" offenses, and other offenses be differentiated? (At the onset, it was decided to delete drug use and possession offenses, but what about drug sales and property offenses? How should these be analyzed?)

(4) What time period should be used in computing crime rates? (monthly, yearly, or for the addiction career?)

(5) Is it feasible to trace crime careers in terms of the predominant type of offense committed? (How can the addicts be classified according to their criminal ways of life?)

(6) How can periods of addiction and periods of regular opiate use be analyzed with respect to crime rates? (With no accepted procedure for computing rates and with the difficulty of combining, or otherwise ordering, addiction and abstinence periods, how could meaningful comparisons be effected?)

The above is a simplified and organized list of some of the measurement problems confronting us at the beginning of the data analysis. In retrospect, it is evident that the difficulties were primarily due to a single methodological problem. An appropriate and efficacious measure of criminality was not available. What was needed was a measure that would provide a feasible means of explaining crime in this population, be scientifically and statistically valid, and yet be reasonably simple to use and understand.

A NEW MEASURE OF CRIMINAL BEHAVIOR: CRIME-DAYS PER YEAR AT RISK

In the present chapter, a new measure of criminal behavior is described and employed in an ongoing research project. The new measure has been termed crime-days per year at risk. A *crime-day* is a 24-hour period in which an individual commits one or more crimes. The number of *crime-days per year at risk* refers to the number of days per year that an individual has committed crimes, from 0 to 365.

This new measure is found to have unique analytical power, since it permits the calculation of uniform crime rates by years at risk and it is not confounded by multiple crimes committed on a given day. Furthermore, it appears to be effective for explaining and understanding the extent of serious criminal behavior, because it relates the number of crimes committed by individuals to a common frame of reference: times per year. The discovery of the average crime-days per year concept was made by the senior author while analyzing detailed life history data pertaining to heroin addicts as part of a follow-up study in Baltimore.

DEFINITION OF TERMS

Crime-Day. A crime-day is defined as a 24-hour period during which one or more crimes are committed by a given individual. Each day of the year, then, is either a crime-day or a noncrime-day.

Heroin Addiction. This term refers to the daily use of opiates (*daily use,* or regular use, is defined as use during at least four days per week for a month, or longer; most subjects in this study were heroin users).

Average Crime-Days Per Year. This measure is defined as the average number of crime-days per year at risk for a given individual. The range is from 0 to 365. Thus, an individual with 1489 crime-days during a seven-year risk period has an average crime-days per year at risk of 213. (Actual computation is by days at risk and number of crime-days.)

Years at Risk. Years at Risk is the number of years an individual is "on the street," or not incarcerated. It is calculated on a cumulative basis by subtracting jail, prison, and hospital time from the years since onset of regular opiate use.

Principal Type of Crime. This is the predominant type of crime engaged in by a given individual during his or her years at risk, as theft (e.g., boosting, burglary), con games, robbery, gambling, drug sales, and so on. This principal type of criminal behavior is the most common offense committed from an actuarial viewpoint. It answers the question, What kind of crime does the individual usually commit? The crimes reported by our sample reflect a broad range of criminal behavior and include larceny (pickpocketing, shoplifting, unauthorized use, burglary), robbery, fencing, assault, con games, pimping, soliciting, gambling, rape, abortions, forging, drug dealing, murder, and loan sharking. Mere possession or use of drugs is not classified as a crime in this analysis.

Criminal Career. This is the criminal behavior pattern an individual has followed while at risk. The two main elements in determining the crime pattern are (1) type of crime and (2) frequency of crime. Examples of crime patterns are: daily theft, daily con games, weekly robbery, weekly forgery, and infrequent assault. In each case, the crime pattern, or career, is the most common, or usual, offense committed during the subject's years at risk and the most frequently committed. Thus, a pattern of daily theft during a four-year period indicates that the individual had as his or her common offense theft of property and that this was carried on most of the time he was at risk. Since the crime pattern is derived for each person from his average crime-days per year and the principal type of crime committed, the actual number and type of crimes is known in each case.

In order to obtain answers to the criminological questions advanced, the study was organized according to the following procedures: (1) A sample of

243 male opiate addicts was selected for study. (2) Periods of addiction and periods of abstinence from opiate dependence were enumerated. (3) The number of crime-days per year at risk was determined for the sample. (4) The addicts were classified by principal type of criminal career pursued from onset of regular opiate use to interview. (5) The extent of crimes committed was analyzed by criminal career types, controlled for addiction and abstinence periods. (6) A correlation analysis of addiction, crime, and demographic variables was undertaken. (7) A stepwise regression of addiction and abstinence periods was undertaken in order to determine the relationship of selected crime and demographic variables to each of these drug use statuses. In the remainder of the chapter, these procedures will be described and the relevant research findings presented.

THE SAMPLE AND INTERVIEW SCHEDULE

This study is based on interview data obtained from 243 Baltimore opiate addicts (most were heroin addicts). The 243 male addicts were a random sample selected from a chronologically stratified list of 4069 known opiate users arrested (or identified) by the Baltimore Police Department between 1952 and 1971. The sample was unselected for criminality, but stratified by race and chronological period. Of the 243 subjects, 109 were white and 134 were black. Analysis of race and cohort differences has been undertaken elsewhere (Nurco and DuPont, 1977).

The selection of the final sample of 243 was accomplished as follows. The initial sample drawn from the police files consisted of 349 individuals, but 57 of these had died by the time of follow-up interview, 2 were in mental hospitals (for psychosis), 6 were unlocated, and 17 refused to participate in the study. Thus, 92 percent of the sample who were alive and not in mental institutions were interviewed (i.e., 267 of 290 subjects).

Of the 267 addicts who were interviewed, 14 claimed never to have been regular users of opiates, 3 used opiates regularly for only one or two months, and the onset of one preceded that of everyone in the sample by 22 years; these 18 were excluded. In addition, a careful review of the remaining 249 cases revealed that 6 interviews had significant discrepancies between their self-reports and FBI records; these 6 were eliminated. (These six claimed no criminal behavior, but their arrest record listed two or more nondrug offenses). The remaining sample consisted of 243 cases. The sample procedure and characteristics of the base population are described more fully elsewhere (Nurco et al., 1975).

Although comprehensive penal, hospital, and other institutional data were collected with respect to the addict sample, the main source of data for the present analysis was personal interviews. Each of the 243 addicts was interviewed between July 1973 and July 1974 by specially trained interviewers who were familiar with the Baltimore addict subculture. The interview lasted some three hours and the questions were focused on six topics: drug use, criminal behavior, work, living arrangements, drug selling, and sources of income.

The interview schedule consisted of six parts: (1) Lifetime prevalence of drug use by specific drugs of abuse (7 pages, completion time about 30 minutes); (2) history of opiate use by addicted and abstinent periods during risk years (3 pages, 30 minutes to complete); (3) preaddiction criminality and circumstances of onset of opiate use (7 pages; 30 minutes); (4) circumstances of first regular use of opiates (i.e., daily use for a month or longer) and each subsequent addiction period. This part includes information on criminality for each period of regular opiate use or abstinence (10 minutes for each addiction period; 7 pages each); (5) marital history, parental background, juvenile delinquency, military service, treatment history, incarceration history, criminal history (16 pages; 60 minutes to complete); (6) interviewer's rating of respondent's attitude, appearance, and overt responsiveness (1 page; 5 minutes).

The validity of the interview data has been the subject of a separate study (Bonito et al., 1976). The findings of this study substantiate the conclusions from prior research concerning the validity of interview data obtained from opiate addicts—namely, that valid data can be obtained if specially trained interviewers who are familiar with the local addict subculture are employed.[4]

THE RESEARCH FINDINGS:
ADDICTION AND ABSTINENCE PERIODS
FOR 243 MALES

The mean age of the 243 males at the time of interview was 35.9 years, and 93 percent of the sample was between 25 and 49 years of age. Since onset of opiate addiction usually had occurred when the subjects were between 15 and 19 years, most of the sample had a post-onset career of 10 or more years (198 had 10 or more years, 37 had 5–9, and 8 had 2–4).

Since a major focus of the lengthy interview was to obtain detailed chronological data pertaining to addiction status from onset of regular opiate use to time of interview, each subject was asked to describe in detail his addiction, abstinent, and incarceration periods. For the entire sample, there were 2340 time periods; 1022 were addiction periods, 488 were abstinent periods, 700 were jail or prison time periods, 52 were hospitalization periods, and 78 periods were unclassified because of insufficient data. (These few unknown periods were omitted from further analysis.) In the present report, attention is directed toward the addiction and abstinent periods, as these were the times during which the subjects were at risk.

All subjects had one or more addiction periods. The average length of an addiction period was found to be two years, although longer periods were common. Each subject was asked about his daily and weekly use of specific drugs during each period (dosage, multiple use, times used per day or week). In this manner, each subject's years, months, and days at risk were classified as addicted to or abstinent from opiates.

The total amount of time that this Baltimore male sample spent addicted to opiate drugs since onset of regular opiate use was 61.6 percent of their risk years; they were off regular opiates 38.4 percent of their risk years. Since they averaged 11.3 years at risk, they were addicted to opiates almost two-thirds of the time and were abstinent somewhat over a third of the time (Figure 2.1). Two further points are pertinent concerning their abstinent

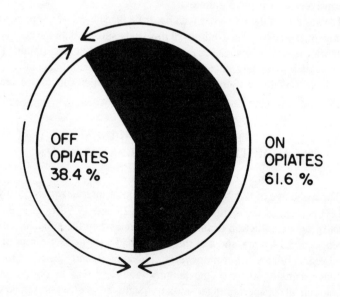

FIGURE 2.1   Time Since Onset Addicted to Opiates or Off Regular Opiate
              Use for 237 Addicts

periods. First, the abstinence from regular opiate use classification included periods of occasional use of opiates as well as periods of frequent use of nonopiate drugs. Second, it is significant that 85 percent of the sample had such abstinent periods.

LIFETIME CRIMINALITY SINCE ONSET OF OPIATE ADDICTION

Although periods of addiction or abstinence during the years at risk provided the chronological frame of reference for the interview, additional detailed data were obtained for each period concerning criminal behavior, employment, income, family life, and other variables. With respect to criminality, each subject was asked about the number and type of crimes he committed on a weekly and daily basis for each addiction or abstinent period. These responses provided the basis for determining the number of crime-days, the principal type of crime, and crime and criminal career pattern for each subject.

The total number of crime-days during the risk years for the 243 addicts is tabulated in Table 2.1. The range in crime-days within the sample was from 0 to 9450—that is, from no crimes committed by six addicts to 9450 crime-days accumulated by one addict during his risk years.

The total number of crime-days amassed by these 243 addicts during their years at risk was 473,738. This total is an underenumeration of the total

TABLE 2.1   Total Crime-Days Amassed by 243 Male Addicts During Years at Risk

Crime-Days	Number of Addicts	Percentage of Addicts
No crime-days	6	2.5
1–99	20	8.2
100–499	31	12.8
500–999	31	12.8
1000–1999	54	22.2
2000–2999	46	18.9
3000–3999	27	11.1
4000–4999	12	4.9
5000–5999	10	4.1
6000–9450	6	2.5
Total	243	100.0

Total crime-days since onset of addiction: 473,738
Mean crime-days per addict: 1,998.9

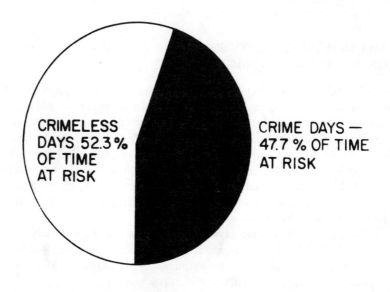

FIGURE 2.2   Percentage of Crime-Days and Crimeless Days While at Risk
              for 237 Addicts

number of crimes committed, as multiple crimes during a crime-day were
common. It is also pertinent to note that most of the crimes reported were for
theft and that drug use or possession was not classified as a crime.

The mean number of crime-days per addict during years at risk was
1998.9. Thus, the majority of these addicts were deeply enmeshed in a
criminal way of life. There were, however, important differences in their
patterns of criminal behavior as well as their frequency of committing
crimes. In order to control for years at risk, crime-days were computed for
each person by years at risk (Table 2.2). The mean number of crime-days per
year at risk for the sample was 178.5. Thus, the total amount of time these
Baltimore addicts spent engaged in daily criminal behavior since their onset
of addiction was almost half of their risk years. To be exact, they were
committing crimes on a daily basis during 47.7 percent of their years at risk
(Figure 2.2).

TABLE 2.2   Crime-Days per Year at Risk for 243 Male Addicts

Crime-Days per Year at Risk	Number of Addicts	Percentage of Addicts
No crime-days	6	2.5
Less than 1 per year	11	4.5
1–49	35	14.4
50–99	26	10.7
100–149	31	12.8
150–199	32	13.2
200–249	25	10.3
250–299	26	10.7
300–349	28	11.5
350–365	23	9.5
Total	243	100.0

Mean crime-days per year at risk: 178.5

CRIMINAL CAREERS OF THE 243 ADDICTS

Each of the 243 addicts was classified as to the common criminal career he had followed since onset of regular opiate use. These criminal career types were determined first on the basis of the principal (or most common) type of crime committed, and second, on the frequency of commission, whether daily, weekly, or less often. Six of the 243 addicts had committed no crimes during their risk periods.

It was found that the 237 addicts who had committed crimes could be classified into nine types of criminal careers: daily theft, daily drug sales, daily other crimes; weekly theft, weekly drug sales, weekly other crimes; infrequent theft, infrequent sales, and infrequent other crimes (Table 2.3). Some two-thirds of the 237 addicts had theft as their principal type of crime. Of these 156 who were career thieves, 41 engaged in daily theft during their year at risk, 58 engaged in weekly theft, and 57 in infrequent theft.

The selling of drugs was the second most favored type of crime committed by these addicts: 45 were principally engaged in selling drugs, or "dealing." Of the 45 dealers, 13 pursued this crime on a daily basis, 18 on a weekly basis, and 14 on an infrequent basis.

The remainder of the sample were engaged in committing other types of crimes on a daily, weekly, or infrequent basis. Of these 36, only 7 were engaged in daily crime, 7 in weekly crime, and 22 in infrequent crime. Confidence games, forgery, gambling, and procuring (pimping) were the principal types of crime committed by these 36 addicts.

TABLE 2.3   Crime-Days per Year at Risk by Type of Criminal Career and
             Addiction Status

Crime Career Type	Number of Addicts	Crime-Days per Year at Risk	Crime-Days per Year at Risk	
			addicted	abstinent
1. Daily theft	41	330.3	347.7	109.7
2. Daily sale of drugs	13	328.0	353.2	88.3
3. Daily other crimes	7	319.4	341.4	151.0
4. Weekly theft	58	189.6	280.9	23.3
5. Weekly sale of drugs	18	181.1	284.0	27.6
6. Weekly other crimes	7	201.9	297.0	70.1
7. Infrequent theft	57	72.4	140.7	7.4
8. Infrequent sales	14	102.4	260.9	10.5
9. Infrequent other crimes	22	46.8	108.2	2.3
No crime	6	—	—	—
Total	243	178.5	248.0	40.8

The classification of the sample into nine criminal career types somewhat obscures the fact that many addicts engaged in more than one type of crime during their years at risk. This situation is especially notable with regard to the 61 addicts who were daily criminals. Thus, 55 of the 61 had engaged in theft during their years at risk, and 43 had engaged in some dealing, although only 13 had this as their principal daily criminal activity. In addition to theft and dealing—the two most common types of crime—33 of the 61 had engaged in other crimes, such as forgery, gambling, confidence games, robbery, and pimping. The complete list of all crimes reported by these daily criminals during their years on the street is: theft (this includes shoplifting; "cracking shorts," burglary, and other forms of stealing), dealing, forgery, gambling, confidence games (flim-flam and so on), pimping, assault, mugging, robbery, armed robbery, and performing illegal abortion. Last, although most of the 61 criminals engaged in more than one type of crime during their years on the street, there still was a marked tendency to focus on one main type of crime—especially theft or dealing. Furthermore, 11 of these 61 males confined themselves exclusively to one type of crime during their years at risk (8 only committed theft, one only sold drugs, one was a confidence man and one a gambler).

THE IMPACT OF ADDICTION UPON
CRIMINAL CAREERS

The extent of criminality among all nine career types was affected by their addiction status. Thus, there was an overall sixfold increase in the number of crime-days per year at risk during addiction, as contrasted with the abstinent periods (Table 2.3). Rather surprisingly, the proportionate increase in crime-days per year at risk when addicted (versus abstinent) was most marked among the criminals who engage in weekly or monthly offenses. Thus, for 5 of these 6 career types (weekly theft, weekly dealing, and the three infrequent types) the extent of criminality increased more than ten times the nonaddicted rate. The greatest increase was for the 22 subjects who committed other crimes on a monthly basis—from 2.3 crime-days per year to 108.2 crime-days per year.

Although the extent of criminality within this addict sample was notably increased when the subjects were addicted to opiate drugs, the nonaddicted crime rate was still quite high. As might be expected, the highest crime rates when not addicted were found among the three criminal career types who had the highest crime rate when addicted (daily theft, daily sales, and daily other crimes). In these three career types, the addicts committed crimes from one to three days per week when not addicted (for these three groups, the rates per year at risk were 109.7, 88.3, and 151.0). In considering the nine career types' rates of criminality when abstinent from opiates, it seems significant that these nine rates vary more (from 2.3 to 151.0) than do the rates when these same subjects are addicted. In a sense, then, one effect of opiate addiction is to raise the number of crimes committed to a threshold or support level, and this occurs for all nine career types. Thus, when addicted, seven of the nine career types commit more than 260 crimes per year and none of the nine career groups falls below 100 crime-days per year at risk.

CORRELATION OF ADDICTION, CRIME, AND DEMOGRAPHIC VARIABLES

In order to investigate the relationship of specific addiction, crime, and demographic variables, we undertook a correlation analysis of ten variables: (1) total number of crime-days accumulated during years at risk (Total CD); (2) total number of crime-days accumulated while addicted during years at risk (CD-H); (3) total number of crime-days accumulated while not addicted during years at risk (CD-off); (4) total number of days addicted during years at risk (H-days); (5) total number of days not addicted during years at risk (off-days); (6) total number of officially recorded arrests during years at risk (arrests); (7) crime committed after age 17 but prior to onset of addiction, by self-report (prior crime, coded as a dichotomy: yes or no); (8) race: white or black; (9) age at onset of opiate addiction (onset age); and (10) age at time of interview (age at interview, or age).

TABLE 2.4 Correlation Matrix for Ten Variables, for 237 Male Addicts

Variable	(1) Total CD	(2) CD-H	(3) CD-Off	(4) H-Days	(5) Off-Days	(6) Arrests	(7) Prior	(8) Race	(9) Onset	(10) Age
1. Total crime-days	—									
2. Crime-days-heroin	.9510	—								
3. Crime-days-off	.3038	-.0056	—							
4. Heroin days	.7303	.7914	-.0768	—						
5. Off days	-.1958	-.2563	.1567	-.2200	—					
6. Total arrests	.3191	.3073	.0852	.2999	-.1488	—				
7. Prior crime	.1493	.1796	-.0706	.2875	.0171	-.0348	—			
8. Race (black)	.2585	.2712	.0003	.2793	-.2105	.0969	.0966	—		
9. Onset age	-.2564	-.2295	-.1221	-.1954	.0518	-.1362	-.0160	.0596	—	
10. Age at interview	.1859	.2130	-.0551	.4124	.2978	.2464	.1278	.2023	.5101	—

Values underlined when $P < .01$

The correlation matrix of Table 2.4 provides an initial delineation of the relationship among these three sets of variables (i.e., addiction, crime, and demographic variables). The first column, total crime-days (variable 1), indicates the overall relationship of criminality to addiction and other variables, but the interpretation of several of these column 1 correlations is ambiguous due to the distinct effect of addiction versus nonaddiction status. This uniqueness of the two addiction statuses is evident in a comparison of columns 2 and 3. Thus, total crime-days when addicted (variable 2) is significantly correlated with all seven variables—H-days, off-day, arrests, prior crime, race, onset age, and age at interview—but not significantly correlated with total crime-days-off (variable 3). Furthermore, total crime-days-off is not significantly correlated with any of these same seven variables (4 through 10). Also underscoring the distinctiveness of the two periods is the absence of correlation between them (i.e., R of $-.0056$ between variables 2 and 3), which indicates that the frequencies of crime committed during addiction and off periods are independent of one another. Thus, the amount of crime committed during addiction periods does not predict the amount of crime committed while off opiates; consequently, a "heroin-day" is a very different kind of day from an "off-day," insofar as crime is concerned.

With respect to criminal history and demographic variables, these are both correlated with total crime-days and crime-days-H, but as noted not with crime-days-off. Specifically, the total number of arrests since onset of addiction is positively correlated with variables 1 and 2. The correlation of arrests with crime-days-H is (.3073). Variable 7, prior crime, is also positively associated with CD-H, but this measure of early criminality poses difficulties with respect to interpretation because it is affected by early onset and prior juvenile delinquency. Nonetheless, it is included in the present analysis as it does measure prior criminality to some extent.

Race (black) is positively correlated with crime-days-H, but again, not with crime-days-off. Age at onset of opiate addiction (variable 9, Table 2.4) is negatively correlated with crime-days-H and crime-days-off, although the latter correlation $(-.1221)$ is not significant. That early age at onset of addiction is correlated with a higher frequency of later criminality is a consistent finding of this study. The moderate positive correlation of age at interview with crime-days-H (.2130) indicates that age (and time at risk) have some relationship to crime-days, but that this issue requires further analysis.

In considering time at risk, or "street" time, it might appear that the high positive correlation between H-days and crime-days-H (.7914) is to be expected, because both of these measures are affected by the amount of time

TABLE 2.5   Stepwise Regression Analysis of Criminality for Addiction and
             Abstinence Periods Among 237 Addicts

Variable	r	Fig. to enter	R^2	R^2 change	Multiple R
A. Dependent Variable: Crime-Days-Heroin					
1. Days-H	.7914	<.001	.6264	.6264	.7914
2. Age at interview	.2130	.002	.6419	.0155	.8012
3. Arrests	.3073	.019	.6503	.0084	.8084
4. Race	.2712	.094	.6545	.0042	.8090
5. Prior crime	.1796	.329	.6659	.0014	.8099
6. Age at onset	−.2295	.495	.6566	.0007	.8103
7. Days-off	−.2563	.717	.6568	.0002	.8105

Variable	r	Fig. to enter	R^2	R^2 change	Multiple R
B. Dependent Variable: Crime-Days-Off					
1. Days-off	.1567	.016	.0246	.0246	.1567
2. Age at onset	−.1221	.043	.0416	.0170	.2039
3. Arrests	.0852	.144	.0503	.0088	.2243
4. Age at interview	−.0551	.129	.0597	.0094	.2444
5. Race	.0003	.295	.0642	.0045	.2533
6. Prior crime	−.0706	.364	.0675	.0034	.2599
7. Days-H	−.0768	.627	.0685	.0010	.2617

at risk. However, considerably more is operating here than time at risk, for if
time at risk were the principal influence, then the two correlations (off-days
with CD-off; and H-days with CD-H) would be about equal in value. (On the
contrary, the marked difference between these two correlations (.1567
versus .7914) indicates that other influences are operating during the addiction periods as contrasted with the off periods. Furthermore, a partial correlational analysis controlling for age at interview revealed that the amount of
crime committed during both the on and the off periods was similar to the
zero-order values. Thus, for the on periods, a partial value of .7907 was
obtained (compared with a zero-order value of .7914) and, for the off periods, a partial value of .1817 (compared with .1567). These results indicate
that age and time at risk are not the principal influences that determined the
number of crime-days accumulated by these 237 addicts.

STEPWISE REGRESSION ANALYSIS OF ADDICTION
AND ABSTINENCE PERIODS

Thus far it has been found that (1) the frequency of crime is strongly
related to the amount of addiction time, and (2) the addiction and nonaddic-

tion (or abstinence) periods are quite distinct experientially, requiring separate analysis. In order to investigate these two major findings with greater precision and analytic power, a stepwise regression analysis of the addiction and abstinence period was undertaken for the 237 male addicts.[5] In this analysis, relevant variables from the correlation matrix are employed.

The stepwise regression analysis of crime-days accumulated while these 237 addicts were addicted yields results that are quite striking (Table 2.5). Thus, there is a strong positive correlation between the number of days addicted and the number of crime-days (.7914). This single variable (H-days) accounts for 63 percent of the variance in criminality during the addiction periods. Two of the remaining variables account for a small additional proportion of the variance; these are age at interview and number of arrests, both positively correlated with crime-days-H.

The stepwise regression analysis of crime-days accumulated during off periods reveals results that are quite different from those of the addiction periods. With respect to criminality during the off periods (as measured by crime-days-off), only two of the seven variables are significantly correlated (Table 2.5). The first of these, off-days, is only weakly correlated with crime-days-off (+.1567). The second variable to enter, age at onset, is negatively correlated with CD-off, indicating the consistent relationship between early age of addiction onset and criminality noted previously. The remaining five variables are not significantly correlated with crime-days-off. Of special interest is the lack of correlation between crime-days-off and H-days. Thus, the amount of crime committed by these heroin addicts while they were not addicted is independent of the amount of their addiction time. This analysis of criminality while not addicted to heroin reveals, then, only a small variance accounted for by the variables studied. In this sense, the findings are similar to those of most criminological research, which show modest correlations between crime and independent variables.

STEPWISE REGRESSION ANALYSIS OF CRIMINALITY FOR THE THREE CAREER GROUPS

Inasmuch as the frequency of crime was found to be related to the criminal careers of these 237 addicts, it was deemed necessary to undertake a separate stepwise regression analysis for each of the three major offender groups: those primarily engaged in theft of property, those who were drug sellers, and those engaged in other types of crimes.

Perusal of Tables 2.6–2.8 reveals that the number of days subjects were addicted is the single most important influence on their criminality during the addiction periods. In this regard, the strongest effect was for the dealers and the weakest was for the other-crimes group. The remaining variables

TABLE 2.6   Stepwise Regression Analysis of Criminality for 156 Addicts
            Engaged in Theft

		A. Dependent Variable: Crime-Days-Heroin			
Variable	r	Fig. to enter	R^2	R^2 change	Multiple R
1. Days-H	.8046	<.001	.6473	.6473	.8045
2. Age at interview	.2825	.011	.6620	.0147	.8136
3. Race	.2570	.081	.6688	.0067	.8178
4. Arrests	.3219	.141	.6735	.0047	.8207
5. Prior crime	.1595	.359	.6753	.0018	.8218
6. Age at onset	−.2119	.417	.6768	.0014	.8227

		B. Dependent Variable: Crime-Days-Off			
Variable	r	Fig. to enter	R^2	R^2 change	Multiple R
1. Days-off	.2537	.001	.0644	.0644	.2537
2. Prior crime	−.1087	.167	.0760	.0116	.2757
3. Age at onset	−.1202	.195	.0862	.0102	.2936
4. Race	.0071	.264	.0938	.0076	.3062
5. Days-H	−.1175	.260	.1014	.0077	.3185
6. Arrests	−.0001	.609	.1030	.0016	.3209
7. Age at interview	−.0591	.615	.1045	.0015	.3233

TABLE 2.7   Stepwise Regression of Criminality for 45 Addicts Engaged in Drug
            Sales (Dealing)

		A. Dependent Variable: Crime-Days-Heroin			
Variable	r	Fig. to enter	R^2	R^2 change	Multiple R
1. Days-H	.8414	<.001	.7080	.7080	.8414
2. Prior crime	.1252	.185	.7201	.0121	.8486
3. Onset age	−.1244	.230	.7299	.0098	.8543
4. Days-off	−.1734	.440	.7339	.0041	.8567
5. Arrests	.1523	.667	.7352	.0013	.8574
6. Age at interview	.4073	.709	.7362	.0010	.8580
7. Race	.3633	.694	.7373	.0011	.8587

		B. Dependent Variable: Crime-Days-Off			
Variable	r	Fig. to enter or remove	R^2	R^2 change	Multiple R
1. Arrests	.3251	.029	.1057	.1057	.3251
2. Age at interview	−.0699	.353	.1241	.1084	.3522
3. Onset age	−.1724	.682	.1277	.0036	.3573
4. Days-H	−.0938	.530	.1364	.0087	.3692
5. Age-removed	−.0699	.979	.1363	<−.0001	.3692
6. Race	.0550	.442	.1492	.0129	.3862

TABLE 2.8   Stepwise Regression of Criminality for 36 Addicts Engaged in Other Crimes

A. Dependent Variable: Crime-Days-Heroin

Variable	r	Fig. to enter	R^2	R^2 change	Multiple R
1. Days-H	.6675	<.001	.4455	.4455	.6675
2. Arrests	.4683	.027	.5229	.0774	.7231
3. Age at interview	−.0551	.066	.5714	.0486	.7559
4. Prior crime	.3597	.278	.5876	.0162	.7666
5. Race	.2969	.310	.6018	.0141	.7757
6. Days-off	−.2637	.700	.6038	.0021	.7771
7. Onset age	−.3219	.406	.6137	.0098	.7834

B. Dependent Variable: Crime-Days-Off

Variable	r	Fig. to enter	R^2	R^2 change	Multiple R
1. Arrests	.4191	.011	.1756	.1756	.4191
2. Age at interview	−.0552	.410	.1926	.0170	.4389
3. Days-off	−.0197	.237	.2277	.0351	.4772
4. Prior crime	.0857	.466	.2410	.0133	.4910
5. Onset age	−.1330	.553	.2500	.0090	.5000
6. Days-H	.0827	.721	.2534	.0034	.5034

added little to the explained variance for the theft and dealer groups, but were more important for the other-crime group. The total variance explained in all three groups was high (i.e., 67.7, 73.7, and 61.4 percent).

The three offender groups were also quite similar with respect to criminality during the off periods, in that substantially less of the variance was accounted for by the variables studied. Thus, for the 156 offenders engaged in theft, the 45 dealers and the 36 involved in other crimes, only from 10 to 25 percent of the variance was accounted for during the off periods.

To recapitulate, these findings suggest that the theft group and the dealers are fairly similar in that their criminality is primarily affected by their drug addiction. During the abstinence period, however, their frequency of crime is not highly explicable by the set of variables investigated in this study. Yet when daily heroin use takes hold, they turn to crime (by theft or dealing) to acquire sufficient resources to support the daily habit.

The "other" group emerges as somewhat unique. Although the impact of daily heroin use is strong, it does not seem to have the same overwhelming effect it does with the other two groups. Consequently, these 36 individuals have a frequency of criminality that is somewhat more predictable during the nonaddiction periods, as indicated by the relatively high R of .5034. While addiction seems to be a factor that definitely increases their crime, at the same time other factors continue to be of consequence in both the addiction and abstinence periods.

REVIEW AND INTERPRETATION OF
THE RESEARCH FINDINGS

In reviewing the research findings of this study, attention will first be directed toward the significance of addiction and nonaddiction periods. Then the frequency, magnitude, and persistence of offenses committed by these 243 addicts will be considered, along with the types of crimes committed during their years at risk. Next, the correlation and stepwise regression analysis will be reviewed. This will be followed by an appraisal of the new measure of criminality utilized in this research—crime-days per year at risk. Last, the broader implications of this study with respect to the control of crime committed by opiate addicts in the United States will be addressed.

It was found that these 243 addicts spent two-thirds of their time addicted to opiates and one-third not addicted. The time under study was their years at risk, or "street" time, and this averaged 11 years per addict from onset of addiction to time of interview. The fact that addiction was not a continuous state of drug dependency seemed significant, for it indicated that there were considerable periods during which changes in the addict's lifestyle might occur. In fact, it was found that these periods of abstention (or lesser use) did have important consequences.[6] In particular, it was found that criminality decreased markedly during the months or years that these addicts were not dependent on heroin and other opiates. The decrease was striking—an 84 percent decline in the crime rate!

One of the major findings of this study was that heroin addicts commit a staggering amount of crime and that this continues fairly much on a daily basis for years and decades. Before turning to an analysis of differences in crime rates by addiction status and other factors, it is meaningful to note the overall amount of crime these 237 males have committed.

The research findings presented in Table 2.1 showed that the average addict has committed one or more crimes during some 2000 days. Taken together, these 237 male opiate addicts have been responsible for committing more than 500,000 crimes during an eleven-year risk period. The exact figure is 473,738 crime-days, but this does not include multiple offenses committed on a given day, so the figure of 500,000 crimes is an underestimate. In this regard, it should be noted that theft was the principal type of crime committed and that drug use and possession were not, themselves, classified as crimes.

This high frequency of criminality among opiate addicts is similar to that reported by other investigators. Thus, Inciardi and Chambers (1972: 59) found that 26 addicts on the street "were responsible on a daily basis for 22 major crimes." In a recent larger study, Inciardi (1979) found that 239 active male heroin users committed 80,644 offenses during a 12-month period. These latter results from addicts in Miami are remarkably similar to the present findings from Baltimore, with respect to both frequency and types of crime committed.

In the present study, it was found that the addicts could conveniently be classified into three major offender types—theft, drug sales, and other crimes—on the basis of the crimes they usually engaged in during their years at risk. This classification proved to be feasible after the concept and measure of crime-days was developed, and it was found that criminal careers for most of the addicts were relatively stable. Thus, 156 addicts were found to be primarily engaged in theft, 45 in drug sales, and 36 in other types of crime.

The measure of average crime-days per year at risk was introduced and employed to determine the frequency of offenses per year for each of the 237 addicts during all of their years at risk. It was found that the mean number of crime-days per year for the 237 addicts was 178.5. However, many addicts had more, or fewer, crime-days for each year at risk. Indeed, the distribution presented in Table 2.2 indicates that 9.5 percent of the addicts had been engaged in crime virtually every day of their lives since they began regular opiate use. Conversely, there were 6 addicts who reported that they had not been engaged in crime at all during their years at risk. But most of the addicts were consistently engaged in a rather high level of crime during their years at risk; two-thirds had from 100 to 365 crime-days per year for all of their years at risk.

A second major finding of the study was that addiction status had a marked influence on criminality among these males. Thus, it was found that the number of offenses increased sixfold when these subjects were addicted. Significantly, this increase occurred for all nine offender types (Table 2.3). Thus, during abstinence, the average crime-days per year varied from 2.3 to 151.0, with an average of 40.8. By contrast, during addiction, the rate was always over 100 crime-days per year and commonly over 250 crime-days per year at risk.

These research findings pertaining to the impact of addiction on criminality were surprising and unexpected. Thus, we did not expect this marked increase, given the known involvement of this population in crime. Conversely, one might say that we were unprepared for the decrease that occurred when addiction ceased.

These findings concerning markedly different crime rates when addicted and when off regular opiates led to a correlational analysis of these data. In this analysis, it was observed that the amount of crime committed during addiction periods was largely a function of opiate use, specifically of the time spent addicted. However, unexpectedly, it was also found that the amount of crime committed when addicted was unrelated to that committed when off opiates. Thus, it may be held that this analysis provides an explanation for high crime rates during addiction, but provides a much less adequate account of criminality during the nonaddiction periods. Although comparatively infrequent, criminality during these off periods deserves further investigation.

The stepwise regression analysis revealed that the impact of addiction on criminality is pervasive and long-lasting. Thus, addiction was the principal force that increased criminality, regardless of the type of crime pursued. Moreover, this relationship between opiate addiction and criminality was not a transitory phenomenon, but an enduring relationship that obtained during an eleven-year risk period.

Before turning to discuss the implications of this study, it is pertinent to comment on the usefulness of the crime-days measure. In this study of subjects with an extensive history of criminality (which involved the computation of offense rates over a decade and more), the introduction of crime-days and crime-days per year at risk was exceedingly efficacious. Indeed, it seems reasonable to conclude that this study could hardly have been completed without the use of a crime-days (or similar) measure. It was found that this measure—crime-days per year at risk—made it possible to compute meaningful and valid rates. It was not only that the rates were appropriate for the data on hand, but the concept of a crime-day proved to have a meaning that facilitated analysis and interpretation of the complex criminal history material.

EXTENSIVE CRIMINALITY AMONG ADDICTS: IMPLICATIONS

The findings of this study concerning the extensive criminality of contemporary opiate addicts in the United States supports similar findings from other research. It is now evident that addicts are responsible for committing an inordinate amount of crime, that many of these offenses are serious in nature, that addicts' criminality is rather firmly enmeshed in their lifestyle, and, therefore, that it is persistent and recurring.

However, this study adds one new ingredient to the picture: Our research findings indicate that it is opiate use itself which is the principal cause of high crime rates among addicts. Once addiction ceases, crime rates drop markedly. This notable decrease in criminality (an overall 84 percent decline) occurs for all types of offenders throughout the risk years. It is apparent, then, that a major means of reducing the amount of crime committed by opiate addicts is within sight. If we can control addiction, it is evident that we will reduce criminality appreciably.

But how can we impact opiate addiction? Three lines of attack come to mind. First, it is imperative that programmatic and research priorities be established to further this specific objective—to impact addiction among persistent offender groups. These two aspects, programs and related research, must be a core component of any major national effort. Research without implementation can hardly be effective, and action programs not based on relevant scientific knowledge are doomed to failure. Indeed, they cannot succeed for logical reasons, since only research can establish success or failure. Therefore, a first priority is to recognize that a major coordinated effort is required that will focus on this single task.

Second, three or four well-designed experimental programs need to be established to reach or impact specific offender populations. These experimental programs should make use of relevant knowledge concerning ongoing programs—such as TASC, methadone maintenance, family therapy, and intensive probation efforts—yet be based on new concepts and new research findings. In this last regard, it is imperative that these new programs be targeted to reach a specific offender population (as contrasted with programs that attempt to serve everyone without regard to need or likelihood of success), and employ means that have either a demonstrated association with the reduction of addiction or a well-developed rationale for effecting this objective.

Finally, let it not be taken amiss if it be suggested that it is time to get on with the task at hand and not be sidetracked by irrelevant ideological, scholastic, or methodological arguments. While it is true that drug abuse may be difficult to define, that alcohol abuse is also a major social problem, that penalties for marijuana use are inconsistent, and that, in fact, there are many unresolved problems and difficulties in conducting research (especially if one seeks perfection and closure), it is also true that existing knowledge and methodology are sufficient to address the problem at hand. We know that criminality is rampant among heroin addicts. We know that addiction markedly increases this criminality. We also know that addiction can be impacted through treatment and control measures.

NOTES

1. Thus Gandossy et al. (1980: 87) note: "The addict career is marked by numerous episodes of remission and relapse from drugs. While we may know very little about the addict life cycle in general, we know even less about these periods of abstention and relapse."

2. In the present study, considerably less than one percent of offenses committed during the risk years resulted in arrest. There were 473,738 crime-days amassed for the sample and 2072 arrests (excluding 797 drug possession arrests). Of the 2072 arrests, 1261 were for theft (60.9 percent).

3. This observation is not meant to denigrate or ignore the significant studies of criminal careers undertaken by Sutherland and others. For recent examples, see Inciardi (1975) and Goldstein (1979).

4. For a discussion of this topic see National Institute on Drug Abuse (1977: 71–97).

5. The ordering of variables was determined by rank order of the partial correlation values. See Nie et al. (1975: Ch. 20).

6. Both Schasne (1966) and Waldorf (1970) report that important changes occur among heroin addicts during periods of abstention; also see Ray (1964). For a theoretical review of cessation and relapse periods, see Lettieri et al. (1980).

REFERENCES

BALL, J.C. (1977) "International survey in 25 nations." Addictive Diseases 3, 1.

––––––– and C.D. CHAMBERS (1970) The Epidemiology of Opiate Addiction in the United States. Springfield, IL: Charles C Thomas.

BALL, J.C. and R.W. SNARR (1969) "A test of the maturation hypothesis with respect to opiate addiction." Bulletin on Narcotics 21, 4: 9–13.

BONITO, A.J., D.N. NURCO, and J.W. SHAFFER (1976) "The veridicality of addicts' self-reports in social research." International Journal of the Addictions 11, 5: 719–724.

CHAMBERS, C.D. (1974) "Narcotic addiction and crime: an empirical overview," Chapter 5 in J.A. Inciardi and C.D. Chambers (eds.) Drugs and the Criminal Justice System. Beverly Hills, CA: Sage.

CHEIN, I., D.L. GERARD, R.S. LEE, E. ROSENFELD (1964) The Road to H. New York: Basic Books.

GANDOSSY, R.P., J.R. WILLIAMS, J. COHEN, and H.J. HARWOOD (1980) Drugs and Crime: a Survey and Analysis of the Literature. Washington, DC: U.S. Department of Justice.

GOLDSTEIN, P.J. (1979) Prostitution and Drugs. Lexington, MA: D.C. Heath.

INCIARDI, J.A. (1979) "Heroin use and street crime." Crime and Delinquency (July): 335–346.

––––––– (1975) Careers in Crime. Skokie, IL: Rand McNally.

––––––– and C.D. CHAMBERS (1972) "Unreported criminal involvement of narcotic addicts." Journal of Drug Issues 2: 57–64.

JACOBY, J.E., N.A. WEINER, T.P. THORNBERRY, and M.E. WOLFGANG (1973) "Drug use in a birth cohort," pp. 300–343 in National Commission on Marijuana and Drug Abuse, Drug Use in America: Problem in Perspective. Washington, DC: Government Printing Office.

KOLB, L. (1925) "Drug addiction and its relation to crime." Mental Hygiene 9: 74–89.

LETTIERI, D.J., M. SAYERS, and H.W. PEARSON [eds.] (1980) Theories on Drug Abuse. Washington, DC: Government Printing Office.

McGLOTHLIN, W.H., M.D. ANGLIN, and B.D. WILSON (1978) "Narcotic addiction and crime." Criminology 16, 3: 293–315.

NASH, G. (1973) "The impact of drug abuse treatment upon criminality." Report, State of New Jersey Division of Narcotic and Drug Abuse Control, December.

National Institute on Drug Abuse (1977) Conducting Followup Research on Drug Treatment Programs. Drug Treatment Monograph Series 2. Rockville, MD: Author.

NIE, N. H., C. H. HULL, J. G. JENKINS, K. STEINBRENNER, and D. H. BURT (1975) Statistical Package for the Social Sciences. New York: McGraw-Hill.

NURCO, D. N., A. J. BONITO, M. LERNER, and M. B. BALTER (1975) "Studying addicts over time: methodology and preliminary findings." American Journal of Drug and Alcohol Abuse 2: 183–196.

NURCO, D. N. and R. L. DuPONT (1977) "A preliminary report on crime and addiction within a community-wide population of narcotic addicts." Journal of Drug and Alcohol Dependence 2: 109–121.

O'DONNELL, J. A. (1969) Narcotic Addicts in Kentucky. Washington DC: Government Printing Office.

———— (1966) "Narcotic addicts and crime." Social Problems 13, 4: 374–385.

PESCOR, M. J. (1943) "A statistical analysis of the clinical records of hospitalized drug addicts." Public Health Reports Supplement 143.

RAY, M. B. (1964) "The cycle of abstinence and relapse among heroin addicts" in H. S. Becker (ed.) The Other Side. New York: Free Press.

ROBINS, L. N. and G. E. MURPHY (1967) "Drug use in a normal population of young Negro men." American Journal of Public Health 57: 1580–1596.

SCHASNE, R. (1966) "Cessation patterns among neophyte heroin users." International Journal of the Addictions 1.

Strategy Council on Drug Abuse (1979) Federal Strategy for Drug Abuse and Drug Traffic Prevention, 1979. Washington, DC: Government Printing Office.

TERRY, C. E. and M. PELLENS (1928) The Opium Problem. New York: Bureau of Social Hygiene.

WALDOLF, D. (1970) "Life without heroin: some social adjustments during long term periods of voluntary abstention." Social Problems 18 (Fall): 228–243.

WEISSMAN, J. C., P. L. KATSAMPES, and T. A. GIACIENTI (1974) "Opiate use and criminality among a jail population." Addictive Disease 1: 269–281.

3

GETTING OVER
Economic Alternatives to Predatory Crime
Among Street Drug Users

PAUL J. GOLDSTEIN

The income of heroin addicts and other drug users is harder to estimate than might be expected. Although the "dope fiend" myth suggests that narcotics users gain a very high income from crime, the data to be presented below suggest that many narcotics users have incomes substantially lower than commonly believed and, further, that much of this income is earned by nonpredatory or even noncriminal means. A major finding emerging from this ethnographic research concerns the wide variety of ways that street opiate users make a living and manage to use drugs.

For street opiate users, economic goal attainment focuses on meeting the demands of daily existence rather than on any long-term career development. Survival presents a daily challenge that is dealt with in whatever fashion appears most appropriate under variable and often difficult circumstances. Predatory crime is often a last resort because it involves a high-risk

AUTHOR'S NOTE: This research was supported by the New York State Division of Substance Abuse Services, by a Public Health Service Award from the National Institute on Drug Abuse, "The Economic Behavior of Street Opiate Addicts" (RO1-DA-01926-01-2), and by an Interagency Agreement, "The Economic Behavior of Nonaddicted Career Criminals," between the

factor. While some may thrive on risk, the majority prefer to generate income in the safest way possible.

The economic successes achieved by street opiate users tend to be discrete and transitory. Subjects in this study perceived and recounted these successes using the processual term, *getting over*. Getting over is a street concept, of course, and not a scientific one. The accounts of how subjects got over tend to blur many of the traditional distinctions social scientists make in this regard, such as legal versus illegal income. Conceptually, legal and illegal income-producing activities may be conceived as extremes on a continuum of economic options. Between these two extremes is a gray area in which many important economic activities are concentrated.

The notion of "getting over" is similar to that of "getting by." Both phrases are most often used to describe an economic state of affairs. However, while "getting by" implies a static state, a mere holding of one's own, "getting over" implies a dynamic process in which some sort of success is achieved. For example, an addict who sells a less experienced user a $5 bag of heroin for $10 says, "I got over on him." An addicted female who dates a drug dealer and receives her narcotics from him declares that she shuns the risks of engaging in theft or street prostitution and would rather "get over" by going out with dealers.[1] Getting over usually involves a degree of scheming or conning.

The phrase has two definitional implications. First, a person is getting over an obstacle (e.g., the rules of a bureaucracy when one fraudulently obtains welfare benefits). Second, a person is getting overly much or something extra (e.g., when one overcharges a peer on a narcotics sale). Getting over is thus further distinguished from getting by in that the latter implies settling for minimal amounts, the bare necessities, whatever one is offered.

Opiate users have a variety of economic options available to them that may be used to finance their drug use and otherwise to sustain themselves in their daily lives. Predatory crime (i.e., essentially all forms of theft in which there is a victim) is one such option. However, an assortment of other options do exist and contribute substantially to the user's total support. Among the alternatives to predatory crime utilized by street opiate users to get over or get by are the following: (1) nonpredatory crime (e.g., selling

National Institute on Drug Abuse (RO1-DA-02355) and the Law Enforcement Assistance Administration (LEAA-J-IAA-005-8), U.S. Department of Justice, under the Omnibus Crime Control and Safe Streets Act of 1968, as amended. Points of view or opinions in this document do not necessarily represent the official position or policies of the U.S. government or the New York State Division of Substance Abuse Services. I wish to thank Bruce Johnson, Ed Preble, and Douglas Lipton for their assistance and critical observations in the preparation of the manuscript.

TABLE 3.1 Demographic Characteristics (n = 51)

	n	Percentage
Race		
Black	31	(61)
Hispanic	14	(27)
White	6	(12)
Sex		
Male	47	(92)
Female	4	(8)
Ever arrested	48	(94)
Ever addicted	43	(84)

NOTE: Mean age = 34. Mean years of use = 12.

drugs), (2) legitimate employment, (3) public support, (4) contributions from friends and/or family, and (5) miscellaneous hustling.

The quantitative data and descriptive accounts of these activities presented below were gathered in the course of a current study of the economic behavior of street opiate users. In this research a storefront office was rented in East Harlem, an area known to be a center of opiate activity. The major methodological approach consists of daily interviews with research subjects. Subjects report to the storefront on a daily basis and are debriefed on their previous day's activities in a fifteen- to twenty-minute structured interview.[2] The initial group of 51 subjects (upon which much of this report is based) reported to the storefront for at least 30 consecutive days. Data reflecting a total of 1883 person-days were collected. Table 3.1 presents basic demographic information on these subjects.

In addition to the regular reporting schedules, field staff spent considerable time with subjects on the streets. Many subjects began to use the storefront as a hangout, even when they were not scheduled to be interviewed. Continuous contact with subjects, and immersion in the social and economic milieux under study, has greatly increased our understanding of the economics of opiate use and provides the basis for this report.

If any single word can describe the essence of how street opiate users "get over," that word is *opportunism*. Subjects were always alert to the smallest opportunity to earn a few dollars. The notion of opportunism is equally relevant to predatory criminality, nonpredatory criminality, employment, and miscellaneous hustling activities.

Many thefts that were reported were the result of sudden, fortuitous circumstances rather than carefully planned capers. A woman's purse was open on the subway. A subject was given money by a stranger to cop (i.e., buy) drugs. A wallet was momentarily left on a department store counter. A truck driver making a delivery failed to lock his truck while inside the store. A purse was left unguarded in a hospital room. A person became inebriated and passed out on the street. A car was left unlocked. All of these events, and others like them, led to thefts.

Predatory crime is the single most important source of cash income for the current sample. Income derived from predatory crime accounted for about 50 percent of total cash income. Nevertheless, many of our subjects were able to survive, and indulge in opiate use, with surprisingly little cash income. The sample as a whole averaged only about $15 per day from predatory crime, although there was considerable variation both among subjects and within the daily activities of individual subjects.

While 47 of the 51 subjects had some income from predatory crime, only 9 or 10 of them could be considered career criminal specialists (e.g., shoplifters, burglars). However, this minority accounted for about 50 percent of the total criminal income. The majority of subjects engaged in theft by "grabbing what they could, when they could."

The practice of bartering, or exchanging services for material goods, is certainly not restricted to opiate users or to urban poverty areas. These practices, however, become even more necessary among individuals who have little or no capital at their disposal, and are widely engaged in by research subjects. Bartering shall be a recurrent theme as the various alternatives to predatory crime are discussed.

In addition to bartering, there are two tactics employed by opiate users that help to alleviate their need for ready cash. In the first, called "getting down," users may pool their cash to make a drug purchase and then share the drugs. For example, Person A has $10 and Person B has $15. A half-quarter of heroin costs about $25. Persons A and B pool their money and "go to the cooker" together. Now, if Person B had had only $12 or $13, but either was a regular customer of a dealer, A and B would probably be able to purchase the half-quarter for their combined $22 or $23. This is called "copping short." Dealers permit regular customers to cop short occasionally, although they may cease to allow it if they believe the customer is doing it too often and abusing the privilege.

NONPREDATORY CRIME[3]

THE DRUG BUSINESS

The major income-producing activity within the category of nonpredatory crime involves working in the drug business. A variety of roles are associated with this enterprise. The examples discussed below are not intended to constitute a complete roster of the role functions found in the drug trade. Rather, they are simply an array of activities that have been observed in the course of the research.

Dealers

While there are individual variations, a rule of thumb regarding payments to street dealers is that for every $100 of heroin sold, the street dealer keeps $40 and returns sixty dollars to "the man" (i.e., the big dealer). For every $100 of cocaine that is sold, the street dealer keeps $25 and returns $75 to "the man." For example, Sonny[4] was paid $30 in cash and 3 ten-dollar bags of heroin for every 10 ten-dollar bags he sold. In this example, Sonny received a combined $60 payment ($30 in cash and $30 in heroin) for every $100 in sales. The reason for this apparent overpayment is that the $30 worth of heroin he received surely did not cost his supplier that amount. According to the rule-of-thumb estimate, it is probable that the heroin in the three bags cost the supplier about $10.[5]

Drug dealing may be engaged in on an infrequent or sporadic basis. It is not necessarily entered into as a full-time or daily occupation. David, for example, was approached by an old friend who was a "big dealer." This dealer told him that one of his regular street dealers had to return to Puerto Rico for a short time and he offered David the street dealer's regular territory. David eagerly accepted, even though he knew the job would only be for a few weeks.

It was not uncommon for big dealers in need of street sellers to approach relatives. Several of the dealing operations that were observed were, at least in part, family operations. Some of the street dealers that were studied worked for their brothers; others worked for cousins. Often, however, these family-drug business relationships were of short duration and involved a "successful" family member throwing some work to a less successful relative who was "down on his luck."

Most subjects in methadone maintenance treatment programs sold some of their dosage at least once during the month they were under study. Ten individuals out of 13 MMTP clients who were observed sold treatment dosages for a total of $935. The street price for methadone was usually $8–$10 a bottle (depending upon the amount of methadone alleged to be in the bottle). Subjects also occasionally swapped their methadone for other drugs, usually cocaine.

Charlie was the only consistent pill dealer that we studied. He went to a doctor once a week and received 30 Valiums and 30 Elavils. He sells the Valiums for 75 cents apiece and the Elavils for 50 cents apiece. He generally buys cheap wine with the proceeds from his pill sales. During a recent week he reported selling 53 of the 60 pills and then getting so drunk that he lost the rest of the pills:

> They must have fell out of my coat. Or I got beat. After I lost my pills I borrowed 4 Elavils from my friend. . . . I can't sleep unless I take Elavils. I'll pay them back Monday when I go to the doctor. Now that I don't have any more pills to sell I'll have to shoplift to get by this weekend.

Pills were sold by other subjects also, but always on a sporadic basis and because some unusual opportunity had presented itself. Steven was offered 500 Valiums for $40. He bought them and quickly resold them for $85. This was his only drug dealing episode in 46 days of daily observation. Keith bought 10 Valiums for $5 and easily resold them for $10.

Holders

Some street dealers will employ other persons physically to hold the drugs that are being sold. They do this to minimize their culpability in case of arrest. Eddie worked for such a dealer. He "held" the drugs while the dealer made the sales. The dealer would take the money and then direct the customers to Eddie. They employed a series of hand signals so that Eddie would know the amount of drugs to dispense. In this way the dealer could never be caught on the streets with drugs in his possession. On a typical day Eddie "held" $200 worth of heroin and $200 worth of cocaine. He received $30 worth of cocaine when all the drugs had been sold.

Touts

"Touts" are persons who spread the word on the streets that a specific dealer's drugs are of high quality. They fulfill an advertising function. They are usually given drugs by the dealer as payment. For example, Frenchy was given a $10 bag of cocaine by a dealer so that he could tell others how good it was. Frenchy said that the cocaine was actually of very poor quality and that while he would tout it to strangers, he would never recommend it to his friends or associates.

Cop Men

There are many reasons why an opiate user will employ another individual to cop (i.e., purchase) drugs for him. Some persons (females and white people especially) may be afraid that if they go to Harlem to buy drugs that they will be "ripped off" (either of their money while on the way to cop, or of their drugs on their way home). Heroin purchasers (especially out-of-towners) frequently do not know which dealers have good-quality heroin, or which can be trusted, and therefore rely on the "cop man's" expertise. Neighborhood opiate users may not want their family, friends, or acquaintances to know that they are using heroin and, therefore, they try to avoid being seen in "copping areas" by utilizing the services of a cop man. The quality of drugs sold by individual dealers varies (usually on a daily basis), and a dealer who had "good stuff" yesterday may be selling "garbage" today. For this reason, many purchasers rely on the cop man to get them good-quality heroin. Some heroin users may be "hot" on the streets and unwilling to leave their apartments (e.g., they have "beaten" somebody and that somebody is after them); therefore they have someone else cop for them.

Individuals who cop drugs for others may be paid at both ends of the transaction. The buyer pays the cop man for his services and the dealer may also. Sometimes the payment is in drugs and sometimes it is in cash. If the buyer and cop man are friends, or close acquaintances, they may "go to the cooker" together (i.e., share the drugs that are purchased).

Cop men have various techniques for maximizing their financial gain in these transactions. Techniques range from modest hustles and conning to outright theft. Cop men may cop short. For example, a buyer gives the cop man $20 to get him two bags of heroin. The cop man buys the two bags for $18 and pockets the extra $2. Or the cop man may inflate the price of the purchase. An individual wishes to buy a quarter of heroin and is told the price is $55. The cop man knows the price is only $50 and will pocket the extra $5. Frenchy was given $65 by a person to buy 13 five-dollar bags of heroin. Frenchy copped 11 bags and slipped in 2 dummies (i.e., bags containing a substance other than heroin), thereby making $10.

Cop men may simply pocket all the money and never return with the drugs. Ulric was given $25 to purchase cocaine. Ulric bought the cocaine, and then used it himself. Isidore was given $200 to cop heroin. He kept the money, saying the would-be purchaser had beaten him for $40 in exactly the same fashion five years earlier and this was a "payback." Paul and two other subjects were given $250 by two "Jersey guys" to cop five quarters of heroin. Our subjects went into a building, ostensibly to buy the drugs, but fled over the roof. They then bought five quarters of heroin and "holed up" for three days in a girl friend's house with two other girls. They shot all the heroin, giving the girls about one quarter. The girls brought them food, cigarettes, and wine.

In order to avoid being victimized, heroin purchasers try to stay on good terms with their cop men. For example, Bobby is a known cop man in the neighborhood. One of his regular customers had somebody else cop for him one day because he could not find Bobby. However, later in the day the two met on the street and the customer gave Bobby a bag of heroin anyway.

Resource Providers

Opiate users may also generate income by providing material resources needed by other addicts, e.g., drug using paraphernalia (such as hypodermic needles and syringes), or a place to "shoot up." Some subjects made money by renting out their "works." Kerwin charged $5 for use of his works, while Bobby charged $3 and Ulric and Vinny charged only $1. Vinny once rented his works to seventeen people in a single day. Ulric obtained possession of some needles and sold thirty of them for $6 to a person operating a "shooting gallery" (i.e., an apartment where narcotics users go to inject drugs). Bat stole ten syringes from a hospital and sold them for $2 apiece. Several subjects permitted their homes to be used as "shooting gallerys," in return for which they usually received a payment in drugs.

Testers

Subjects also received heroin and cocaine in conjunction with testing drugs. Some dealers were not drug users themselves and, hence, could not be certain of the quality of the drugs they possessed. This is an important factor, because if the drugs were of high purity then they could be "hit" or "stepped on" (i.e., diluted) additional times, thus increasing the dealer's profit. Several subjects were given half-quarters of heroin to try in order to report to the dealer on the quality. A current subject functions as a "house connection." She stays in an apartment and distributes drugs to the five "runners" who work for her on the street and who have direct contact with the heroin purchasers. Every morning "the man" comes to the apartment and drops off the daily allotment of drugs. Our subject injects some of the heroin to determine its quality and then informs "the man" how many times it may be "stepped on." She does the cutting and bagging in the apartment and receives both heroin and cash as payment for her work.

OTHER NONPREDATORY CRIME

In addition to the drug business, opiate users engaged in a number of other nonpredatory criminal activities. They are frequently able to get over by acting as middlemen in assorted illicit ventures. Their activities as cop men were described above. Other types of middleman activities relate to the disposal of stolen merchandise. Ulric's friend had just stolen a TV set and did not know what to do with it. Ulric put his friend in touch with a fence and received $10 for his efforts. On another occasion Ulric simply phoned a fence for a friend who had just stolen a stereo and received $10 for this service. Ulric has also served as a "tip-off" man. For example, on one occasion he told two friends that a certain man had money and could be "taken off." His friends committed the robbery, taking $86. Ulric was later given $10 for the tip.

Keith acted as a middleman on a credit card theft. The thief had stolen a woman's purse which contained a credit card. But the thief did not know any woman capable of using the card in stores. Keith supplied a woman for this endeavor and received $100 (the woman received $50 and the original thief earned $100). In another credit card episode a girl stole the card and gave it to Keith and a friend. She told them to get her $40 and to keep whatever else they could get. Keith and his friend used the card to purchase a record player (bought for $229 and sold for $110) and a television set (bought for $120 and sold for $65). They gave the girl the agreed-upon $40 and gave another friend $5 for helping them carry the merchandise. They were left with $130, which they split. Keith thus earned $65.

Bobby steered two people who had stolen a social security check worth $156 to somebody who would cash it. He was given $20.

Selling merchandise that others have stolen is a fairly safe method of getting over, though these opportunities are few because most thieves are able to dispose of their own loot. Steven sold a painting that a friend had stolen for $100 and received $35. Kerwin helped DC sell some meat that she had shoplifted and earned $2. Keith bought a box of stolen kites for $25 and resold them for $100. Frank sold $180 worth of food stamps for a friend and received $60.

Subjects earned money by "watching the backs" of persons engaged in various sorts of dangerous activities. Brad watches the back of a street prostitute he knows and earns between $10 and $30 per day on a fairly regular basis. Brad will also "lay chicky" (be a lookout) for thieves. George earned $20 as a lookout on a truck heist. Vinny earned $20 as a lookout for a shoplifter. Frank earned $25 for watching the back of a street prostitute on a single occasion.

The gambling business is another source of cash for opiate users. Ubie and Dubie both earn at least $10 per day for steering people to "numbers joints." Dubie does this on a fairly regular basis. Quincy occasionally serves as a dealer in illegal card games, earning about $30 each time.

LEGITIMATE EMPLOYMENT

Subjects worked for a total of 254 days (13 percent) of the 1883 person-days studied. Only five subjects had full-time jobs—three as porters, one as a florist, and one as a cab driver. Cab-driving was described as an excellent occupation for an opiate addict. The cab driver is mobile and can easily get to a copping area if in need of drugs. Further, he has sufficient autonomy to take the time to purchase and inject the drugs, and also to "nod out" if the drugs are of good quality.

An additional seventeen subjects worked occasionally at odd jobs (primarily painting apartments, helping people move, and washing cars). Frenchy established a sort of "squatter's rights" to a specific fire hydrant on the block. Other persons knew that this was "his hydrant." He would arrive with his bucket, soap, and brush, and solicit drivers to have their car washed. Street car washes cost between $5 and $15. The majority of subjects doing odd jobs worked two days or less during the study period. Twenty-nine subjects did no legitimate work at all during the study period.

"Legitimate" employment was occasionally colored with illegality. For example, Vinny and one of his friends were approached by a person from Connecticut that had come to New York City to purchase heroin. Vinny copped 28 ten-dollar bags for this person and received 6 ten-dollar bags of heroin as payment for his efforts. Vinny and his friend drove the buyer home to Connecticut and then stole his car. They returned to New York with the car, which they operated as a "gypsy cab" for three days. Vinny earned about $50 during this period. This anecdote aptly illustrates the complex economic realities of street life. In a single episode this subject moved smoothly from nonpredatory crime (copping) to predatory crime (auto theft) to employment (cab-driving). He seized the opportunities available to him at each stage of the episode and got over.

Another example of legitimate employment tainted with illegality concerns Cathy, a young woman who uses large quantities of cocaine and works as a part-time teacher. Cathy's main source of income is shoplifting. She specializes in stealing leather goods, such as pocketbooks and briefcases. She states that she maintains her teaching position for two reasons. First, as a legitimation for her income; second, and more important, as an outlet for stolen goods. She offers the merchandise that she has stolen to the parents of children in her class and thus has a pool of potential buyers that increases each year. She claims that she hardly ever goes to a fence and can generally get better prices from the parents.

Frenchy worked in a menial capacity for two drug dealers. He cleaned their apartment, cooked their meals, and brought them sodas and coffee when they were dealing on the streets. He was paid in heroin for these services.

PUBLIC SUPPORT

Fourteen subjects (27 percent) received public support during the study period. The total amount received by the fourteen was $1800, or an average of $131 over about a month. Persons receiving public support may pool their resources. Eddie, an addict who received disability payments, lived with two women (nonaddicts) who were crippled and also received public support. He would give them his entire check when it arrived and they gave him a daily allowance. The women benefited from having a man around the house and from the contributions taken from his check toward food, rent, and other living expenses. Eddie benefited from having a permanent place to stay and regular meals. His allowance provided him only a small amount of spending money, so he financed his drug use by engaging in both predatory crime (mainly shoplifting) and nonpredatory crime (copping).

A few subjects believed that they got over on welfare through their participation in methadone maintenance treatment programs. In New York, addicts who apply for welfare must be enrolled in treatment as a prerequisite for receiving such payments. Some subjects enrolled for the sole purpose of collecting welfare checks. Bat is an extreme example of this phenomenon. He claims that he *never* consumes his methadone, because he is afraid of getting addicted to it. He brings an empty cup with him to the program and substitutes it for the full cup that he is given. After walking out of the program with the methadone he either sells it or throws it away. He is currently receiving a 70 mg. dosage. He stays on the program because it continuously qualifies him for public assistance. He says that the program is starting to reduce his dosage and that he will start taking the methadone when they cut him down to 20 or 25 mgs.

CONTRIBUTIONS FROM FRIENDS AND FAMILY

Familial and friendship networks provide many basic economic necessities that enable street opiate users to survive with little in the way of cash resources. Free rooms were provided to subjects on 40 percent; free meals on 43 percent; free cigarettes on about 8 percent; and free alcohol was provided on 11 percent of the person-days studied. Other sorts of contributions (e.g., a roll of toilet paper supplied by a friendly local merchant) were given on 1 percent of the person-days.

Many subjects received drugs as a gift. Sometimes an individual would make a "big score," purchase a large quantity of drugs, and invite friends to share with him. A friend of Victor's mugged somebody, purchased a quarter of heroin, and invited Victor to join him. Special occasions, such as birthdays, sometimes elicited a gift of drugs. Friends or relatives who were "doing well" (especially those who were dealing drugs) might bestow a drug gift as an expression of caring and conspicuous generosity. Edith received as a present from her cousin, a "big dealer," eight quarters of heroin (worth about $400) on one occasion. Spouses and lovers were common sources of small gifts of drugs.

While heroin and cocaine, because of their relatively high expense, constituted the most substantial drug gifts, marijuana was the drug most frequently given. A total of $429 worth of marijuana was bestowed on friends or relatives on 166 person-days. Gifts of $1059 worth of heroin (on 37 person-days) and $711 worth of cocaine (on 44 person-days) were given. Further, $100 worth of methadone (on 16 person-days) and $44 worth of pills (on 23 person-days) were given as gifts.

It is difficult to place a cash value on a room provided for the night by a sister or a meal cooked by a girlfriend. However, approximately $175 worth of cigarettes, $450 worth of alcohol, and $250 worth of other contributions were provided to subjects during the study period. It has already been shown that over $2300 worth of drugs were given to subjects by friends or family.

In addition to the material contributions of friends and family, subjects also received direct financial assistance from them. For example, Bobby reported being sick (i.e., in need of heroin) one day until 10:00 p.m. He finally told his brother that he was sick and had not been able to get over all day. His brother asked him how much he would need to "get straight." Bobby said he would need $10, which his brother gave to him. During the study period, subjects received cash contributions of $1241 from friends, $1031 from relatives, and $484 from spouses or paramours—a total of $2756.

MISCELLANEOUS HUSTLING

A subject in our current study has earned the nickname "Señor Go-Go" for his unceasing hustling activities. Any person on his way to pick up or cash a check (employment, welfare) is likely to find himself accompanied by Señor Go-Go. When we decided to modify our sampling procedures and only interview persons who resided on specific blocks, Señor Go-Go volunteered to recruit such persons for a "finder's fee" of $5. He was quite helpful to us in this respect (though we did catch him occasionally trying to sneak in some people from blocks not in the sample). However, one day he began to grumble that $5 was an inadequate payment and he wanted to receive $10 henceforth. When he was told that this was impossible he asked angrily how we expected him to buy a bag of dope for only $5!

Another form of miscellaneous hustling refers to "pimping with a small p." It was found that male subjects often described behaviors in which they "ran a game" on women and obtained some money as a result as "pimping off of them" even though no prostitution was involved. For example, Kenny occasionally dated a nurse. He knew the day that she received her paycheck and he would invariably visit her in the hospital on that day with a story designed to extract money from her (e.g., he needed money to pay back a loan or some guys would kill him). Another subject borrowed money from several women on a fairly continuous basis, always promising to pay it back but never doing so.

Since liquor sales are prohibited on Sundays, several of our subjects earned money by selling wine on that day. They would purchase one or two cases during the week at the regular price and then resell them on Sunday, usually for a markup of $.25 to $.35 a bottle.

Only a few subjects admitted to panhandling, and the proceeds from this activity were never very great. Subjects engaged in panhandling on 17 person-days. The total income derived from this activity was only $61.

BARTERING AND IN-KIND PAYMENTS

It has been noted throughout the preceding discussion of alternatives to predatory crime how bartering, or receiving in-kind payments of drugs for services, is a common occurrence in the lives of our subjects. In fact, approximately 26 percent of all heroin consumed, and 14 percent of all cocaine, was obtained without any cash outlay. Tables 3.2 and 3.3 reveal the cash equivalent amounts of heroin and cocaine received for specific activities, the proportions of total consumption that these amounts represent, and the number and proportion of person-days of drug use on which each activity-for-drugs occurred during the 1883 person-day study period.

Most activities for which payment was made in drugs have been described previously. Dealing drugs and touting or copping for drugs were the major activities in this regard. Drugs were occasionally given to thieves by fences as payment for stolen property. This type of drug bartering rightly belongs in the category of predatory crime as, of course, does stealing heroin or cocaine. Both categories are included in Tables 3.2 and 3.3 to show the full range of behaviors by which drugs may be obtained without cash outlay.

Frenchy stole four women's dresses (worth $28 apiece) and exchanged them for $40 worth of heroin. Keith mugged a person for $7 in cash and a wristwatch, which he exchanged for a half-quarter of heroin (worth $25). Gail, an expert shoplifter, reported an arrangement that she had had previously with a fence but which was no longer in effect during the study period. The fence would give her all the drugs she wished on a daily basis "on credit," and she would turn over all the merchandise she stole to him. At the end of the week there would be an accounting. If Gail had turned over $500 worth of merchandise and received only $450 worth of drugs, the dealer-

TABLE 3.2   Activities for Which Heroin Was Received Without Cash Outlay

	Cash Equiva-lent	Percentage of Total Heroin Consumed	Number of Person-Days	Percentage of Person-Days of Heroin Use
Payment for dealing, touting, or copping	$3626	17.0	131	18.0
Gift	$1059	5.0	37	5.0
Copping short	$ 194	1.0	36	5.0
Stole heroin	$ 175	0.8	3	0.4
Payment for noncriminal activity	$ 160	0.7	14	2
Payoff from fence	$ 158	0.7	3	0.4
Testing heroin	$ 125	0.6	5	0.7
Allowed home to be used as shooting gallery	$ 98	0.5	6	0.8
Use of works	$ 30	0.1	3	0.4
Total	$5625	(26)	238	(33)

TABLE 3.3   Activities for Which Cocaine Was Received Without Cash Outlay

	Cash Equiva-lent	Percentage of Total Cocaine Consumed	Number of Person-Days	Percentage of Person-Days of Cocaine Use
Payment for dealing, touting, or copping	$1745	7.0	72	8.0
Gift	$ 711	3.0	44	5.0
Payoff from fence	$ 380	2.0	6	0.7
Copping short	$ 155	0.7	26	3.0
Allowed house to be used as shooting gallery	$ 115	0.5	4	0.4
Stole cocaine	$ 90	0.4	1	0.1
Payoff for noncriminal activity	$ 70	0.3	5	0.6
Testing cocaine	$ 30	0.1	3	0.3
Watching someone's back	$ 10	0.04	1	0.1
Steering person to somebody selling works	$ 5	0.02	1	0.1
Total	$3311	(14)	163	(18)

fence would give her the remainder in cash. Conversely, if she had received more drugs than the value of the goods she had turned over, then she would be required to pay the difference in cash.

DISCUSSION

Among the street opiate users who were interviewed and observed in this study, predatory crime constituted the largest single source of cash income. However, subjects were shown to have the ability to survive, and to engage in opiate use, with relatively little cash income. Subjects frequently received rooms and meals from friends or relatives at no cost. Subjects also received cash, alcohol, and drugs as gifts from friends or relatives. The bartering of services (especially in the drug business) was shown to be an important vehicle for obtaining drugs (mainly heroin).

With regard to employment, most subjects worked at odd jobs when the opportunity presented itself. Few subjects looked for work in a serious fashion. Rather, a friend or acquaintance might need help moving or painting an apartment. Sometimes the opportunity to work was parlayed into an opportunity to steal, as in the case of the subject who was asked to help somebody move and managed to walk away with an air conditioner in the process.

Conventional wisdom, and much of the social scientific literature on substance use, indicates that narcotics users should be under daily physiological compulsion to obtain sufficient money to support an opiate habit. In fact, our research on the streets of East Harlem challenges traditional thinking in this regard. We have previously reported that observed patterns of opiate consumption do not conform to stereotypical expectations:

> Most heroin users did not use heroin on a daily basis. . . . The dollar amounts of heroin consumed varied greatly from day to day. . . . The concepts of physical dependence, tolerance, and habit size were not particularly useful in helping to understand the varied patterns of daily use. These terms . . . imply a degree of stability in daily use or steady escalation in heroin dosage that is not present in the case histories of these research subjects [Johnson et al., 1979: 24–25].

Further, subjects recruited for the study were given a life history interview (LHI) in which special attention was paid to the year immediately preceding the interview. Data collected on the LHI regarding drug use were then compared with similar data collected from the daily interviews. The vast majority of subjects estimated their average heroin use per day for the previous year to be higher than what they reported on the daily interviews. In fact, the mean daily heroin use reported for the previous year was about four times greater than that reported on current daily interviews. While it is possible that most respondents used substantially less heroin this year than last year, it appears far more likely that daily ethnographic data collection elicited more accurate data than those methods requiring subjects to recall heroin consumption over extended periods of time.

When addicts are asked how much heroin they have used during the course of a year, or longer, they may very well respond in terms of the "ideal" addict—the one they would like to be but, in fact, approximate only infrequently. They may forget about those days when they were not able to get over and, as a result, used little or no heroin. An opiate user who likes to use $50 worth of heroin per day, but may only do so one or two days a week, may still maintain the self-image of a $50-a-day addict, even though his actual consumption may average out to $20 per day or less. Thus, the generally erratic and unstable patterns of generating income and getting over exhibited by subjects in this study are complemented by generally erratic and unstable patterns of heroin consumption.

These observations raise questions regarding the direction of the relationship between criminal activity and drug use. The traditional interpretation is that individuals commit crimes as the result of a drug-induced compulsion. However, the data suggest that, in many cases, subjects who have opportunistically and successfully seized a chance to get over simply use their gains to purchase drugs. Many of these subjects have little in the way of living expenses, are not oriented toward putting money in the bank or making expensive purchases, and really have limited choice in the way they spend illicit earnings. Drug use is a major form of conspicuous consumption among society's outsiders.

At this time it is impossible for us to separate the amount of crime caused by drug use from the amount of drug use caused by the existence of a criminal income. Clearly, the relationship goes in both directions, often for the same individual and perhaps even on the same day. For example, a heroin addict may shoplift some merchandise because of a need for heroin. Having gotten straight from the proceeds of the shoplifting, he may later be asked by some friends to join them in a burglary. He does so, but not out of need for heroin. He has already taken care of his need. Yet, with the proceeds from the burglary he may well purchase and use more drugs (perhaps heroin mixed with cocaine this time).

Careful and probing research is needed to explicate the dynamics underlying both drug use and crime, and the multifaceted relationship between the two phenomena. Ethnographic techniques may well hold the most promise in this regard. Interviewing subjects in institutional settings, or perusing official statistics, is a poor substitute for being with subjects on a daily basis. Participant observation research would probably yield the greatest gains, but there are risks and impracticalities that outweigh the potential gains.

There are few social scientists who could blend into, or adapt to, the dangerous and illicit world of street opiate users. Most researchers would prefer not to be present at a mugging, armed robbery, or drug transaction. Both legal and bodily risk is involved. Further, most subjects prefer to engage in these activities without an audience. They argue that even if they trusted the observer fully, his or her presence might distract them, causing them to make a mistake and suffer physical or legal harm. Finally, subjects' associates (e.g., partners in crime, drug dealers, or customers) might be made uncomfortable by an observer's presence. Our own research methods have evolved in a process of trial and error. We have found that a fixed location (presently a storefront), staffed by a mixture of social scientists and indigenous fieldworkers, and providing a congenial atmosphere, has excellent potential for generating valid and reliable data on a host of issues connected to drug use and crime.

A major question in this research, and one that is intrinsic to most ethnography, relates to generalizability of findings. How representative are the above-described subjects of the universe of opiate users? How representative are they of opiate users in New York City? Indeed, how representative are they of opiate users in East Harlem? In addition to the question of representativeness of subjects is the question of representativeness of situation. For example, much of this research was done at a time when narcotics users were bemoaning the poor quality of heroin that was available on the streets. Some opiate users claimed that the potency was so low that it was possible to ingest $100 worth of heroin and not even feel it; or that they could use $50 to $100 worth of heroin daily for an extended duration and not get "strung out" (i.e., physically dependent). It is possible that during times of heightened heroin potency many narcotics users would exhibit more of the conventional symptoms of addiction (e.g., escalation of daily dosage) and stereotypical concommitant behaviors (e.g., increased predatory criminal activity).

It is evident from over two years of research on the streets of East Harlem that the subjects described in this report are fairly typical of the universe of East Harlem opiate users. No claims can be made, however, as to their representativeness in terms of larger universes. Nevertheless, the foregoing data portray at least a stratum of narcotics users that do not conform to conventional expectations of opiate use patterns and criminality. The empirical question that remains concerns how large this stratum is in the universe of opiate users. In the future we shall be concentrating on introducing new sampling techniques in order to increase the generalizability of our data and address this critical issue. New research operations will begin in dissimilar socioeconomic areas in order to generate comparative data.

In summary, the street opiate users that have been observed thus far tend to engage in drug use and criminal activity on a relatively erratic basis. Opportunism is the key notion. When the opportunities are there, most subjects are sufficiently astute to seize them. When the opportunities are not there, most subjects survive. A regular or substantial cash income is not necessary because many necessities of life, such as food, are frequently provided by friends or relatives and, further, the bartering of goods or services is a common facet of everyday existence. Factors such as these reduce the compulsion of street opiate users to engage in income-generating predatory crime.

NOTES

1. For a full discussion of this phenomenon, see Goldstein (1979: 45–52 and passim).

2. Special credit for data collection must be extended to Tom Miller, Senior Community Worker.

3. No in-depth examination of predatory crime will be undertaken in this report. It was the subject of a previous paper (Goldstein and Duchaine, 1979), and the wide scope of that topic necessitates omission at this time. Included in the category of nonpredatory crime are such activities as selling drugs or performing functions within the drug business, the so-called victimless crimes (e.g., prostitution, gambling), and acting in certain secondary roles associated with predatory crime (e.g., selling goods that someone else has stolen).

4. All names used in this report are fictitious.

5. Opiate-using prostitutes sometimes cite this factor as a reason for refusing to accept payment in drugs for sexual services. They argue that if their services cost $20, and they are offered two $10 bags, they are "getting beat" because the two bags probably did not cost the customer $20. If he is a dealer, those two bags may only have cost him $5 or $10.

REFERENCES

GOLDSTEIN, P. J. (1979) Prostitution and Drugs. Lexington, MA: D. C. Heath.
———— and N. S. DUCHAINE (1979) "Daily criminal activities of street drug users." Presented at the meetings of the American Society of Criminology, Philadelphia.
JOHNSON, B. D., P. J. GOLDSTEIN, and N. S. DUCHAINE (1979) "What is an addict? theoretical perspectives and empirical patterns of opiate use." Presented at the meetings of the Society for the Study of Social Problems, Boston.

4

WOMEN, CRIME, AND DRUGS

SUSAN K. DATESMAN

The relationship between drug use and crime has been the focus of innumerable studies. While our knowledge of this relationship is far from exact, it has been developed, for the most part, through the study of male populations. Relatively few studies exist in this area that have used female populations, and most of these have appeared within the past decade. Although both drug use and crime are considered to be major social problems, the implicit reference has usually been to male drug use and crime. The most obvious reason for this relative neglect of women is that the vast majority of known drug users and criminals are men. According to the FBI's Uniform Crime Reports, women accounted for only 16 percent of the total arrests in 1977 and made up only 13.9 percent of the arrests for drug abuse violations (Federal Bureau of Investigation, 1978).

It is not just a matter of numbers, however. In the latter part of the nineteenth century, when the majority of addicts were middle-class white women, addiction was not regarded as a social problem of any consequence. Beginning with the Harrison Act in 1914, however, a series of events occurred that linked addiction with crime. As the addict population became typified by lower-class black males, moral hostility increased and "the image of the addict changed from a sick to a contemptible deviant" (Conrad and Schneider, 1980: 128). Addiction had become a social problem.

In addition to statistical insignificance, female drug use and crime have not been considered as major social problems because of the nature of their drug use and criminal activity. A number of studies have found that males are more likely to use drugs obtained illegally, while females are more likely to use drugs obtained legally (O'Donnell, 1969; Williams and Bates, 1970; Suffet and Brotman, 1976). One survey of New York State residents reported that the drugs with the lowest percentages of female users were methedrine, solvents and inhalants, heroin, cocaine, and marijuana, including hashish (Chambers, 1972). The highest percentages of female users were reported for diet pills, nonheroin narcotics, stimulants other than amphetamines and cocaine, antidepressants, and relaxants or minor tranquilizers. Since female drug use has involved primarily licit substances, it has not evoked the same degree of public concern as illicit drug use, with its presumed direct connection to crime.

Similarly, the public generally reacts less severely to crimes typically associated with women than to those typically associated with men. The public seems to view male law violation as "real" crime which is dangerous, serious, often organized, and injurious to the social order. Female crimes, on the other hand, are commonly seen as victimless, most harmful to the offender, and having minimal impact on the social order. According to official statistics, women are involved mostly in nonviolent and property crimes. For example, UCR data for 1977 indicate that the female percentage of arrests exceeded their overall arrest rate of 16 percent only in the categories of larceny, forgery and counterfeiting, fraud, embezzlement, prostitution, disorderly conduct, vagrancy, curfew, and running away from home (FBI, 1978).

The fact that female drug use and crime have not typically been considered as social problems has implications for the amount of research attention devoted to these subjects. Traditional social scientists have tended to concentrate their research in those areas that have been officially recognized as social problems. A practical reason for this focus is that research funds tend to be more readily available when a problem area has been officially identified. The failure to become a major social problem has meant that monies to study female drug use and crime have been limited, which in turn has been at least partly responsible for the lack of interest in these topics. When research monies have been allocated to study female drug use, they have most often been to examine the effects of female drug use on sexual behavior, pregnancy and children.[1]

The women's movement that emerged in the late 1960s has been linked by some to increases in the rates of female drug use and crime, particularly crime that is serious and violent (see, for example, Adler, 1975; Suffet and

Brotman, 1976). According to the UCR, however, the percentage of total arrests accounted for by females increased only about 5 percent between 1960 and 1977.[2] Moreover, the largest increases in the female percentage of arrests have occurred for nonviolent and property crimes, mostly larceny and fraud, and, to a lesser extent, forgery and counterfeiting and embezzlement. The female percentage of arrests for drug abuse violations, on the other hand, has remained relatively stable since 1960. At the same time, arrests for drug abuse violations have increased as a percentage of total female arrests, making up only 1 percent of all female arrests in 1960 but 5.5 percent in 1977.

The available evidence does not indicate that the women's movement has had a significant impact on the observed changes in female crime (Datesman and Scarpitti, 1980: 355–376). These changes can more likely be attributed to other factors, including increased opportunities for shoplifting and welfare fraud, the willingness of merchants to prosecute shoplifting and employee theft, and especially greater economic pressures on women. The women's movement has, however, been influential in creating an interest in studying female drug use and crime, along with other areas in which women had not previously been studied or inadequately studied. While the relationship between female drug use and crime is still an understudied area, most of the studies that do exist have appeared since 1970. The remainder of this chapter will review and critique these contemporary studies, after first placing female drug use and crime in historical context. Data will also be presented from a large, ongoing study of drug use and crime that includes women as research subjects in an effort to provide a more complete picture of female addiction and crime. A final section will assess the current state of our knowledge in this area and identify future research needs.

HISTORICAL CONTEXT OF
FEMALE DRUG USE AND CRIME

Prior to the passage of the Harrison Act in 1914, the majority of addicts were women. Cuskey et al. (1972) reviewed a number of studies covering the period before the Civil War to about 1920, all showing the high ratio of female to male addicts (1972: 10–11). During this period, over-the-counter medicines with a very high narcotic content were readily available. Medical journals frequently reported cases of fatal opium poisoning caused by popular medicines such as Mrs. Winslow's Soothing Syrup and Dr. Bull's Cough Syrup (Haller and Haller, 1974: 285). Furthermore, physicians freely prescribed narcotics for a wide variety of ills. A leading crusader against opium addiction in the late nineteenth century estimated that over 80 percent of these cases could be attributed to prescription drugs (Haller and Haller, 1974: 291). Ironically, many of the so-called cures for addiction also had a high opium content (Terry and Pellens, 1928: 88; Haller and Haller, 1974: 294).

F. E. Oliver, a physician during this period, linked the high incidence of female addiction to the stigma attached to alcohol use compared with the relative respectability of using medicines that contained opium. "As teeto-talers," Oliver said, "[women] avoided the disdain of husbands and friends by pointing to the delicious syrups, nervines, and tonics made from roots, herbs, and barks, or rich in animal organisms, that supplied all their extra nutritional needs" (Haller and Haller, 1974: 279). Primary among the rea-sons for women's addiction, according to a report by the Michigan state board of health in 1878, was "to relieve painful menstruation and diseases of the female organs of generation" (Terry and Pellens, 1928: 96). Housewives used opium to relieve household cares (Haller and Haller, 1974: 281) while society women used it "to calm their shattered nerves" after "a trying season of parties and social functions" (Terry and Pellens, 1928: 114). The high addiction rate among women was also blamed on "their more nervous orga-nization and tendency to hysterical and chronic diseases" (Haller and Haller, 1974: 282). A further cause of addiction among women, according to F. E. Oliver, was the "vicious mode of life" as a prostitute, while another observer noted that "almost every brothel has its victims" (Terry and Pellens, 1928: 94, 114).

Female addiction has been most often linked with crime in the form of prostitution, which typically has been regarded as the female equivalent of crime. Lombroso (1911: 192), for example, stated that "prostitution largely takes the place of crime in women, thus explaining why women seem less criminal than men." The relationship between addiction and prostitution has been frequently pointed to in the historical literature. In 1880, for example, a study of opium use among the customers of fifty Chicago druggists found that females outnumbered males three to one, and that the largest group of women addicts were prostitutes. This latter finding was also reported by the Michigan and Massachusetts state boards of health and by the Chicago Vice Commission (Haller and Haller, 1974: 282). Further, Emma Goldman, while imprisoned on Blackwell's Island in New York, noted that the prison received a large influx of women prisoners in March 1894, nearly all prosti-tutes and nearly all habitual users of narcotics (1931: 141).

In the early nineteenth century, it became widely believed that drugs were frequently employed to lure innocent and unsophisticated young girls into prostitution (Lemert, 1951: 254–255). Bingham Dai, in his investigation of drug abuse in Chicago during the early 1930s, stated that it was "a matter of common knowledge" that a pimp attempting to entice a girl into prostitution "not seldom 'dopes' her and makes her an addict so that she will have to depend on him for her drug and thereby becomes his woman" (1937: 136). This variant of the white slavery myth has since been repudiated by numerous researchers. MacNamara and Sagarin, for example, state that many women remain in prostitution because of dependence on drugs, but that "their activities are sufficiently voluntary to distinguish these individuals from [white slaves]" (1977: 117–118). Lemert (1951: 255) suggested that prostitutes themselves may have played a part in propagating this myth in order to arouse sympathy in their clients and discount responsibility for their own involvement in prostitution. The myth of white slavery also fits well with the stereotype of the weak and submissive female and the notion that no woman would make a deliberate, rational choice to enter into such a life (Goldstein, 1979: 88).

It has also been suggested that female addicts may be forced into prostitution to support an expensive drug habit. One observer of the drug scene during the 1930s stated:

> Logically, criminality is bound to begin in a case of morphanism the moment the economic margin above living expenses is not sufficient to cover the purchase of the habitual amount of the drug. . . . Prostitution in women, stealing in one form or another in men, are the rule (cited in Inciardi, 1980: 215).

Others noted that prostitutes might also use drugs to "help them endure the strain of their unpleasant business" (Woolston, 1921: 56; see also Terry and Pellens, 1928: 499).

CONTEMPORARY PERSPECTIVES ON FEMALE DRUG USE AND CRIME

As noted earlier, the majority of addicts at present are male. The transition from female to male predominance in opiate use occurred after the passage of the Harrison Act in 1914 (Cuskey et al., 1972: 12). The purpose of the Harrison Act was ostensibly to make the process of drug distribution in the United States a matter of record (Lindesmith, 1965: 3–8). Addicts were required to obtain their drugs from physicians registered under the Act and records of transactions had to be kept. The Harrison Act was broadened, however, by a series of three Supreme Court decisions that linked addiction with crime. These Court decisions made illegal the prescription of drugs for addicts by physicians and the possession of drugs by addicts. Among the consequences of criminalizing addiction were the emergence of an addict subculture, the creation of a criminal drug underworld, the promotion of the image of the dope fiend, and a change in the population of addicts (Conrad and Schneider, 1980: 116, 143). While the typical nineteenth-century addict was middle-aged, rural, middle-class, white, and female, the typical twentieth-century addict is young, urban, lower-class, a member of a minority group, and male. When addiction became associated with crime, male addicts began to outnumber female addicts, since women, because of social role and lack of opportunity, could not as easily obtain illegal drugs.

As was the case historically, addiction and prostitution continue to be linked in the contemporary literature. A literature search revealed that estimates of the proportion of female addicts that are prostitutes ranges from about 30 percent to as high as 90 percent (see, for example, Ellinwood et al., 1966; Chambers et al., 1970; Chambers and Inciardi, 1971; Cushman, 1971, 1972; Inciardi and Chambers, 1972; File et al., 1974; Rosenbaum, 1975; Weissman and File, 1976; Binion, 1977; Haskell and Yablonsky, 1978). There is some evidence, however, that addicts who engage in prostitution frequently engage in other criminal activities as well. File et al. (1974), for example, found that a third of their sample of addicted female arrestees had been arrested for both prostitution and serious crimes, while 7 percent had only prostitution charges and the remainder had only nonprostitution charges.

Further, several studies have shown that the criminal involvement of addicts who engage in prostitution may differ from that of addicts who do not engage in prostitution. In the File et al. study, the arrest rate for addict/ prostitutes was almost three times as high as that for addicts. Addict/ prostitutes were more likely than addicts to be arrested at least once for larceny, robbery, assault, or homicide, while approximately equal percentages had been arrested for burglary, weapons offenses, and gambling. The percentage of addicts ever arrested exceeded that of addict/prostitutes for only two offenses, drug possession or sale and liquor offenses.

Similar findings were reported in another study by James et al. (1976, 1979). In general, addict/prostitutes were much more likely than addicts to be criminally involved both as juveniles and as adults. Juvenile arrests were reported by about 64 percent of the addict/prostitutes but only by about 40 percent of the addicts. In addition, 10 percent of the addict/prostitutes had more than six juvenile arrests as compared with less than 2 percent of the addicts. As adults, addict/prostitutes were more involved in shoplifting, forgery, and larceny than addicts. This study also found that prostitution was the most frequent charge for addict/prostitutes, while addicts were most often arrested on drug charges.

The high incidence of prostitution among female addicts has led several researchers to examine the direction of involvement between addiction and prostitution, that is, whether addiction precedes prostitution or prostitution precedes addiction. The sequence of involvement between addiction and prostitution is not altogether clear, however. One observer has stated that "many prostitutes become heroin addicts and vice versa. It is impossible to say which is the more prevalent life course" (Maglin, 1974: 162). Similarly, Winick and Kinsie (1971: 68), in their comprehensive study of prostitution in the United States, stated that "it is not possible to say with any certainty what proportion of prostitutes became drug addicts before or after their entrance into the vocation." They estimated that half of the prostitutes in large cities were addicts and that many had become addicted simultaneously with entry into prostitution.

Two more recent studies also report mixed findings on the sequential relationship between addiction and prostitution. Of the 50 addict/prostitutes interviewed by James, 48 percent reported addiction concurrent with prostitution, and 38 percent reported addiction after prostitution. She concluded, therefore, that "one cannot argue that prostitution leads to addiction or vice versa" (1976: 610). Similarly, of the 27 addict/prostitutes interviewed by Goldstein (1979: 72), 48 percent were addicted prior to prostitution, 41 percent were addicted following prostitution, and 7 percent were addicted concurrently with prostitution.

The more general question of whether crime precedes addiction among women or vice versa has also been investigated. One study of 54 women who had been patients at the Lexington Hospital found that only 7 percent had been arrested before addiction, while 26 percent had been arrested after addiction (O'Donnell, 1966). In another study of 52 female addicts certified to the New York State Narcotic Addiction Control Commission, 10 percent had been arrested prior to addiction and 65 percent had been arrested following addiction; some 60 percent had been arrested for drug law violations since becoming addicted (Chambers, 1974).

Other research has extended the investigation of the crime and addiction sequence among women to include various kinds of drugs. For example, Voss and Stephens (1973) found that only 12 percent of their sample of 217 female addicts at the Lexington Hospital admitted arrest prior to their first use of drugs, including alcohol and marijuana. When the use of alcohol and marijuana were excluded, however, 34 percent admitted arrest before the use of other drugs. Finally, 39 percent admitted arrest before the use of narcotics, including heroin.

Further information on the sequence of crime and drug use among female

TABLE 4.1

	Addicts	Addict/Prostitutes
First criminal involvement	12.0	10.9
First juvenile arrest	14.3	13.7
First drug use	15.9	15.6
First narcotics use	20.1	18.3
Addiction	21.1	20.0
First adult arrest	21.8	20.4

addicts and addict/prostitutes was presented by James et al. (1976, 1979). A comparison of the mean ages at the various stages of crime and drug use showed the sequence given in Table 4.1. Although the sequence was the same for both addicts and addict/prostitutes, it generally occurred somewhat earlier for addict/prostitutes than for addicts.

Any conclusions or implications drawn from the above studies, however, must be viewed as tentative at best. The relevance of much of this research to any generalizations about the relationship among women, crime, and drugs is weakened by certain methodological problems. A major limitation of most of this research is that the populations under study were typically addicts under arrest or clients of treatment programs. This focus is understandable, since such users are more identifiable and accessible to researchers than are addicts in the community. It is unclear, however, to what extent identified users are representative of active users. For example, do active users engage in the same kinds of crimes and follow the same sequence of crime and drug use as users identified by criminal justice and treatment agencies?

The biases involved in identifying arrest and treatment populations have been well documented. Arrests, for example, reflect only crimes that become known to the police and cannot take into account what victimization surveys have shown to be large amounts of unreported crime (see Law Enforcement and Assistance Administration, 1977). In addition, arrests are biased by the exercise of discretion by police officers and by the relative efficiency of police agencies. Clearance rates vary widely for different types of crimes, and addict criminality has been shown to be heavily biased in the direction of those crimes that have the lowest clearance rates, such as robberies and property offenses (Research Triangle Institute, 1976: 59–63). Clients of treatment programs may also not be representative of active users. For example, studies of drug users in jails, prisons, and criminal justice diversion programs indicate that substantial numbers have never been in treatment (Research Triangle Institute, 1976: 90).

Moreover, most studies of women, crime, and drugs have not only relied on users identified by criminal justice and treatment agencies, but have also used the statistics generated by those agencies as a measure of criminal activity. Arrest statistics, as noted above, reflect only known crimes that have been acted upon by the police and, thus, are an unknown and unrepresentative estimate of an individual's criminal activity. For example, one study of the unreported criminal behavior of drug addicts found that only one crime was cleared by arrest for every 120 offenses committed (Inciardi and Chambers, 1972: 57). Finally, it is widely recognized that arrest statistics may be at least as responsive to organizational and political needs and demands as to "real" criminal activity, and may, in fact, be a more accurate measure of the former than of the latter.

Other limitations of much of the research done to date include using fairly small samples and collecting only a small amount of information, so that only a limited number of questions concerning the relationship between addiction and crime among women can be addressed.

A study is now in progress that attempts to overcome the more serious shortcomings of previous studies and provide a more complete picture of the relationship between female addiction and crime.[3] The following section focuses on data collected as part of that study.

FEMALE DRUG USE AND CRIME IN MIAMI, FLORIDA

The findings reported here are based on interviews conducted in Miami, Florida, during 1978 with 153 female heroin users who were active in the community. Contacts within the Miami drug community were used as starting points for the interviews. At some point during the interview, after rapport had been established, the interviewer requested the names of other active heroin users known to the respondent. These users were then approached for an interview and the process was continued until that particular network of users had been exhausted. Another known user was then contacted and the process was repeated. In this way, former users and those only peripherally connected to the drug community were eliminated and respondents were restricted to currently active users.

Because of the problems with official statistics discussed above, the data in this study were all derived from self-reports. In general, studies have shown that self-report data obtained from drug users tend to be both reliable and valid (see Ball, 1967; Stephens, 1972; Amsel et al., 1976). Measures used in the present study to encourage valid and reliable reporting included (1) using experienced interviewers familiar with the Miami drug community; (2) assuring respondents of complete confidentiality and anonymity; (3) enhancing respondent recall through interviewing techniques and ques-

TABLE 4.2

Lifetime Arrests	Percentage of Total
Prostitution and person and/or property crime	36.6
Prostitution only	15.0
Person and/or property crime only	28.8
Other crime only	19.6
Total	100.0

tionnaire construction; (4) building intraquestionnaire reliability checks into the interview schedule; and (5) reinterviewing a sample of users to check for interquestionnaire reliability as well as to detect the falsification of interview schedules by interviewers.

Because of the emphasis in both the historical and the contemporary literature on the link between addiction and prostitution, the analysis is presented for three female user groups created on the basis of their self-reported involvement in prostitution during the twelve months prior to interview:

- Group I (users/nonprostitutes)—users who reported no involvement in prostitution during the twelve months prior to interview;

- Group II (users/prostitutes)—users who reported between 1 and 125 acts of prostitution during the twelve months prior to interview (25.4 median);

- Group III (users/prostitutes)—users who reported 126 or more acts of prostitution during the twelve months prior to interview (252.1 median).

The findings are divided into two sections. The first deals with the types of offenses committed by the female addicts in this sample, while the second deals with their sequence of drug use and criminal behavior.

TYPES OF OFFENSES

Initially, the pattern of association between prostitution and other offenses was examined for the total sample of female addicts. The results (see Table 4.2) were obtained based on the arrest histories of the women. As can be seen, only a small percentage of these female addicts had been arrested exclusively for prostitution, while the largest percentage had been arrested for both prostitution and serious crimes. This latter group also had the highest mean number of lifetime arrests (7.84), followed by those arrested only for prostitution (6.17), serious crimes (4.32), and other crimes (0.60). When only arrests for person and property offenses were considered, however, the mean number of lifetime arrests was slightly higher for those

TABLE 4.3

Current Criminal Activity	Percentage of Total
Prostitution and person and/or property crime	67.3
Prostitution only	3.9
Person and/or property crime only	20.9
Other crime only	7.8
Total	100.0

addicts arrested for only serious crimes (2.61) than for those also arrested for prostitution (2.36).

Somewhat different results were obtained, however, when admitted criminal activity during the twelve months prior to interview was used as the basis for classification rather than arrest histories. The results are given in Table 4.3. On the basis of current criminal activity, a full two-thirds of the sample admitted involvement in both prostitution and serious crimes, while less than 4 percent limited their criminal activities to prostitution. Again, those addicts involved in both prostitution and serious offenses had the highest mean number of lifetime arrests, while those involved in only serious crimes had been arrested slightly more often for person and property offenses.

Table 4.4 shows the current criminal activity of the women for each of 22 specific types of illegal behavior. About 29 percent of the sample reported no involvement in prostitution during the twelve months prior to interview (users/nonprostitutes), while about 71 percent reported at least one instance of prostitution (users/prostitutes). As can be seen, the most frequent offense for users/nonprostitutes and users with lower involvement in prostitution was drug sales, which constituted over half of the total offenses reported by the former group and about two-fifths of those reported by the latter group. Drug sales was the second most frequent offense for users with higher involvement in prostitution, but accounted for only 15.9 percent of their total offenses. Prostitution was the most frequent offense for this latter group, making up over half of their total offenses, and was ranked third for users with lower involvement in prostitution, accounting for about a fifth of their total offenses. Shoplifting also accounted for about a fifth of the offenses of users with lower involvement in prostitution and 16.2 percent of the offenses for users/nonprostitutes, but only 10.4 percent of those of users with higher involvement in prostitution.

These data also show that all of the users/prostitutes and 86.4 percent of the users/nonprostitutes engaged in criminal activity during the twelve months prior to interview. In general, the participation rates of users/

TABLE 4.4 Current Criminal Activity of Active Female Heroin Users in Miami, Florida (1978)

Involvement in Prostitution: Offense	Percentage of Total Offenses			Percentage of Sample Involved		
	I (n=44)	II (n=54)	III (n=54)	I (n=44)	II (n=54)	III (n=54)
Robbery	1.9	0.5	1.5	18.2	24.1	13.0
Assault	0.2	0.1	<0.1	9.1	7.4	11.1
Burglary	1.5	0.5	0.3	20.5	20.4	24.1
Vehicle theft	0.1	<0.1	<0.1	6.8	1.9	3.7
Theft from vehicle	0.4	0.3	0.6	15.9	13.0	31.5
Shoplifting	16.2	21.4	10.4	54.5	77.8	83.3
Picking pockets	0.6	0.1	2.9	2.3	5.6	9.3
Prostitute theft	0.0	3.1	4.8	0.0	61.1	72.2
Other theft	0.6	2.2	1.4	11.4	31.5	20.4
Forgery	6.4	1.5	1.3	25.0	31.5	31.5
Con games	1.2	1.1	0.5	6.8	25.9	24.1
Receiving stolen goods	3.9	4.4	2.6	22.7	50.0	42.6
Prostitution	0.0	19.2	52.7	0.0	100.0	100.0
Procuring	11.5	2.8	2.3	9.1	31.5	16.7
Drug sales	53.7	39.5	15.9	65.9	88.9	81.5
Arson	<0.1	0.0	0.1	2.3	0.0	3.7
Vandalism	<0.1	<0.1	<0.1	2.3	3.7	3.7
Fraud	0.6	<0.1	0.2	6.8	3.7	9.3
Gambling	0.9	3.1	2.2	18.2	27.8	25.9
Extortion	0.0	<0.1	0.1	0.0	3.7	5.6
Loan-sharking	0.0	<0.1	0.0	0.0	1.9	0.0
Alcohol offense	0.0	0.1	<0.1	0.0	3.7	9.3
Other offense	0.3	0.0	<0.1	4.5	0.0	1.9
Total	100.0	100.0	100.0	86.4	100.0	100.0

prostitutes were higher than those of users/nonprostitutes. Excluding prostitution offenses, the highest proportions of all users, regardless of prostitution status, admitted involvement in drug sales and shoplifting. About two-thirds of the users/nonprostitutes, as compared to 88.9 percent of the users with lower involvement in prostitution and 81.5 percent of those with higher involvement, reported selling drugs. Similarly, only 54.5 percent of the users/nonprostitutes, but 77.8 percent of the users with lower involvement in prostitution and 83.3 percent of those with higher involvement, admitted engaging in shoplifting. Users/prostitutes also had higher participation rates than users/nonprostitutes for prostitute theft, receiving stolen goods, other theft, forgery, con games, and gambling.

SEQUENCE OF DRUG USE AND CRIME

Table 4.5 shows the mean ages of initiation into the various stages of drug use and crime for the female addicts in the sample. Those users who were more heavily involved in prostitution at the time of interview were somewhat older than the other users when they first used alcohol and became intoxicated. Users with current involvement in prostitution were also older than users/nonprostitutes when they first used drugs and marijuana, although they were somewhat younger when they first tried barbiturates and cocaine. Heroin use and continuous heroin use occurred at aproximately the same ages for all three user groups. The largest differences occurred with respect to the mean age at first crime, with the users who were currently less involved in prostitution not committing their first crime until about two years after those with greater involvement in prostitution, and about a year and a

TABLE 4.5   Mean Ages at Initiation into Drug Use and Crime of Active
Female Heroin Users in Miami, Florida (1978)

Involvement in Prostitution:	I (n = 24)	II (n = 40)	III (n = 43)
First alcohol use	13.7	13.4	14.4
First alcohol intoxication	13.8	13.7	14.4
First drug use	14.3	15.1	15.0
First marijuana use	14.5	15.2	15.2
First crime	15.5	17.1	15.0
First barbiturate use	17.9	17.4	17.1
First arrest	17.5	18.8	17.8
First heroin use	18.8	19.0	19.1
First cocaine use	20.0	19.6	19.0
First continuous heroin use	19.4	19.5	19.7

half after the users/nonprostitutes. A similar but weaker difference can be seen for mean age at first arrest, with users less involved in prostitution experiencing a first arrest about a year after the other users.

With respect to the sequence of drug use and crime, there was a progression from alcohol use to drug use to crime to arrest to heroin use among users/nonprostitutes and those less involved in prostitution. Among those more involved in prostitution, however, alcohol use occurred first, followed by first drug use concurrent with first crime, then arrest and heroin use.

Table 4.6 shows the percentages of the female users who committed their first crimes prior to, concurrent with, or following their use of various drug classes. The patterns for alcohol intoxication and drug use were similar for users/nonprostitutes and users reporting heavier current involvement in prostitution. Approximately half of these women had committed their first

TABLE 4.6   Percentage of Crime Occurring Before and After Drug Use Among Active Female Heroin Users in Miami, Florida (1978)

Involvement in Prostitution:	I (n = 24)	II (n = 40)	III (n = 43)
	Alcohol Intoxication		
Crime before drug use	37.5	10.0	37.2
Crime concurrent with drug use	12.5	10.0	11.6
Crime after drug use	50.0	80.0	51.2
Total	100.0	100.0	100.0
	Drug Use		
Crime before drug use	20.8	10.0	34.9
Crime concurrent with drug use	25.0	20.0	14.0
Crime after drug use	54.2	70.0	51.2
Total	100.0	100.0	100.0
	Heroin Use		
Crime before drug use	70.8	67.5	81.4
Crime concurrent with drug use	12.5	7.5	7.0
Crime after drug use	16.7	25.0	11.6
Total	100.0	100.0	100.0
	Continuous Heroin Use		
Crime before drug use	70.8	67.5	83.7
Crime concurrent with drug use	20.8	7.5	4.7
Crime after drug use	8.3	25.0	11.6
Total	100.0	100.0	100.0

crime either before or concurrent with alcohol intoxication or drug use (excluding alcohol and marijuana), or else afterwards. On the other hand, those users with lesser involvement in prostitution were much more likely to have committed their first crime after they first became intoxicated or tried drugs. When only heroin use is considered, however, then crime is clearly a post-drug phenomenon. The vast majority of these female addicts had already committed their first crimes by the time they tried heroin.

DISCUSSION

At this point, certain tentative conclusions concerning the relationship between female drug use and crime can be drawn from the available evidence. First, the evidence indicates that female drug users commit a significant amount of crime, primarily of a nonviolent and income-generating nature. Female drug users tend to be involved primarily in prostitution, drug sales, and shoplifting, although they do engage in a wide variety of other offenses as well. This general conclusion is supported whether the female addicts are arrestees, patients in treatment, or active users in the community. It appears, however, that most studies using arrest or treatment populations have tended to overstate the relationship between female drug use and prostitution. In the Miami study, only 4 percent of the active female users were involved exclusively in prostitution during the twelve months prior to interview. Prostitution offenses accounted for about 37 percent of the total offenses of these women, followed by drug sales, which constituted about 27 percent, and shoplifting, which made up about 14 percent. They tended to avoid the violent crimes of robbery and assault, which together accounted for only about 1 percent of their total offenses.

Female addicts, then, like female criminals in general, tend to commit crimes that are consistent with traditional female roles. For example, Rosenblum (1975) suggests that the attributes of prostitution are present in the nondeviant female sex role. She maintains that women in general are socialized to use their sexuality for gain in nonsexual interaction, and that prostitution requires only an exaggeration of this situation. In addition, prostitution can be seen as one response to the double standard whereby society tolerates nonmarital sexuality to a greater extent for males than for females. Prostitution provides an outlet for male sexuality by creating a group of women who are willing to exchange their sexuality for payment at the risk of both moral and legal censure. Legal censure also reflects the double standard, in that prostitution laws often apply to or are enforced against only female prostitutes and not against male prostitutes or male clients (Rosenbleet and Pariente, 1973). Ethnographic studies have found that addict/prostitutes engage in prostitution only as an expedient means to support their drug habits and do not have a commitment to prostitution as a lifestyle (James, 1976; Goldstein, 1979).

Shoplifting and drug sales also reflect certain aspects of the traditional female role. For example, since women have the primary responsibility for buying most family necessities, they have a greater opportunity to shoplift than men. Dependence as an aspect of the female role is also present when female addicts who shoplift rely on an "old man" for protection or to dispose of the stolen items (Sutter, 1970; File, 1976). Similarly, there is some evidence that female addicts who sell drugs are usually involved in a dealing partnership with a male with whom they have some kind of personal relationship, again for protection (File, 1976).

While addicts and addict/prostitutes appear to engage in the same types of criminal behavior, there does appear to be some utility in distinguishing between these two groups. In general, both arrest and self-report data indicate that addict/prostitutes are more involved in criminal behavior than addicts, even when prostitution offenses are excluded. In the Miami data, however, the female users currently reporting involvement in only serious crimes were slightly more likely to have been arrested for person and property crimes than those reporting current involvement in both prostitution and serious crimes. In addition, the Miami data suggest that the extent of involvement in prostitution may also be a potentially discriminating factor. For example, users/nonprostitutes and users with lesser involvement in prostitution both reported drug sales as their most frequent current criminal activity, whereas those with higher involvement most often reported prostitution.

Conclusions regarding the temporal sequence of drug use and crime among women are more ambiguous and less certain. The female addicts studied by James et al. (1976) reported a progression from crime to drug use to addiction to arrest. Among the active female heroin users in Miami, however, alcohol and drug use occurred first, followed by crime, then arrest, and finally addiction. The sequence was somewhat modified for the users reporting more involvement in prostitution, with drug use and crime occurring concurrently. At this point, the safest conclusion would be that for the vast majority of female addicts, crime precedes the onset of addiction. As with male drug use and crime, however, it does not appear that a simple cause-and-effect relationship exists. Freda Adler (1975: 77), for example, has suggested that addiction and prostitution may be merely simultaneously occurring elements of a deviant lifestyle.

There is obviously a need for further research in the area of female drug use and crime. As discussed earlier, there are serious methodological problems that restrict the validity of much of the previous work in this area. Studies of the sort currently being conducted in Miami need to be replicated with other populations in order to obtain a better understanding of the relationship between female drug use and crime. Among the most obvious issues for future investigation are the following:

(1) The extent and nature of criminal behavior among female addicts. For example, in what ways do patterns of drug use and crime differ between males and females? Are there specific crime patterns associated with the use of various types of drugs by women, and with polydrug use? How much of the crime committed by female addicts is drug-related? What are the effects of periods of nondrug use on female crime?

(2) The sequence of drug use and crime among female addicts. For example, what is the direction and extent of preaddiction and postaddiction criminality among female addicts? Is there a definite sequence of drug use and crime among women? Are female drug use and crime merely correlated, or can a causal relationship be shown? What other factors impact on this relationship? Does the sequence of drug use and crime differ for males and females?

(3) The impact of treatment on female drug use and crime. For example, do treatment programs reduce the amount of crime or change the nature of crime among female addicts? What is the impact of various types of treatment programs on female drug use and crime? Are the effects of treatment programs on female drug use and crime short-term or long-term? What factors are related to treatment outcome for female addicts?

(4) The impact of the legal and penal systems on female drug use and crime. For example, how does contact with the criminal process affect the extent and nature of female drug use and crime? What effect does incarceration have on subsequent drug use and crime among women?

(5) The relationship between female drug use and crime and traditional female roles. For example, what is the relationship between the female role and the extent and nature of drug use and crime among women? What roles do female addicts play in drug and criminal subcultures? Does the female role affect the sequence of female drug use and crime? To what extent do treatment personnel hold stereotyped perceptions about women, and do these influence treatment outcomes of female addicts? How do family and child care responsibilities affect female drug use and crime?

The drug policies in effect at the present time have not been markedly successful. While there is some evidence of a remedicalization of addiction, the criminal approach continues to predominate as it has for the past five decades (Reasons, 1975; Conrad and Schneider, 1980). Most assessments agree that this approach has not only been relatively ineffective in deterring drug use, but that it is also associated with significant social costs (Weissman, 1978). More careful and critical study of the issues raised above, using both male and female populations, should contribute to a more effective and enlightened drug policy.

NOTES

1. Over half of the citations in the Women and Drugs bibliography published in August, 1978, by the Drug Abuse Epidemiology Data Center examined the effects of female drug use on pregnancy, children, or sexual behavior. Only about 7 percent studied the relationship between female drug use and crime while the remainder dealt with various other aspects of drug use among women.

2. The UCR trend data presented here are analyzed in Datesman and Scarpitti (1980: Pt. I).

3. These data were generated by DHEW Grant 1-R01-DA-0-1827-03, from the Division of Research, National Institute on Drug Abuse. I would like to thank the principal investigator, James A. Inciardi, for the use of these data.

REFERENCES

ADLER, F. (1975) Sisters in Crime. New York: McGraw-Hill.

AMSEL, Z., W. MANDELL, L. MATTHIAS, C. MASON, and I. HOCHERMAN (1976) "Reliability and validity of self-reported illegal activities and drug use collected from narcotic addicts." International Journal of the Addictions 11 (April): 325–336.

BALL, J. C. (1967) "The reliability and validity of interview data obtained from 59 narcotic drug addicts." American Journal of Sociology 72 (May): 650–654.

BINION, V. J. (1977) "A description of selected variables of women admitted to demonstration treatment programs of the National Women's Drug Research Project from September, 1975, through February, 1976." Ann Arbor, MI: Institute for Social Research.

CHAMBERS, C. D. (1972) "An assessment of drug use in the general population." Pp. 50–123 in J. Susman (ed.) Drug Use and Social Policy. New York: AMS Press.

——— (1974) "Narcotic addiction and crime: an empirical Review," pp. 125–142 in J. A. Inciardi and C. D. Chambers (eds.), Drugs and the Criminal Justice System. Beverly Hills, CA: Sage.

CHAMBERS, C. D. and J. A. INCIARDI (1971) "Some aspects of the criminal careers of female narcotic addicts." Presented at the annual meeting of the Southern Sociological Society.

——— R. K. HINESLEY, and M. MOLDESTAD (1970) "Narcotic addiction in females: a race comparison." International Journal of the Addictions 5 (June): 257–278.

CONRAD, P. and J. W. SCHNEIDER (1980) Deviance and Medicalization: From Badness to Sickness. St. Louis: Mosby.

CUSHMAN, P., Jr. (1971) "Methadone maintenance in hard-core criminal addicts." New York State Journal of Medicine 71 (July 15): 1768–1774.

——— (1972) "Methadone maintenance treatment of narcotic addiction." New York State Journal of Medicine 72 (July 1): 1752–1755.

CUSKEY, W. R., T. PREMKUMAR, and L. SIGEL (1972) "Survey of opiate addiction among females in the United States between 1850 and 1970." Public Health Reviews 1: 6–39.

DAI, B. (1937) Opium Addiction in Chicago. Montclair, NJ: Patterson Smith. (This edition published in 1970.)

DATESMAN, S. K. and F. R. SCARPITTI [eds.] (1980) Women, Crime, and Justice. New York: Oxford.

ELLINWOOD, E. H., W. G. SMITH, and G. E. VAILLANT (1966) "Narcotic addiction in males and females: a comparison." International Journal of the Addictions 1 (June): 33–45.

Federal Bureau of Investigation (1978) Uniform Crime Reports. Washington, DC: Government Printing Office.

FILE, K. N. (1976) "Sex roles and street roles." International Journal of the Addictions 11 (April): 263–268.

_____ T. W. McCAHILL, and L. D. SAVITZ (1974) "Narcotics involvement and female criminality." Addictive Diseases 1: 177–188.

GOLDMAN, E. (1931) Living My Life, Volume I. New York: Da Capo Press. (This edition published in 1970.)

GOLDSTEIN, P. J. (1979) Prostitution and Drugs. Lexington, MA: D. C. Heath.

HALLER, J. S., Jr. and R. M. HALLER (1974) The Physician and Sexuality in Victorian America. Urbana: University of Illinois Press.

HASKELL, M. R. and L. YABLONSKY (1978) Criminology: Crime and Criminality. Skokie, IL: Rand McNally.

INCIARDI, J. A. (1980) "Women, heroin, and property crime," pp. 214–222 in S. K. Datesman and F. R. Scarpitti (eds.) Women, Crime, and Justice. New York: Oxford.

_____ and C. D. CHAMBERS (1972) "Unreported criminal involvement of narcotic addicts." Journal of Drug Issues 2 (Spring): 57–64.

JAMES, J. (1976) "Prostitution and addiction: an interdisciplinary approach." Addictive Diseases 2: 601–618.

_____, C. T. GOSHO, and R. WATSON (1976) "The relationship between female criminality and drug use," pp. 441–455 in Drug Use and Crime: Report of the Panel on Drug Use and Criminal Behavior. Springfield, VA: National Technical Information Service.

_____ (1979) "The relationship between female criminality and drug use." International Journal of the Addictions 14, 2: 215–229.

Law Enforcement Assistance Administration, U.S. Department of Justice. (1977) Criminal Victimization Surveys in Washington, D.C. Washington, DC: Government Printing Office.

LEMERT, E. M. (1951) Social Pathology. New York: McGraw-Hill.

LINDESMITH, A. R. (1965) The Addict and the Law. Bloomington: Indiana University Press.

LOMBROSO, C. (1911) Crime, Its Causes and Remedies (H. P. Horton, trans.). Boston: Little, Brown.

MacNAMARA, D. E. J. and E. SAGARIN (1977) Sex, Crime, and the Law. New York: Free Press.

MAGLIN, A. (1974) "Sex role differences in heroin addiction." Social Casework 55 (March): 160–167.

O'DONNELL, J. A. (1966) "Narcotic addiction and crime." Social Problems 13 (Spring): 374–385.

_____ (1969) Narcotic Addicts in Kentucky. Washington, DC: Government Printing Office.

REASONS, C. E. (1975) "The addict as a criminal: perpetuation of a legend." Crime and Delinquency 21 (January): 19–27.

Research Triangle Institute (1976) Drug Use and Crime: Report of the Panel on Drug Use and Criminal Behavior. Springfield, VA: National Technical Information Service.

ROSENBAUM, M. (1975) "Sex roles among deviants: the woman addict." Presented at the annual meeting of the American Sociological Association.

ROSENBLEET, C. and B. J. PARIENTE (1973) "The prostitution of the criminal law." American Criminal Law Review 11 (Winter): 373–427.

ROSENBLUM, K. E. (1975) "Female deviance and the female sex role: a preliminary investigation." British Journal of Sociology 26: 169–185.

STEPHENS, R. (1972) "The truthfulness of addict respondents in research projects." International Journal of the Addictions 7 (Fall): 549–558.

SUFFET, F. and R. BROTMAN (1976) "Female drug use: some observations." International Journal of the Addictions 11 (February): 19–33.

SUTTER, A. G. (1970) "A hierarchy of drug users," pp. 666–676 in M. E. Wolfgang, L. Savitz, and N. Johnson (eds.) The Sociology of Crime and Delinquency. New York: John Wiley.

TERRY, C. E. and M. PELLENS (1928) The Opium Problem. Montclair, NJ: Patterson Smith. (This edition published in 1970.)

VOSS, H. L. and R. C. STEPHENS (1973) "Criminal history of narcotic addicts." Drug Forum 2 (Winter): 191–202.

WEISSMAN, J. C. (1978) "Understanding the drugs and crime connection: a systematic examination of drugs and crime relationships." Journal of Psychedelic Drugs 10 (July–September): 171–192.

———— and K. N. FILE (1976) "Criminal behavior patterns of female addicts: a comparison of findings in two cities." International Journal of the Addictions 11 (December): 1063–1077.

WILLIAMS, J. E. and W. A. BATES (1970) "Some characteristics of female narcotic addicts." International Journal of the Addictions 5: 245–256.

WINICK, C. and P. M. KINSIE (1971) The Lively Commerce. Chicago: Quadrangle Books.

WOOLSTON, H. B. (1921) Prostitution in the United States. Montclair, NJ: Patterson Smith. (This edition published in 1969.)

5

DRUGS AND VIOLENCE

DUANE C. McBRIDE

For the last century, researchers, clinicians, and policy makers have focused on the relationship between criminal and drug using behavior. In the early part of the twentieth century many observers concluded that drug abuse led to moral degradation and crime (see Terry and Pelens, 1928). The assumption that there was a linkage between drug abuse and crime played a major part in the passage of the 1914 Harrison Act. As Reasons (1975) has documented, the fundamental national policy and approach to drug abuse established in the early 1900s has been within the context of drugs causing crime. During this time period, the Federal Bureau of Narcotics was very active in describing the drug addict as behaving in a bizarre, unpredictable, often violent manner. The pre-World War II popular media influenced by the Bureau of Narcotics portrayed drug users quite literally as monsters and fiends (see Lindesmith, 1940).

While in recent years portrayals of the drug abuser have become less sensational, the record implies that federal intervention and treatment policy still rests on the assumed linkage between crime and drugs. The establishment of the Special Action Office for Drug Abuse Prevention (SAODAP) in 1971 and of the National Institute on Drug Abuse in 1974 was justified on the basis of the drug-crime connection. In his message to Congress on June 17,

1971, President Nixon stated that the drug abuse problem and resulting crime had reached a national epidemic. Nixon's response was the establishment of SAODAP. Shortly after the establishment of NIDA, the federal strategy report stated that "the crime rate, the deaths, the discussion and the fear all culminated in focusing national attention on drug abuse." During the 1970s, when expenditures for other social programs were being reduced, the drug abuse treatment budget was rapidly increasing. Drug abuse treatment services and research formed one of the very few growth areas among social service programs. Drug abuse has competed very successfully for national attention and resources. For example, the NIDA budget is about 30 percent larger than the budget of the National Institute on Alcohol Abuse. Yet, even at the most generous estimates, NIDA's target population is only 10–15 percent as large as the target population of NIAAA. The assumed linkage between drug abuse and crime has played a significant role in the public concern for and fear of drug abusers in the establishment and continued strong funding of NIDA.

The focus on drugs and crime has always included a concern with the relationship between drugs and violence. Particularly in the years during and prior to World War II, the Federal Bureau of Narcotics attempted to portray narcotics, marijuana, and other drugs as directly and immediately producing bizarre, violent, fiendish behavior. A host of written and visual material was produced within this framework. The film *Reefer Madness* is perhaps the best known product of that era. In this film a marijuana smoker is portrayed as turning into a werewolf-like creature after inhaling marijuana smoke (see Lindesmith, 1940, for an overview and critique of this approach). While these simplistic notions have become considerably modified over the last few decades, the concern about the effects of drugs on violent behavior has remained. Whenever a drug user engages in violence, the media are apt to describe the incident in such a manner as to imply the continued existence and danger of drug fiends.

The basic purpose of the report is to examine the relationship between drug use and violence. Specifically, this will be done by

(1) reviewing the literature on the types of crimes engaged in by various types of drug users, to determine if certain types of drug use are associated with violent behavior;

(2) examining the potential role of violence in a drug abuser's life through (a) briefly reviewing the literature on the pharmacological effects of specific drugs that may cause violent behavior, (b) examining the role of violence in the routine daily interaction of drug abusers; and

(3) presenting new data on the relationship between type of drug use and type of crime.

A METHODOLOGICAL NOTE

In any focus on drug abuse and crime, perhaps the first issue revolves around the definition of terms. The terms *drugs* and *crime* are often used imprecisely, and it can be difficult to ascertain which drug and what crimes are related or not related in a specific study or paper. As Voss (1976) noted, "in much of what is written on the topic, the term *drug* is used without a precise definition and may refer to many things." At times the term *drug addict* has meant a heroin user; at other times it has been applied to LSD or marijuana users; and most recently, professionals have begun to use the term in describing the abuse of prescription central-nervous-system depressants. In recognition of the problem of the meaning of *drugs,* SAODAP established a committee to recommend a typology of drugs (Bateman, 1975). The initial SAODAP Committee was followed by two other committees established by NIDA in 1975 and 1978 (see Elinson and Nurco, 1975; Rittenhouse, 1978). These committees recommended to researchers that, at a minimum, nine categories be used in drug abuse research. These categories are

(1) narcotic and nonnarcotic analgesics
(2) sedatives
(3) antipsychotic agents (tranquilizers)
(4) stimulants (perhaps cocaine separately)
(5) cannabis
(6) hallucinogens
(7) solvents (inhalants)
(8) nicotine
(9) alcohol

The basic intent of the committees recommending the use of these categories was to provide a general taxonomic, conceptual framework within which the term *drug* could be understood. In focusing on the relationship between drugs and violence, it is important to keep in mind these categories and to understand the relationship in terms of each of the categories of drugs as they may relate to violent behavior.

The term *crime* is also often used in a general, imprecise way. The title of this chapter implies that some procedure has been used to divide crime into a categorical scheme and that one category, violent crime, has been chosen for attention. There are a variety of taxonomies used in criminology. Typological constructions have been developed on the basis of legal categories (Federal Bureau of Investigation, 1976), the perceived severity ranking of legal categories (Rossi et al., 1974), the social and psychological characteristics of offenders (Duncan et al., 1953; Rich, 1956), or combinations of the

preceding (Clinard and Quinney, 1967). As was the case with the term
drugs, it is important to have some type of categorical scheme of crime in
mind when examining the relationship between crime and drugs. Essentially, this chapter focuses on drugs and violent crime. For purposes of this
analysis, the term *violent crime* refers to all crimes against persons, including homicide, manslaughter, rape, assault, battery, and child molestation.

LITERATURE ON TYPE OF DRUG
AND TYPE OF CRIME

The relationship between crime and drugs has been around from a variety
of perspectives. Researchers have examined the statistical and causal nature
of the relationship, economic issues, the role of drug laws in creating a
statistical relationship, ecological impingements, and the relationship between specific types of drugs and types of crime (see Kozel et al., 1972;
O'Donnell et al., 1976; Weissman, 1978; McGlothlin, 1979; McBride and
McCoy, 1980, 1981).

While academics have tended to focus on a variety of theoretical, methodological, and substantive issues in studying crime and drugs, policy
makers have tended to focus on the relationship between type of crime and
type of drug use. This was a major focus of a crime-drugs panel established
by the National Institute on Drug Abuse in 1975 and a panel established by
the Law Enforcement Assistance Administration in 1978. As Weissman
(1978: 171) has noted, "a presumed direct connection between narcotics use
and the commission of property-acquisitive crime has been a time honored
principal of American drug control policy." Weissman also notes that this
position has frequently been broadened to include other psychoactive drugs.

In the 1950s and 1960s, most drug abuse research focused primarily on
heroin or other narcotics use. Thus, interest in crime and drugs tended to
focus on heroin and type of crime. In one of the major post-World War II
studies of the crime-drug relationship, Finestone (1957) found that heroin
users primarily engaged in nonviolent property crimes. Further, he claimed
that as rates of heroin addiction increased in a given area, crimes against
person decreased and property crimes increased. From Finestone's perspective, heroin addicts concentrated their activities on behaviors that would
result in the most monetary gain in order to enable them to purchase heroin.
Noneconomically productive activities such as assault were avoided. Finestone's observations and conclusions have provided a stimulus and framework for many other studies. Subsequent studies have tended to confirm
Finestone's findings that heroin addicts concentrate their activities on acquisitory property crimes.

In the early 1970s, Inciardi and Chambers (1972) examined the types of crimes committed by a population of heroin addicts in New York City. In their analysis, they also found that heroin addicts were more likely to commit property crimes than crimes against person. Specifically, they found that in their sample of heroin addicts, property crimes were about five times greater than the number of crimes against persons. In the latter part of the 1970s, Inciardi (1979) replicated this study and obtained similar results.

Researchers examining crime-drug relationships in the normal population have also found a relationship between drug use and property crime. Elliott and his colleagues (1976), in a major longitudinal study of delinquent behavior, have found a strong correlation between the use of all types of illicit drugs—particularly marijuana—and property crime. Other general population surveys, by O'Donnell and his colleagues (1976), Jacoby et al. (1973), and Johnston et al. (1976), have all found that all types of illicit-drug users are more likely to commit property crimes than other types of crime, and that drug users are more likely to commit property crimes than are nondrug users.

Researchers who have studied criminal justice populations have reported similar findings. In a survey of drug use patterns among a probability sample of one year's felony arrests in Dade County, Florida, McBride (1976) found that all categories of illicit drug users in general, and heroin users particularly, were overrepresented in the property charge categories. Those who currently used illicit drugs were found to constitute 52.9 percent of the sample and over 56 percent of those charged with property crimes. The narcotics users who constituted 16 percent of the population were underrepresented in crimes against person, whereas 26 percent of all those charged with armed robbery and 19 percent of those charged with property crimes were using heroin at the time of arrest. A similar overrepresentation in property crimes was found by Barton (1976) and Kozel and Dupont (1977). These studies also found that illicit-drug users were underrepresented in crimes against person. Nondrug users were more likely to commit crimes against person than were all types of drug users.

The national panels initiated by the National Institute on Drug Abuse and the Law Enforcement Assistance Administration concluded in their examinations of the literature that illicit-drug abuse appeared to be related to acquisitory property crimes. The expenses of regular drug use appeared to demand a focus on activities that would yield the most monitory return (Crime and Drugs, 1976; Gandossy et al., 1980; Greenberg and Adler, 1973). The conventional wisdom has been that the economic demands of many types of drug use result in property crime. Researchers have tended to conclude that illicit-drug users are not driven toward violence by the use of drugs and are, in fact, less violent than nondrug using criminals, because of the economic demands of drug use.

There have been in the last few years some voices dissenting from the general notion that crime among drug users is nonviolent. In studying New York City samples of heroin users, Zahn and Bencivengo (1974) and Stephens and Ellis (1975) have argued that the criminal behavior patterns of heroin users are changing. These researchers suggest that, while older co-horts of heroin users, who initiated use from 1955–1970, may have been relatively nonviolent, new, initiating cohorts of heroin users are increasingly engaging in crimes against person. The implication is that researchers should begin to focus on the relationship between drugs and violent crime in new initiating cohorts.

DRUGS AND VIOLENCE

A brief review of the literature and issues in crime and drugs indicates that, traditionally, researchers have not seen a relationship between drugs and violence. Generally, the existing research suggests that drug abuse is related to nonviolent behavior and that, in fact, drug abusers who are in-volved in violent crime will become less violent after initiation into drug use. It has been suggested that such a relationship occurs because drug abusers, such as heroin or cocaine users, must focus on crimes that will produce the income necessary to obtain these drugs. Also, it has been noted that, phar-macologically, many of the most commonly abused drugs act as central-nervous-system depressants. Clinically, these drugs may produce less ag-gressive and violent behavior. However, while the traditional research wisdom implies a lack of violence associated with drug use, recent conclu-sions by Stephens and Ellis, Zahn, and the popular media (Schorr, 1979) would imply the importance of reexamining the drugs-violence issue. In this reexamination of the relationship between drugs and violence, two compo-nents will be included: (1) the pharmacological effects of drugs that produce aggressive or violent behavior, and (2) violence as a part of the drug-using subculture behavior

PHARMACOLOGICAL EFFECTS

As was noted earlier, many of the most common drugs of abuse are strong nervous-system depressants and are specifically used to produce a tranquil-ized, euphoric effect (Agar, 1973). However, there are drugs abused that have often been perceived as producing bizarre behavior. These have pri-marily been the hallucinogenic drugs, such as LSD and PCP or amphetamines and other stimulants. The popular media are replete with the horrors produced by all of these substances. Aggressive and violent behavior have usually been seen as possible behavioral effects of these drugs. While most of the literature on the effects of LSD and PCP is based on fairly isolated case studies, there does appear to be some initial evidence that the hallucinogenic drugs may so strongly affect perceptions or the chemistry of the brain that bizarre, aggressive, and violent behavior may well occur (Tinklenberg and Woodrow, 1974; Burns and Lerner, 1976; McBride and Russe, 1979). It should be noted that neither researchers nor the popular media have argued that hallucinogenic drugs produce violent crime in the sense of crimes planned and carried out against persons. Rather, the evidence is that the violent behavior these drugs produce is to a large extent unpredictable in its specific direction; it is, rather, unpremeditated and random in its course.

The literature on the relationship between violence and amphetamine use has been extensive. Ellinwood (1971), in a study reported in the *American Journal of Psychiatry,* focused on thirteen individuals who had committed homicides while under the influence of amphetamines. His clinical conclusion was that amphetamine use led directly to the commission of the murders. Ellinwood argued that the use of amphetamines led to paranoid thought patterns and delusions, consequently to violent behavior directed at supposed persecutors. Smith (1972), in another study during the same period, also concluded that amphetamines had a direct effect in producing a subculture of violence among users. In a recent case-study report, Asnis and Smith (1978) drew similar conclusions regarding the effects of amphetamine use on violence. They examined three amphetamine users who had committed homicides. Similar to Ellinwood (1971), they described the development of delusional paranoia and social isolation resulting in extreme violence.

Studies that have focused on the effects of amphetamine use, from the inception of use in the drug revolution of the 1960s to current reports, have consistently concluded that regular amphetamine use produces paranoia delusions, which produce violent individual behavior and an amphetamine-using subculture characterized by paranoid delusion and violence. While researchers have noted that the violent behavior is generally mediated by personality characteristics and situational context, the conclusions have consistently focused on the direct role of amphetamines in causing the violence (Griffith, 1966; Carey and Mandel, 1968; Rawlin, 1968; Smith, 1969; Grinspoon and Hedblom, 1975).

The tradition of amphetamine research was criticized by Greenberg in 1976. She basically claimed that the conclusions regarding the effects were based on clinical observations of a few individuals who had manifested violent behavior, not on carefully designed, large-scale investigations.

Greenberg argued that existing data imply that amphetamine users are not more likely to be involved in crimes against person than are other types of drug users or nondrug users (see Eckerman et al., 1971).

While, as Greenberg has noted, definitive, carefully designed research studies have not been completed, the clinical evidence and observations. cannot be so easily dismissed. Concepts of the direct causative effect of amphetamine use on violent behavior may be simplistic, and certainly should be examined within the context of other personality and social variables. However, in increasing the complexity of our understanding of the relationship, the clinical evidence suggesting the causal relationship between amphetamine use and violent behavior cannot be ignored.

In the overall patterns of drug use in our society, epidemiological data suggest that the use of drugs such as LSD, PCP, or amphetamines is relatively rare (National Institute on Drug Abuse Annual Survey, 1979). While the evidence may suggest violence as an almost pharmacological effect of these drugs, these particular substances are not subject to the dominant patterns of use in our society. In addition, when they are used, it is usually within the context of a multiple drug use pattern (see McBride and Russe, 1979).

LIFESTYLE AND VIOLENCE

Attempts to understand the relationship between drug use and crime have often exhibited a very narrow perspective. Traditionally, the focus has been on the criminal activities drug users engage in to support a drug use pattern. The conclusions that drug abusers are not violent criminals often derive from a limited focus on the daily life of a drug abuser. Obtaining funds to purchase drugs is one important aspect of a drug abuser's life, and this frequently does involve acquisitory property crimes. However, as ethnographic researchers have documented, drug abusers must also focus on finding and maintaining a dependable source of drugs (see Agar, 1973). It is within the context of the drug deal that violence occurs.

Buying and selling drugs requires a face-to-face interaction in which the dealer is trying to sell the lowest quality at the highest price, while presenting the drug as the highest quality at the lowest price. Meanwhile, the buyer is attempting to obtain the best-quality drugs at the lowest price. As the ethnographic researchers have documented (Agar, 1973), the fear of being "burned"—of obtaining poor-quality drugs at high prices—is a major concern in the world of the street addict. The dealer, possessing the desired drug, is afraid of being "ripped off"—of having the drug stolen from him by the buyer during the transaction. Thus, the economic transaction of the drug deal involves mutually suspicious individuals, each of whom has a strong motivation to obtain as much as possible and give as little as possible. This setting, on both small and large scales, is usually seen as the basis for the violence in the drug abuser's world. As Fiddle (1976: 556) noted, "much of the interaddict violence springs from sellers purveying completely adulterated bags of heroin or from addicts stealing from pushers."

In the last few years violent death associated with or resulting from a drug deal that went bad has become well documented. Fitzpatrick (1974) has reported that one-quarter of the deaths of federal drug-treatment program clients are due to homicides. In a follow-up study of heroin addicts seeking treatment in Dade County, Florida, McCoy and his colleagues (1978) found that murder was the single largest cause of death. Two-thirds of those who died were murdered, and the police records showed that the murders took place either during a drug deal or as the result of the deal.

The relationship between homicide and drug use in a community was clearly documented by Monforte and Spitz (1975). These researchers examined autopsy toxicology reports and police investigation records for 207 homicide cases in Wayne County, Michigan. On the basis of their analysis, Monforte and Spitz concluded that about two-thirds of the homicide victims were involved with other illicit drug dealing or using. Often researchers focusing on crime-drug issues have attempted to account for property-crime rates by the price of heroin (Silverman and Spruill, 1977). Monforte and Spitz's study implies that drug abuse may have a much stronger relationship with the occurrence of homicide.

Most of the studies on drugs and violent death have focused on heroin use, though it is usually noted that heroin users also use other drugs. While the heroin deal may traditionally have the most violence associated with it, any purchase of illegal drugs, for reasons already outlined, certainly has the potential for violence. All purchases of illegal drugs involve mutual suspicion and the temptation to sell drugs of inferior quality or to rip off the dealer. Fitzpatrick (1974) implies that the illegal situation generates an environment in which violence or murder is used to eliminate local competitors and informers, and to maximize profits for the seller or minimize expenses for the buyer. The purchase of all illegal drugs is often within this context.

Most of the concern with drugs and violence has focused on the local street scene. However, because of the extremely large amounts of money involved, violence often emerges within the context of the control of markets. While this has probably always been a part of the drug scene at higher levels, the recent increase in the use of cocaine has apparently stimulated extensive and visible violence. The media (Schorr, 1979) has, in recent years, focused on the extent of cocaine dealer violence. Many communities, particularly in New York and South Florida, have been the scene of spectacular machine gun shootouts between cocaine importers and distributors. The events have been reminiscent of the media portrayal of the Prohibition years and Al Capone.

Any attempts to understand the relationship between drugs and crime must have a broader focus than an individual drug user's attempt to obtain money to purchase drugs. The interactional situation of the drug transaction and the economics of the drug market must be considered. Such a focus shows a great potential for violence, and existing data strongly imply that violence is a frequent and routine part of a drug user's life on the street and an integral part of the illegal drug importation and marketing system. Monforte and Spitz's study particularly implies that drug abuse may account for much of the extreme violence in a community.

TRENDS IN THE RELATIONSHIP
BETWEEN TYPE OF DRUG
AND TYPE OF CRIME

As was shown earlier, research has consistently found that drug users, particularly narcotics users, are more likely to commit property crimes than nondrug-using criminals. However, a study by Stephens and Ellis (1975) suggests that those findings may have been due to a cohort effect. That is, the relationship between type of drug use and type of crime may have been an artifact of the heroin-epidemic-initiating cohort of 1969–1971. Stephens and Ellis indicate that for those initiating heroin use in the postepidemic years, violent crime rates were higher than among those who initiated heroin use in the epidemic. There is also a second piece of evidence that suggests the importance of reexamining the relationship between type of drug use and type of crime. That evidence is that violence appeared to be associated with cocaine distribution and use (Schorr, 1979) and the rapid increase in cocaine use in our society (NIDA Annual Survey, 1979).

Many of the existing data on the relationship between crime type and drug type were collected during the early to middle 1970s and probably did primarily involve individuals who initiated use during the epidemic years (see Crime and Drugs, 1976; Gandossy et al., 1980).

Largely because of the implications of the Stephens and Ellis report, data were analyzed from a survey of all county jail inmates in an east-central Florida county. Data were collected on sociodemographic and socioeconomic characteristics, as well as on drug use histories and criminal behavior. The sample was composed of 292 individuals, 76 percent of whom were white and 17 percent of whom black. The sample was also 85 percent male. The inmates of the county jails consisted of all of those sentenced to a year or less by the county courts, those awaiting trial on serious charges, and those awaiting transfer to another jurisdiction.

Data presented in Table 5.1 show the relationship between type of drug used and the primary charge of arrest. Primary charge of arrest was determined by using the seriousness index implied by the FBI Uniform Crime Reports and by Rossi and his colleagues (1974). Only the most serious charge is presented in Table 5.1. Serious crimes against persons are ranked the highest, and income-producing, victimless crimes are ranked the lowest. Data are presented in terms of column and row percentages. The column percentages reflect the proportion of users of alcohol, marijuana, and the like who were arrested for each category of crime. For example, the upper lefthand cell shows that 5.8 percent of the alcohol users were arrested for serious crimes against persons. Row percentages, which are presented in parentheses, describe the proportion of those primarily arrested for each category of crime who used each type of drug. Again, the upper lefthand corner of the table shows that of those who were arrested for serious crimes against person, 59.1 percent also used alcohol.

Before proceeding it is important to define the crime categories used:

(1) Serious crimes against person: This includes murder, manslaughter, rape, and aggravated assault.
(2) Less serious crimes against person: This includes assault and battery, and simple assault.
(3) Robbery: This includes all forms of robbery.
(4) Property crime: This includes all types of burglary, theft, larceny, fraud, or arson.
(5) Drug law violations: This includes the sale or possession of narcotics or other dangerous drugs.
(6) Income-producing, victimless crime: This includes gambling and prostitution.
(7) Other: This includes vagrancy, resisting arrest, desertion, and parole or probation violations.

The drug categories represent regular drug use—weekly for a six-week period—and conform to those categories suggested in the literature (see Voss, 1976).

An examination of the marginals around Table 5.1 is important for understanding the frequency distribution of types of crime and types of drugs and for comparing the rates in each cell with the average rate for that row or column. The most frequent arrest charge, as the table shows, involved a

TABLE 5.1 Type of Drug and Type of Crime

Crime Type	Drug Type													
	Alcohol $n=224$	Marijuana $n=213$	Hallucinogens $n=56$	Sedatives/ Tranquilizers $n=69$	Barbiturates $n=65$	Methaqualone $n=75$	Amphetamines $n=92$	PCP $n=46$	Inhalants $n=23$	Cocaine $n=104$	Dilaudid $n=46$	Other Opiates $n=29$	Heroin $n=40$	Total
Serious crimes against persons	5.8 (59.1)	7.5 (72.7)	7.1 (18.2)	7.9 (22.7)	7.8 (22.7)	4.1 (13.6)	7.6 (31.8)	10.9 (22.7)	17.8 (18.2)	8.7 (40.9)	15.2 (31.8)	13.8 (3.4)	12.5 (22.7)	7.6 $n=22$
Less serious crimes against persons	4.0 (75.0)	4.2 (75.0)	3.6 (16.7)	1.6 (8.3)	3.1 (16.7)	4.1 (25.0)	3.3 (25.0)	8.7 (33.3)	— (—)	5.8 (50.0)	8.7 (33.3)	3.4 (8.3)	7.5 (25.0)	4.2 $n=12$
Robbery	12.5 (87.5)	9.9 (65.6)	3.6 (6.3)	7.9 (15.6)	10.9 (21.9)	8.1 (18.8)	10.9 (31.3)	6.5 (9.4)	8.7 (6.3)	11.5 (37.5)	13.0 (18.8)	20.7 (18.8)	12.5 (15.6)	11.1 $n=32$
Property crime	47.8 (81.1)	50.5 (81.1)	57.1 (24.2)	55.6 (26.5)	51.6 (25.0)	54.1 (30.3)	48.9 (34.1)	52.2 (18.2)	39.1 (6.8)	44.2 (34.8)	39.1 (13.6)	41.4 (9.1)	50.0 (15.2)	45.1 $n=132$
Drug law violations	8.9 (76.9)	9.9 (80.8)	14.3 (30.8)	11.1 (26.9)	6.3 (15.4)	13.5 (38.5)	13.0 (46.2)	8.7 (15.4)	8.7 (7.7)	14.4 (57.7)	13.0 (23.1)	3.4 (3.8)	10.0 (15.4)	9.0 $n=26$

TABLE 5.1 (Continued)

Crime Type	Drug Type													Total
	Alcohol $n=224$	Marijuana $n=213$	Hallucinogens $n=56$	Sedatives/ Tranquilizers $n=69$	Barbiturates $n=65$	Methaqualone $n=75$	Amphetamines $n=92$	PCP $n=46$	Inhalants $n=23$	Cocaine $n=104$	Dilaudid $n=46$	Other Opiates $n=29$	Heroin $n=40$	
Income-producing victimless crimes	2.7 (50.0)	2.8 (50.0)	— (—)	1.6 (8.3)	3.1 (16.7)	2.7 (16.7)	2.2 (16.7)	— (—)	4.3 (8.3)	1.0 (8.3)	2.2 (8.1)	3.4 (8.3)	— (—)	4.2 n=12
Other	18.3 (77.4)	15.1 (60.4)	14.3 (15.1)	14.3 (17.0)	17.2 (20.8)	13.5 (18.9)	14.1 (24.5)	13.0 (11.3)	21.7 (9.4)	14.4 (28.3)	8.7 (7.5)	13.8 (7.5)	7.5 (5.7)	18.3 n=53
Total	(77.5)	(73.4)	(19.4)	(21.8)	(25.6)	(26.4)	(31.8)	(15.9)	(8.0)	(36.0)	(15.9)	(10.0)	(13.8)	

117

property crime. About 46 percent of primary arrests were for this type of crime. Other types of crime constituted the second largest category, 18.3 percent, robberies were next at 11.1 percent, followed by drug law violations at 9.0 percent, serious crimes against persons at 7.6 percent, less serious crimes against persons at 4.2 percent, and victimless crime at 4.2 percent.

Table 5.1 also presents the distribution of regular drug use type in the incarcerated population. Regular drug use was defined as use at least twice a week over a six-week period in the previous year. As the data show, 77.5 percent regularly used alcohol and 73.4 percent regularly used marijuana. Cocaine was the next most commonly used drug, with use reported by 36 percent of the population. Of the narcotic drugs, 15.9 percent of the total population used Dilaudid, 13.8 percent used heroin, and 10 percent used other narcotics. Unlike primary charge of arrest, drug use is not indexed and a given individual appears in as many categories of drugs as he or she uses. While there are many ways to present this relationship, it was felt that in this preliminary effort it was best to examine the relationship of each type of drug use with a seriousness index of crime which is essentially based on extent of violence against persons.

The data in Table 5.1 *are not consistent* with most of the previous literature which suggests that narcotics and cocaine users are overrepresented in property crime categories (see Gandossy et al., 1980). For example, Dilaudid users constituted 15.9 percent of the total population and 18.8 percent of robbery charges and 13.6 percent of all property crimes. Thus, Dilaudid users were not more likely to be arrested for robbery or property crime than would be suggested by their proportion of the population. Heroin users, as well as cocaine users, are also not overrepresented in property crime categories. Heroin and cocaine users constitute 13.8 percent and 36 percent of the population, and 15.2 percent and 34.8 percent of those charged with property crimes.

An examination of the distribution in Table 5.1 shows that Dilaudid, heroin, and cocaine users are overrepresented in the crimes against person categories. Dilaudid and heroin users made up 15.9 percent and 13.8 of the total population, respectively. Of those charged with serious crimes against person, 33.3 percent were Dilaudid users and 22.7 percent were heroin users. Similar overrepresentation occurs for cocaine, PCP, and inhalant users. These data clearly suggest that these types of drug users are more likely to commit violent crimes than are those who do not use these drugs. *This is not consistent with the literature. It may be an isolated idiosyncratic case or it may represent the trend that Stephens and Ellis saw, beginning five years ago, of increasing violence among narcotics users.*

TABLE 5.2   Multiple Regression of Drug Use Type on a Serious Crime Index

	Simple R	Multiple R	R Square	R Square Change
Dilaudid	.22	.22	.05	.05
Amphetamines	−.06	.24	.06	.01
Hallucinogens	−.06	.25	.06	—
Methaquaalone	−.06	.26	.07	.01

In an attempt to elaborate on the relationship of type of drug use and type of charge, a dummy variable stepwise multiple regression technique was employed. Each type of drug used was regressed on the crime index. The results of the multiple regression analysis are shown in Table 5.2.

The data in Table 5.2 show that narcotics users had the strongest relationship to the crime index. In fact, it was the only variable with a positive relationship. For the other variables entered, those who did not use amphetamines, hallucinogens, or methaquaalone were more likely to be charged with a serious crime than those who did use these substances. In the multiple regression program, Dilaudid and heroin use had such a strong correlation (r = .67) that after Dilaudid use was entered, heroin use did not explain any additional variance.

Consistent with the analysis presented in Table 5.1, the data in Table 5.2 indicate that narcotics users are more likely to engage in violence than are those who do not use narcotics or who use other types of drugs. *While these data have to be considered preliminary, they do indicate an increasing violence associated with the criminal behavior of narcotics users.*

SUMMARY AND CONCLUSIONS

It has been the purpose of this chapter to examine the relationship between drug use and violence. This was done by a review of the literature on the relationship between drug use and type of crime committed, an examination of the possible violence-inducive pharmacological effects of drugs, an evaluation of the role of violence in the daily life of the drug abuser, and a presentation of recent data on the relationship between type of drug used and violent crime. Major conclusions are the following:

(1) The existing data and literature indicate illicit-drug users, particularly narcotics users, are more likely to commit property crimes than crimes against person; further that drug users are more likely to commit property crimes than are nondrug users, and that after the initiation of drug use, the user is likely to reduce violent crimes and increase the commission of property crimes. Conventional wisdom has usually concluded that the relation-

ship between drug use and property crime occurs because of the monetary cost of drug use and the need to commit property crimes that produce the funds necessary to obtain drugs. From this perspective, crimes of violence, because they are risky without aiding the obtainment of desired drugs, are avoided.

(2) The majority of the most popular drugs of abuse are central-nervous-system depressants, and, as ethnographers have noted, users seek these drugs in order to produce a sedated, euphoric effect. The literature, however, also suggests that some types of drugs, such as stimulants, amphetamines, and hallucinogens, can produce paranoia or distorted perceptions of reality that result in violent behavior. However, the relatively low incidence of use of these substances implies that whatever violence may be caused by these drugs does not have a major societal impact.

(3) An examination of the literature describing the daily life of the drug abuser suggest that the interactional context of the drug deal is very likely to produce violence. The dealer is attempting to sell low-quality drugs at high prices, and the user is attempting to obtain high-quality drugs at the lowest price. The dealer "burning" the buyer and the buyer "ripping off" the dealer appears to result in a high level of violence in illicit-drug-using groups. Existing data suggest that homicide is a major cause of the death of drug users, particularly narcotics users, and that drug abusers account for a large proportion of homicide victims in urban areas. Additionally, conflict over distribution and markets also appears to create a good deal of violence among large importers and dealers. It is suggested that any attempt to understand the relationship between drugs and crime must include a focus on the daily life and interaction of the user—particularly within the context of the drug deal—not just on the activities undertaken to obtain the money for drugs.

(4) A presentation of recent data on the relationship between type of drug used and type of crime indicated that narcotics, cocaine, PCP, and inhalant users were overrepresented in crimes against person than other types of drug users or nondrug users. It was suggested that these data may represent a new trend of increased violence among narcotics users.

Overall, the information and data presented in this chapter imply that violence is very much a part of drug abuse, from the marketing system to the street buy, and that it is increasingly a part of the criminal behavior of the drug abuser.

REFERENCES

AGAR, M. H. (1973) Ripping and Running: A Formal Ethnography of Urban Heroin Addicts. New York: Academic Press.

ASNIS, S. and R. SMITH (1978) "Amphetamine abuse and violence." Journal of Psychedelic Drugs 10: 317–377.

BARTON, W. I. (1976) "Heroin use and criminality: survey of inmates of state correctional facilities, January," in Research Triangle Institute, Drug Use and Crime. Springfield, VA: National Technical Information Service.

BATEMAN, M.(1975) "Functional taxonomy of drugs," pp. 12–16 in J. Elinson and D. N. Nurco (eds.) Operational Definitions in Socio-Behavioral Drug Use Research. NIDA Monograph Series 2. Rockville, MD: National Institute on Drug Abuse.

BURNS, S. R. and S. E. LERNER (1976) "Perspectives: acute phencyclidine intoxication." Clinical Toxicology 9: 477–501.

CAREY, J. and J. MANDEL (1968) "The Bay Area speed scene." Journal of Health and Social Behavior 9: 164–174.

CLINARD, M. B. and R. QUINNEY (1967) Criminal Behavior Systems: A Critique. New York: Holt, Rinehart & Winston.

Crime and Drugs (1976) "Drug use and crime." Springfield, VA: National Technical Information Service.

DUNCAN, O. D., L. E. OHLIN, A. J. REIS, and H. E. STANTON (1953) "Formal devices for making selection decisions." American Journal of Sociology 58: 537–584.

ECKERMAN, W. C., J. D. BATES, J. V. RACHAL, and W. K. POOLE (1971) Drug Usage and Arrest Charges. Washington, DC: Drug Enforcement Administration.

ELINSON, J. and D. NURCO (1975) Operational Definitions in Socio-Behavioral Drug Use Research. Rockville, MD: National Institute on Drug Abuse.

ELLINWOOD, E. (1971) "Assault and homicide associated with amphetamine abuse." American Journal of Psychiatry 127: 90–95.

ELLIOTT, D. S. and A. R. AGETON (1976) Subcultural Delinquency and Drug Use. Boulder, CO: Behavioral Research Institute.

Federal Bureau of Investigation (1976) Uniform Crime Reports. Washington, DC: Government Printing Office.

FIDDLE, S. (1976) "Sequences in addiction." Addictive Diseases 2: 553–568.

FINESTONE, H. (1957) "Use of drugs among persons admitted to a county jail." Public Health Reports 90: 504–508.

FITZPATRICK, J. P. (1974) "Drugs, alcohol and violent crime." Addictive Diseases 1: 353–367.

GANDOSSY, R. P., J. R. WILLIAMS, J. COHEN, and H. J. HARWOOD (1980) Drugs and Crime: A Survey and Analysis of the Literature. Washington, DC: National Institute of Justice.

GANDOSSY, R. P. et al. (1980) "A survey and analysis of the extant crime/drug literature." Methodological Issues, Patterns of Drug Use and Criminal Behavior, Life Cycles, Economic Issues and Drug Treatment. Research Triangle Park, NC: Research Triangle Institute.

GREENBERG, S. (1976) "The relationship between crime and amphetamine abuse: an empirical review of the literature." Contemporary Drug Problems 5: 101–130.

————— et al. (1974) "Crime and addiction: an empirical analysis of the literature." Contemporary Drug Problems 3: 221–270.

GRIFFITH, J. (1966) "A study of illicit amphetamine traffic in Oklahoma City." American Journal of Psychiatry 123: 560–568.

GRINSPOON, L. and P. HEDBLOM (1975) "The speed culture: amphetamine use and abuse in America." Cambridge, MA: Harvard University Press.

INCIARDI, J. A. (1979) "Heroin use and street crime." Crime and Delinquency 25: 335–346.

_____ and C. D. CHAMBERS (1972) "Unreported criminal involvement of narcotic addicts." Journal of Drug Issues 2: 57–64.

JACOBY, J. E., N. WEINER, T. THORNBERRY, and M. WOLFGANG (1973) "Drug use and criminality in an age cohort." Appendix to National Commission on Marijuana and Drug Abuse, Drug Use in America: Problem in Perspective. Washington, DC: Government Printing Office.

JOHNSTON, L. D., P. M. O'MALLEY, and L. K. EVELAND (1976) "Nonaddictive drug use and delinquency: a longitudinal analysis," in Research Triangle Institute, Drug Use and Crime. Springfield, VA: National Technical Information Service.

KOZEL, N. J. and R. L. DuPONT (1977) Criminal Charges and Drug Use Patterns of Arrestees in the District of Columbia. Washington, DC: Government Printing Office.

_____ and B. BROWN (1972) "Narcotics and crime: a study of narcotic involvement in an offender population." International Journal of the Addictions 7: 443–450.

LINDESMITH, A. R. (1940) "The drug addict as a psychopath." American Sociological Review 5: 914–920.

McBRIDE, D. C. and McCOY, C. B. (1981) "Crime and drugs: the issues and the literature." Journal of Drug Issues.

_____ (1981) "The ecology of crime and drugs." Criminology.

_____ (1976) "The relationship between type of drug use and arrest charge in an arrested population," pp. 409–418 in Research Triangle Institute, Drug Use and Crime. Springfield, VA: National Technical Information Service.

McBRIDE, D. C. and B. R. RUSSE (1979) "The social characteristics of PCP users." Addictive Diseases.

McCOY, C. B. et al. (1978) "The social cost of treatment denial." Final Report to the National Institute on Drug Abuse.

McGLOTHLIN, W. (1979) "Drugs and crime," in R. L. DuPont et al. (eds.) Handbook on Drug Abuse. Rockville, MD: National Institute on Drug Abuse.

MONFORTE, J. R. and W. U. SPITZ (1975) "Narcotic abuse among homicides in Detroit." Journal of Forensic Sciences 20: 186–190.

National Institute on Drug Abuse (NIDA) Annual Survey (1979) National Institute on Drug Abuse Annual Household Survey. Washington, DC: Government Printing Office.

O'DONNELL, J. A., H. L. VOSS, R. R. CLAYTON, G. T. SLATIN, and R. G. W. ROOM (1976) Young Men and Drugs: A Nationwide Survey. NIDA Monograph Series 5. Washington, DC: Government Printing Office.

RAWLIN, J. W. (1968) "Street level abuse of amphetamines," in J. R. Russo (ed.) Amphetamine Abuse. Springfield, IL: Charles C Thomas.

REASONS, C. E. (1975) "The addict as criminal." Crime and Delinquency: 19–27.

RICH, J. (1956) "Types of stealing." Lancet 2: 496.

RITTENHOUSE, J. D. (1978) "Report of the Task Force on Comparability in Survey Research on Drugs." Technical Paper, National Institute on Drug Abuse, Rockville, Maryland.

ROSSI, P. H., E. WAITE, C. E. BOSE, and R. E. BERK (1974) "The seriousness of crimes: normative structure and individual differences." American Sociological Review 31: 324–337.

SCHORR, M. (1978) "Gunfights in the cocaine corral." New York 11: 48–57.

SCHUR, E. (1969) Our Criminal Society. Englewood Cliffs, NJ: Prentice-Hall.

SILVERMAN, L. P. and N. L. SPRUILL (1977) "Urban crime and price of heroin." Journal of Urban Economics 4: 80–103.

SMITH, R. (1972) "Speed and violence: compulsive methamphetamine abuse and criminality in the Haight-Ashbury District in drug abuse," pp. 435–448 in C. Zarsfonetis (ed.) Proceedings of the International Conference. Philadelphia: Lee & Febiger.

———— (1969) "The world of the Haight-Ashbury speed freak." Journal of Psychedelic Drugs 2: 77–83.

STEPHENS, R. C. and R. D. ELLIS (1975) "Narcotic addicts and crime: analysis of recent trends." Criminology 12: 474–488.

TERRY, C. R. and M. PELLENS (1928) The Opium Problem. New York: Bureau of Social Hygiene.

TINKLENBERG, J. R. and K. M. WOODROW (1974) "Drug use among youthful assaultive and sexual offenders," in S. H. Frazier (ed.) Aggression: Proceedings of the 1972 Annual Meeting of the Association for Research in Nervous and Mental Disease. Baltimore: Williams & Wilkins.

VOSS, H. R. (1976) "Problems of definition and measurement in survey research on drugs." Appendix to NIDA Task Force Report on Crime and Drugs. Springfield, VA: National Technical Information Service.

WEISSMAN, J. C. (1978) "Understanding the drugs and crime connection: a systematic examination of drugs and crime relationships." Journal of Psychedelic Drugs 10: 171–192.

ZAHN, M. A. and M. BENCIVENGO (1974) "Violent death: a comparison between drug users and non-drug users." Addictive Diseases 1: 283.

6

CRIMINAL INVOLVEMENTS OF
MINORITY GROUP ADDICTS

CARL D. CHAMBERS, SARA W. DEAN,
and MICHAEL F. PLETCHER

When one reviews the literature relevant to the criminal involvements of narcotic addicts, one finds an emerging consensus on several conclusions. For example, most researchers have reached *at least* general agreement on *at least* the following:

(1) The criminal involvements of narcotic addicts are extensive and varied, and most of their crimes go unreported and/or unsolved (see Inciardi and Chambers, 1972).

(2) The criminal involvements of narcotic addicts are greater than their criminal involvements prior to the onset of addiction, and they are more involved than criminals who are not addicted (see Chambers, 1974; Cushman, 1974; File et al., 1974; Plair and Jackson, 1970; Weissman et al., 1974).

(3) In order to place the criminal involvements of narcotic addicts in an appropriate perspective, one must control for the race, sex, and age of the addicts (see

AUTHORS' NOTE: The studies discussed herein—of active Black male addicts in Philadelphia, active Black male addicts in Washington, D.C., active Black female addicts in Philadelphia, active Black female addicts in Washington, D.C., active Mexican-American male addicts

Ball, 1970; Ball and Lau, 1970; Chambers and Moffett, 1970; Chambers et al., 1970a, 1970b; File et al., 1974; James, 1976).

(4) Although the mainstays of the narcotic addict's crime repertoire are still property crimes, vice crimes, and selling drugs to other addicts, addicts have become increasingly involved in the commission of crimes against persons when these "personal" crimes produce an immediate financial return (see Chambers, 1974; Greenberg and Adler, 1974; Inciardi and Chambers, 1972; Preble and Casey, 1969; Weissman et al., 1974).

(5) The specific criminal involvements of narcotic addicts probably vary by both time and place (see Ball, 1970; U.S. Bureau of Narcotics and Dangerous Drugs, 1971).

Unfortunately, most of the literature from which this consensus has emerged is based on data obtained from addicts once they have been arrested, become incarcerated, or entered a rehabilitation program for their addiction. A notable exception to this can be found in the work done by Preble and Casey (1969).

This chapter was conceptualized by the authors to contribute to the better understanding of the criminal involvements of at least the Black and Mexican-American narcotics addicts by reporting data on the following:

(1) A contemporary, comparative assessment of the differences in criminal involvements of felons who abused heroin versus those who did not. This comparison was accomplished among *incarcerated Mexican-American felons* in San Antonio and records all of their crimes during the year which preceded their arrest.

(2) A contemporary assessment of the crimes being committed by *Black male active addicts* in Philadelphia.

(3) A contemporary assessment of the crimes being committed by *Black female active addicts* in Philadelphia.

(4) A contemporary assessment of the crimes being committed by *Black male active addicts* in Washington, D.C.

(5) A contemporary assessment of the crimes being committed by *Black female active addicts* in Washington, D.C.

(6) A contemporary assessment of the crimes being committed by *Mexican-American male active addicts* in Phoenix.

(7) A contemporary assessment of the crimes being committed by *Mexican-American female active addicts* in Phoenix.

in Phoenix, and active Mexican-American female addicts in Phoenix—were conducted under the direction of Carl D. Chambers and funded solely by the Personal Development Institute, Geneva, Florida, as part of a larger effort to produce information on the evolution of heroin addiction among minorities in the United States.

COMPARATIVE CRIMINAL INVOLVEMENTS OF
MEXICAN-AMERICAN ADDICT AND NONADDICT FELONS

During 1977–1978, White et al. (forthcoming) conducted an extensive interview study among Mexican-American felons incarcerated in San Antonio's county jail. A major focus of this study was to compare the criminal involvements of 95 Mexican-American felons who were heroin abusers with 61 Mexican-American felons who did not abuse heroin. At one level, all these Mexican-American felons were drug "users" in that they were or had been marijuana smokers. For our purposes here, we are reporting only those data relating to a comparison between those who did and those who did not use heroin.

When the investigators compared Mexican-American felons who used heroin with those who did not, they encountered a number of both expected and unexpected differences between the two groups. As criminals, those who used heroin were found to be significantly different from nonusers in several respects. Consider the following general demographic differences:

(1) There was a higher proportion of women in the heroin-abusing population of incarcerated felons than among those felons who had not abused heroin (11.6 percent versus 4.9 percent). One would expect heroin-abusing women to be more liable for arrest and incarceration than women felons who did not abuse heroin.

(2) The heroin abusers tended to be an older group of felons. While 29.4 percent of the heroin abusers were above age 30, only 13.1 percent of the nonabusers were that old.

(3) The heroin-abusing felons were not found to be different in education attainment or in marital status.

(4) Although the heroin-abusing felons and nonabusing felons had acquired essentially the same occupational skills, the heroin users were less likely to be using them. For example, 22.1 percent of the heroin abusers reported crime as their *only* source of income, and 87.4 percent reported at least partial support from crimes. This compared to 4.9 percent of the nonabusers whose *only* source of income was crime and 60.7 percent who derived at least some income from committing crimes. Interestingly, 12.6 percent of the heroin abusers and 4.9 percent of the nonabusing felons considered themselves to be "career" criminals.

As criminals, those who had been heroin abusers were found to be significantly different from those who had not been, in several respects: (1) Heroin-abusing felons had begun their crime careers earlier. Both, however, normally began these careers by committing property crimes. (2)

Heroin-abusing felons had experienced an arrest earlier in their crime careers. (3) Probably an artifact of having been criminals longer, the heroin-abusing felons had experienced more arrests and had spent more time incarcerated.

When the investigators controlled for the crimes that had been committed during the *year* preceding the current arrest and incarceration, it became obvious that those Mexican-Americans who abused heroin were much more involved in committing crimes than felons who had not abused heroin: (1) A greater proportion of heroin abusers were involved in committing almost every type of crime during the past year than had been the case with nonabusing felons. (2) In addition to being involved in more types of crimes, once involved, the heroin-abusing felons committed a greater number of crimes within each type. (3) A greater proportion of the heroin-abusing felons were found to have carried or used a weapon while committing their crimes. The weapon most frequently carried by these heroin-abusing crimi-

TABLE 6.1   Comparative Criminal Involvements of Mexican-American Addicts and Nonaddicts (SAN ANTONIO, 1977/1978): Types of Crimes Committed Last 12 Months

Type of Crime	Percentage of Addict Sample Committing This Type of Crime (n=95)	Percentage of Nonaddict Sample Committing This Type of Crime (n=61)
Burglary	26.3	24.6
Shoplifting	37.9	11.5
Forgery	14.7	1.6
Theft from auto	40.0	16.4
Auto theft	15.8	14.8
Picking pockets	3.2	0
Con games	12.6	3.3
Arson	4.2	0
Extortion	3.2	0
Prostitute thefts	9.5	0
Fencing stolen goods	39.0	19.7
Other thefts	21.1	6.6
Assault and robbery	12.6	23.0
Armed robbery	29.5	19.7
Gambling	5.3	3.3
Prostitution (women only)	85.7	33.3
Procuring (men only)	13.6	3.5
Loan-sharking	1.1	4.9
Drug sales	10.5	26.2

TABLE 6.2 Extent of Involvement in Specific Types of Crimes Committed
During Last 12 Months: Mexican-American Addicts and
Nonaddicts (SAN ANTONIO, 1977/1978)

	95 Addicts		61 Nonaddicts	
Type and Number of Crimes	n	%	n	%
1. Armed Robberies				
None	67	70.5	49	80.3
1–5	21	22.1	11	18.0
6–10	3	3.2	1	1.6
11–20	1	1.0	0	0
21 or more	3	3.2	0	0
2. Burglaries				
None	42	44.2	38	62.3
1–5	18	19.0	14	33.0
6–10	9	9.4	4	6.6
11–20	6	6.3	4	6.6
21 or more	20	21.1	1	1.6
3. Shoplifting				
None	59	62.1	54	88.5
1–5	8	8.4	5	8.2
6–10	9	9.4	1	1.6
11–20	2	2.1	0	0
21 or more	17	17.9	1	1.6

TABLE 6.3 Comparative Use of Weapons During the Commission of Crimes
by Mexican-Americans

	Addicts (n=95)	Nonaddicts (n=61)
Carried A Weapon	50.5	24.6
	(n=48)	(n=15)
Type of Weapon Carried Among Those Who Carried One		
Gun	70.8	66.7
Knife	20.8	20.0
Gun and knife	6.3	6.7
Other	2.1	6.7
Total	100.0	100.0

TABLE 6.4   Proportion of Total Criminal Involvement to Support
            Drug Use Among 95 Mexican-American Addicts

Proportion	n	Percentage		
0– 10%	14	14.7		
11– 20%	2	2.1	22.1	
21– 30%	5	5.3		41.1
31– 40%	3	3.2		
41– 50%	15	15.8		
51– 60%	2	2.1		
61– 70%	2	2.1		
71– 80%	21	22.1		59.0
81– 90%	11	11.6	54.8	
91–100%	20	21.1		
Total	95	100.0		

nals was a gun. Of all those who carried weapons, 77.1 percent carried at
least a gun. Some also carried knives at the same time. Of note, *39.0 percent
of these heroin-abusing felons had carried a gun during their search for
money in support of their drug use*. (4) As one would expect, a significant
portion of the crimes committed by these heroin-abusing felons was directly
related to their drug use.

CRIMINAL INVOLVEMENTS OF CONTEMPORARY
ACTIVE BLACK MALE ADDICTS

ACTIVE BLACK MALE ADDICTS
IN PHILADELPHIA

During October 1976, 70 active Black male addicts were identified and
interviewed in Philadelphia. The identification and interviews were accomplished by a Black male, a former heroin addict who had been active in the
heroin subculture of the city and had been an acquaintance of the investigator
for some ten years. Three criteria had to be met before an addict could be
included in the study: (1) The addict had to have been active "on the street"
for at least the past 30 days, i.e., not in a treatment program, not in the
hospital, and not in jail. (2) The addict had to have used heroin on three
successive days during the past 7 days. (3) The addict had to have committed
at least one crime during the past 30 days to obtain money to be used for
heroin.

The interviews were directed toward determining (1) what types of
crimes were being committed by these addicts, (2) what types of crimes were

the *primary* crimes being committed, and (3) what proportion of one's total monthly income was being derived from the crimes being committed.

The respondents were paid a fee for the interview.

Findings

These 70 Philadelphia active Black male addicts were found to be committing a wide variety of specific crimes within the four general categories of crimes, and very few could be considered as specialists in a specific crime: (1) If one rank orders the *specific crimes* by the proportion of the 70 addicts who committed those crimes during the last 30 days, the most frequent are burglaries, drug selling, shoplifting offenses, armed robberies, and assaultive robberies. (2) If one rank orders each specific crime by the proportion of the 70 addicts who identified that crime as the one they viewed as their *primary crime*, the rank order changes with only burglaries, armed robberies, drug sales, and shoplifting, being indicated by many. (3) Committing crimes is the primary means whereby these active addicts support their drug use and obtain monies for other "living expenses." Seventy percent derive essentially all of their monthly income from committing crimes. Of those who had at least *some* legitimate income (n = 21 or 30.0 percent), 57.1 percent were working at legal jobs, 9.5 percent had working spouses, and 33.3 percent were receiving welfare monies either directly or through their spouses.

ACTIVE BLACK MALE ADDICTS IN WASHINGTON, D.C.

During the period December 1977 to January 1978, 25 active Black male addicts were identified and interviewed in Washington, D.C. The same procedures and criteria described for the study in Philadelphia were employed here as well. These interviews were expanded, however, to permit additional assessments.

Findings

These 25 Washington, D.C., Black male addicts were found to be more involved in committing a wide variety of specific crimes than the Black male addicts in Philadelphia. In addition, these Washington, D.C., addicts were more likely to be committing crimes against persons.

(1) If one rank orders the *specific crimes* by the proportion of the 25 addicts who committed that crime during the last 30 days, addicts are most often involved in the commission of assaultive robberies, burglaries, drug sales, armed robberies, and thefts from autos.

(2) If one rank orders the specific crimes being committed by the *number of crimes* in each, they are most often involved in procuring, drug sales, burglaries, assaultive robberies, and shopliftings.

(3) Although the *total dollar return* was approximately the same for property crimes and robberies, the *average dollar return* for the individual robbery offenses was three times greater than for individual property crimes.

(4) Of special note are the prevalence and characteristics of the robbers who are in this study population. Consider the following:

- 56.0 percent of all these addicts reported committing at least one robbery during the 30 days, and the average was 3.5 robberies;

- 20.0 percent of all these addicts reported robbery as the *only* type of crime they had committed during the 30 days; and

TABLE 6.5   Criminal Involvements of 70 Black Male Addicts
(Philadelphia, 1976): Types of Crimes Committed Last 30 Days

Type of Crime	Percentage of Sample Committing This Type of Crime	Percentage of Sample for Whom This Was the Primary Crime
Burglary	60.0	37.1
Shoplifting	32.9	12.9
Forgery	2.9	0
Theft from auto	2.9	0
Auto theft	2.9	0
Purse snatching	1.4	0
Picking pockets	1.4	0
Con game	4.3	2.9
Other property	0	0
Assault and robbery	17.1	4.3
Armed robbery	27.1	21.4
Other personal	0	0
Gambling	18.6	0
Procuring	4.3	0
Other vice	0	0
Drug sales	60.0	17.1

Any property crime 82.9%	Only property crime 17.1%
Any personal crime...............38.6%	Only personal crime 1.4%
Any vice crime 21.4%	Only vice crime................... 0
Any drug selling 60.0%	Only drug selling 8.6%

- of those who committed robberies, 78.6 percent assaulted their victims, 57.1 percent derived *more* of their income from robberies than from all the other crimes they committed during the same period, and 36.0 percent committed only robberies.

TABLE 6.6   Proportion of Total Monthly Income Derived from Criminal Activity Among 70 Black Male Addicts

Proportion	n	Percentage
1– 25%	1	1.4
26– 50%	7	10.0
51– 75%	13	18.6
76–100%	49	70.0
Total	70	100.0

TABLE 6.7   Criminal Involvements of 25 Black Male Addicts (WASHINGTON, D.C., 1977/1978): Crimes Committed Last 30 Days

Type of Crime	Percentage of Sample Committing This Type of Crime	Total Number of This Type of Crime Committed in 30 Days
Burglary	36.0	62
Shoplifting	16.0	27
Forgery	8.0	6
Theft from auto	28.0	20
Auto theft	12.0	4
Purse snatching	16.0	7
Picking pockets	0	0
Con games	12.0	4
Other "property" crimes	12.0	20
Assault and robbery	44.0	34
Armed robbery	32.0	15
Other "personal" crimes	0	0
Gambling	12.0	30
Procuring	8.0	260
Other vice crimes	8.0	13
Drug sales	36.0	175

Any property crime	64.0%	Only property crime	12.0%
Any personal crime	56.0%	Only personal crime	20.0%
Any vice crime	24.0%	Only vice crime	0
Any drug selling	36.0%	Only drug selling	0

TABLE 6.8 Comparative Monetary Return for Different Types of Crimes Committed During a 30-Day Period: 25 Black Male Addicts

Type of Crime	Total Crimes Committed		Total Approximate Dollar Return*	Percentage of Total Dollar Return	Average Dollar Return Per Crime
	n	%			
Property crimes	150	22.2	$11,600	35.6	$ 77.33
Personal crimes	49	7.2	11,150	34.2	227.55
Vice crimes	303	44.8	3,500	10.7	11.55
Drug sales	175	25.8	6,350	19.5	36.29
Total	677	100.0	$32,600	100.0	$ 48.15

*The self-reported dollar amount for each crime was rounded to the nearest $50 prior to summing.

TABLE 6.9 Criminal Involvements of Various Age Cohorts of 25 Black Male Addicts: Crimes Committed During 30-Day Period

Age Cohort	Property		Personal		Vice		Drug Sales		Total	
	n	%	n	%	n	%	n	%	n	%
15–19 (4)	26	45.6	11	19.3	0	0	20	35.1	57	100.0
20–24 (6)	36	66.7	10	18.5	3	5.6	5	9.3	54	100.0
25–29 (6)	73	21.9	6	1.8	240	71.9	15	4.4	334	100.0
30–34 (6)	4	2.2	22	12.0	23	12.5	135	73.4	184	100.0
35–39 (1)	1	12.5	0	0	7	87.5	0	0	8	100.0
40–44 (1)	4	11.8	0	0	30	88.2	0	0	34	100.0
45–49 (1)	6	100.0	0	0	0	0	0	0	6	100.0
Total (25)	150	22.2	49	7.2	302	44.6	175	25.9	677	100.0

Age Cohort	Property		Personal		Vice		Drug Sales		Total	
	n	%	n	%	n	%	n	%	n	%
15–19 (4)	26	17.3	11	22.5	0	0	20	11.4	57	8.4
20–24 (6)	36	24.0	10	20.4	3	1.0	5	2.9	54	8.0
25–29 (6)	73	48.7	6	12.2	240	79.2	15	8.6	334	49.3
30–34 (6)	4	2.7	22	44.9	23	7.6	135	77.1	184	27.2
35–39 (1)	1	.7	0	0	7	2.3	0	0	8	1.2
40–44 (1)	4	2.7	0	0	30	9.9	0	0	34	5.0
45–49 (1)	6	4.0	0	0	0	0	0	0	6	.9
Total (25)	150	100.0	49	100.0	303	100.0	175	100.0	677	100.0

(5) The 25 Black male addicts ranged in age from 19 to 48, with an average age of 27.1 (median was 28). The types of crimes committed were found to be related to age. Of special relevance, a greater proportion of the total crimes committed by addicts under the age of 25 were for crimes against persons than for those over age 25. No one over the age of 35 had committed a crime against a person. The data suggest that as Black male

addicts become older, they are much more likely to be committing vice crimes or selling drugs.

CRIMINAL INVOLVEMENTS OF CONTEMPORARY ACTIVE BLACK FEMALE ADDICTS

ACTIVE BLACK FEMALE ADDICTS IN PHILADELPHIA

During October, 1976, 26 active Black female addicts were identified and interviewed in Philadelphia. The identification and interviews were accomplished by a Black female former heroin addict who had been active in that subculture for some ten years prior to entering a methadone maintenance program. The interviewer had been an acquaintance of the investigator for some eight years. This study was a companion study, in progress simultaneously with the study of active Black male addicts. The procedures and criteria described above for that study were employed with this study as well.

Findings

As was the case with the active Black male addicts interviewed during the same time period in the same subculture, these 26 active Black female addicts were found to be committing a wide variety of different specific crimes within the four general categories of crimes, and very few could be considered specialists in any one specific crime.

(1) If one rank orders the *specific crimes* by the proportion of the 26 addicts who committed those crimes during the preceding 30 days, one finds these women are most frequently involved in the commission of shoplifting offenses, drug selling, prostitution, and robberies.

(2) If one rank orders the specific crimes by the proportion of the 26 addicts who identified the particular crime as the one they viewed as their *primary crime*, the rank order remains the same: shoplifting, selling drugs, prostitution, and robberies. In fact, these four specific crimes were the only crimes identified as primary crimes.

(3) If one rank orders the *categories of crimes* by the proportion of the 26 addicts who committed crimes within the category, these Black female addicts were committing property crimes, selling drugs, and committing vice crimes (prostituting themselves); only a minority committed crimes against persons.

(4) Committing crimes is the primary means these female addicts utilize to support their drug use and to obtain monies for other "living expenses."

Some 92 percent derive at least half of their total monthly income from crime, and 38.5 percent derive virtually all their income from crimes. Of those who had at least *some* legitimate income (n = 17 or 65.4 percent), 88.2 percent were receiving some form of welfare monies and 11.8 percent were working.

When one compares the criminal involvements of the Black females with the Black males active in the same heroin subculture at the same time, the following generalizations seem appropriate:

(1) About the same proportion of female and male addicts are involved in committing property crimes and in having property crimes as their primary crime. However, the specific property crimes they commit are different. Black females shoplift and Black males commit burglaries.

(2) Black males appear more "opportunistic," committing just about whatever crime presents itself. Black females appear more focused in the crimes they commit.

(3) Black males are much more involved in committing assaultive robberies and armed robberies than are Black females. In addition, the Black male is much more likely to commit robberies as his primary crime but neither Black male nor Black female is likely to commit robberies only.

(4) Both Black males and Black females are heavily involved in the selling of drugs, but the females are much more likely to sell drugs as their primary crime. Approximately 1 in 10 of the active addicts of both sexes sells drugs exclusively.

ACTIVE BLACK FEMALE ADDICTS IN WASHINGTON, D.C.

During the period December 1977 to January 1978, 15 active Black female addicts were identified and interviewed in Washington, D.C. The procedures and criteria described for the other studies in Philadelphia and Washington, D.C., were employed here as well. The one difference in this study was the interviewer, who when recruited was not a long-time personal acquaintance of the investigator. She was a former addict who had successfully completed treatment and was employed as an outreach worker in a local drug rehabilitation program.

Findings

These 15 Washington, D.C., Black female addicts were found to be much more involved in committing a wide variety of specific crimes than the Black female addicts in Philadelphia. In addition, these Washington addicts were much more involved in the committing of robberies and in prostitution, but much less involved in the selling of drugs, than their Philadelphia counterparts.

The following characterize the types and amount of crimes being committed by these active Black female addicts in the Washington, D.C., heroin subculture:

(1) If one rank orders the *specific crimes* by the proportion of the 15 addicts who committed those crimes during the previous 30 days, one finds these women are most frequently involved in the commission of prostitution, shoplifting offenses, "other" property crimes (usually prostitute thefts or mailbox theft), assaultive robberies, and forgeries.

(2) If one rank orders the specific crimes by the *total number of times the crime was committed* during the 30-day period, the Black female addicts most frequently prostitute themselves, sell drugs, commit "other" property crimes (usually thefts from prostitution customers or from mailboxes), and shoplift. No other crime approaches the prevalence of these four crimes.

(3) If one rank orders the *crime type categories* by the proportion of addicts who report at least some crimes in that category, these addicts most frequently committed property crimes, followed by vice crime, crimes against persons, and drug sales. Very few of these Black female addicts specialized in a specific crime, but 40.0 percent specialized in only one of the four categories of crimes (most frequently property crimes or prostitution).

(4) If one rank orders the *crime type categories by the total dollar return* for the crimes committed within each category, these Black female addicts derived the greatest proportion of their illegal monies from property crimes, followed by prostitution, drug sales, and robberies. However, the average dollar return per crime was the highest for robberies. The average return for a robbery was more than two and a half times greater than for the average property crime.

(5) Of special note are the prevalence and characteristics of the assaultive and armed robbers in this study population of 15 active Black female addicts. Consider the following:

- One-third of these female addicts committed at least one assaultive or armed robbery during the 30-day study period, and the average was 3.4 such robberies;

- 6.7 percent reported robbery as the only type of crime they had committed during that time period; and

- of those who committed robberies, 80.0 percent assaulted their victim, 20.0 percent derived *more* of their total illicit income from robberies than from all the other crimes they had committed, and 20.0 percent committed only robberies.

(6) The 15 Black female addicts ranged in age from 19 to 43, with an average age of 28.9 (median was 27). The types of crimes committed were found to be related to age. Crimes against persons were being committed

TABLE 6.10   Criminal Involvements of 26 Black Female Addicts
             (Philadelphia, 1976): Types of Crimes Committed Last 30 Days

Type of Crime	Percentage of Sample Committing This Type of Crime	Percentage of Sample for Whom This Was the Primary Crime
Burglary	3.9	0
Shoplifting	69.2	46.2
Forgery	0	0
Theft from auto	0	0
Auto theft	0	0
Purse snatching	0	0
Picking pockets	3.9	0
Con game	0	0
Other property	3.9	0
Assault and robbery	0	0
Armed robbery	11.5	3.9
Other personal	0	0
Gambling	0	0
Prostitution	34.6	11.5
Other vice	0	0
Drug sales	50.0	38.5

Any property crime . . . . 69.2%   Only property crime 15.4%
Any personal crime . . . . 11.5%   Only personal crime   0
Any vice crime . . . . 34.6%   Only vice crime 7.7%
Any drug selling . . . . 50.0%   Only drug selling 11.5%

TABLE 6.11   Proportion of Total Monthly Income Derived from Criminal
             Activity Among 26 Black Female Addicts

Proportion	n	%
1– 25%	0	0
26– 50%	2	7.7
51– 75%	14	53.9
76–100%	10	38.5
Total	26	100.0

TABLE 6.12   Criminal Involvements of 15 Black Female Addicts
(Washington, D.C., 1977/1978): Crimes Committed Last 30 Days

Type of Crime	Percentage of Sample Committing This Type of Crime	Total Number of This Type of Crime Committed in 30 Days
Burglary	20.0	5
Shoplifting	40.0	66
Forgery	26.7	19
Theft from auto	0	0
Auto theft	13.3	3
Purse snatching	6.7	2
Picking pockets	13.3	7
Con games	13.3	6
Other "property" crimes	40.0	101
Assault and robbery	26.7	14
Armed robbery	13.3	3
Other "personal" crimes	0	0
Gambling	0	0
Prostitution	60.0	296
Other vice crimes	0	0
Drug sales	26.0	220

Any property crime . . . . 73.3%   Only property crime 13.3%
Any personal crime . . . . 33.3%   Only personal crime 6.7%
Any vice crime . . . . 60.0%   Only vice crime 13.3%
Any drug selling . . . . 26.7%   Only drug selling 6.7%

TABLE 6.13   Comparative Monetary Return for Different Types of Crimes
Committed During a 30-Day Period: 15 Black Female Addicts

Type of Crime	Total Crimes Committed n	%	Total Approximate Dollar Return*	Percentage of Total Dollar Return	Average Dollar Return per Crime
Property crimes	209	28.2	$ 8,050	49.8	$ 38.52
Personal crimes	17	2.3	1,750	10.8	102.94
Vice crimes	296	39.9	4,000	24.8	13.51
Drug sales	220	29.6	2,350	14.6	10.68
Total	742	100.0	$16,150	100.0	$ 21.77

*The self-reported dollar amount for each crime was rounded to the nearest $50 prior to summing.

TABLE 6.14   Criminal Involvements of Various Age Cohorts of 15 Black
Female Addicts: Crimes Committed During Last 30 Days

Age Cohort	Property		Personal		Vice		Drug Sales		Total	
	n	%	n	%	n	%	n	%	n	%
15–19 (1)	15	55.6	9	33.3	3	11.1	0	0	27	100.0
20–24 (5)	23	18.1	7	5.5	97	76.4	0	0	127	100.0
25–29 (2)	79	72.5	0	0	20	18.3	10	9.2	109	100.0
30–34 (3)	25	11.9	0	0	175	83.3	10	4.8	210	100.0
35–39 (2)	47	31.8	0	0	1	.7	100	67.6	148	100.0
40–44 (2)	20	16.5	1	.8	0	0	100	82.6	121	100.0
Total (15)	209	28.2	17	2.3	296	39.9	220	29.7	742	100.0
15–19 (1)	15	7.2	9	52.9	3	1.0	0	0	27	3.6
20–24 (5)	23	11.0	7	41.2	97	32.8	0	0	127	17.1
25–29 (2)	79	37.8	0	0	20	6.8	10	4.5	109	14.7
30–34 (3)	25	12.0	0	0	175	59.1	10	4.5	210	28.3
35–39 (2)	47	22.5	0	0	1	.3	100	45.5	148	20.0
40–44 (2)	20	9.6	1	5.9	0	0	100	45.5	121	16.3
Total (15)	209	100.0	17	100.0	296	100.0	220	100.0	742	100.0

almost entirely by female addicts under the age of 25, while drug sales were
being committed almost entirely by those female addicts above the age of
35. Female addicts in the age ranges of 20–24 and 30–34 were primarily
prostituting themselves.

CRIMINAL INVOLVEMENTS OF CONTEMPORARY
ACTIVE MEXICAN-AMERICAN MALE ADDICTS

ACTIVE MEXICAN-AMERICAN MALE
ADDICTS IN PHOENIX

During the period December 1977 to January 1978, 25 Mexican-
American male active addicts were identified and interviewed in Phoenix.
The same procedures and criteria were used in Phoenix that were used in the
studies with Black addicts in Philadelphia and Washington, D.C. These
procedures and criteria have been described earlier in this chapter. The
interviewer for this study was a former heroin user and "dealer" who had
been an acquaintance of the investigator for twelve years and had been an
interviewer on several prior studies with the investigator.

Findings

The 25 active Mexican-American male addicts were found to be "opportunistic" criminals committing a wide variety of different crimes in their quest for money. The following characterize the types of crimes these active addicts committed during the 30-day study period, and their success as criminals.

(1) If one rank orders the *specific crimes* by the proportion of the 25 addicts who committed them, the addicts are most frequently involved in the commission of burglaries, robberies (both assaultive and armed), thefts from autos, and the selling of drugs.

(2) If one rank orders the specific crimes by the *total number of times the crime was committed,* these Mexican-American male addicts most frequently sold drugs, committed burglaries, stole things out of automobiles, committed "other" property crimes, and committed robberies.

TABLE 6.15 Criminal Involvements of 25 Mexican-American Male Addicts (Phoenix, 1977/1978): Crimes Committed Last 30 Days

Type of Crime	Percentage of Sample Committing This Type of Crime	Total Number of This Type of Crime Committed in 30 Days
Burglary	52.0	47
Shoplifting	8.0	11
Forgery	4.0	2
Theft from auto	32.0	44
Auto theft	8.0	4
Purse snatching	20.0	6
Picking pockets	0	0
Con games	4.0	1
Other "property" crimes	16.0	33
Assault and robbery	32.0	20
Armed robbery	32.0	10
Other "personal" crimes	0	0
Gambling	8.0	15
Procuring	4.0	20
Other vice crimes	0	0
Drug sales	28.0	366

Any property crime . . . . 76.0%   Only property crime 20.0%
Any personal crime . . . . 52.0%   Only personal crime 20.0%
Any vice crime . . . . 12.0%   Only vice crime   0
Any drug selling . . . . 28.0%   Only drug selling 4.0%

TABLE 6.16   Comparative Monetary Return for Different Types of Crimes
Committed During a 30-Day Period: 25 Mexican-American
Male Addicts

| Type of Crime | Total Crimes Committed | | Total Approximate Dollar Return* | Percentage of Total Dollar Return | Average Dollar Return Per Crime |
	n	%			
Property crimes	148	25.6	$10,850	41.7	$ 73.31
Personal crimes	30	5.2	6,150	23.7	205.00
Vice crimes	35	6.0	1,550	6.0	44.29
Drug sales	366	63.2	7,450	28.7	20.36
Total	579	100.0	$26,000	100.0	$ 44.91

*The self-reported dollar amount for each crime was rounded to the nearest $50 prior to summing.

TABLE 6.17   Criminal Involvements of Various Age Cohorts of 25
Mexican-American Male Addicts: Crimes Committed
During Last 30 Days

| Age Cohort | Property | | Personal | | Vice | | Drug Sales | | Total | |
	n	%	n	%	n	%	n	%	n	%
15–19 (3)	28	73.7	1	2.6	0	0	9	23.7	38	100.0
20–24 (10)	63	70.8	20	22.5	5	5.6	1	1.1	89	100.0
25–29 (7)	35	37.6	8	8.6	20	21.5	30	32.3	93	100.0
30–34 (4)	22	6.2	0	0	10	2.8	326	91.1	358	100.0
35–39 (0)	0	0	0	0	0	0	0	0	0	0
40–44 (1)	0	0	1	100.0	0	0	0	0	1	100.0
Total (25)	148	25.6	30	5.2	35	6.0	366	63.2	579	100.0
15–19 (3)	28	18.9	1	3.3	0	0	9	2.5	38	6.6
20–24 (10)	63	42.6	20	66.7	5	14.3	1	.3	89	15.4
25–29 (7)	35	23.6	8	26.7	20	57.1	30	8.2	93	16.1
30–34 (4)	22	14.9	0	0	10	28.6	326	89.1	358	61.8
35–39 (0)	0	0	0	0	0	0	0	0	0	0
40–44 (1)	0	0	1	3.3	0	0	0	0	1	.2
Total (25)	148	100.0	30	100.0	35	100.0	366	100.0	579	100.0

(3) If one rank orders the *crime type categories* by the proportion of
addicts who report at least some crimes in that category, these addicts most
frequently committed property crimes, followed by crimes against persons,
drug sales, and, finally, vice crimes. Interestingly, these Mexican-American
male addicts were as likely to "specialize" in crimes against persons (robberies) as they were to concentrate only on property crimes.

(4) If one rank orders the *crime type categories by the total dollar return* for the crimes committed within each category, these Mexican-American male addicts derived the greatest proportion of their illegal monies from property crimes, followed by the selling of drugs, the commission of robberies, and only incidentally from vice crimes. As we had come to expect, however, the average dollar return per crime was the highest for robberies. The average return for a robbery was almost three times higher than for the average property crime, and ten times higher than for the average drug sale.

(5) Based on our findings with Mexican-American addicts in San Antonio, we had expected to find a high prevalence of crimes against persons being committed by the cohort in Phoenix. Such was the case:

- More than half of these active male addicts in Phoenix had committed at least one assaultive robbery or armed robbery during the 30-day study period, and the average was 2.3 such robberies;

- 20 percent of the total study population reported robbery as the *only* type of crime they had committed during the 30-day period; and

- of those addicts who committed robberies, 61.5 percent admitted assaulting the victim during the commission of the robbery, 53.8 percent derived more of their illegal income from robberies than from all other crimes they committed, and 38.5 percent committed *only* robberies.

(6) The 25 Mexican-American male addicts ranged in age from 17 to 40, with an average age of 25.0 (median was 23). The types of crimes committed were related to age:

- Addicts 15–19 were almost exclusively committing property crimes or selling drugs.

- Addicts 20–24 were almost exclusively committing property crimes or robberies.

- Addicts 25–29 were "opportunistic" criminals committing all types of crimes.

- Addicts 30–34 were almost exclusively drug sellers.

CRIMINAL INVOLVEMENTS OF CONTEMPORARY ACTIVE MEXICAN-AMERICAN FEMALE ADDICTS

ACTIVE MEXICAN-AMERICAN FEMALE ADDICTS IN PHOENIX

During the period December 1977 to January 1978, 20 active Mexican-American female addicts were identified and interviewed in Phoenix. The same procedures and criteria were used in Phoenix that were used in the studies with Black addicts in Philadelphia and Washington, D.C. These procedures and criteria have been described earlier in this chapter. The interviewer for this study was a former heroin addict who had been an acquaintance of the investigator and had worked on similar projects with him for more than five years.

Findings

The 20 active Mexican-American female addicts were found to be generally opportunistic in their criminal involvement, committing a wide variety of specific types of crimes. When compared with active male addicts in the same city, they were more involved in committing shoplifting offenses and forgeries than were the males, but less likely to be involved in the commission of robberies. As drug sellers, however, they were as likely to be involved as were the males.

(1) If one rank orders the *specific crimes* by the proportion of the 20 female addicts who committed them, these women were most frequently prostituting themselves, followed by equal involvements in robberies, shopliftings, and forgeries.

(2) If one rank orders the specific crimes by the *total number of times each was committed* during the 30-day study period, prostitution offenses were the most prevalent, followed by shoplifting offenses, drug sales, forgeries, and robberies.

(3) If one rank orders the *crime type categories* by the proportion of female addicts reporting some crimes in that category, one finds most often property crimes, followed by vice crimes, crimes against persons, and drug selling, in that order. Interestingly, there was considerable specialization within crime categories. For example, 20.0 percent of the women committed *only* property crimes, 15.0 percent committed *only* vice crimes, 15.0 percent were *only* drug sellers, and 10.0 percent committed *only* crimes against persons (assaultive and/or armed robberies).

(4) If one rank orders the *crime type categories by the total dollar return* for the crimes committed within each category, the Mexican-American female addicts derived the greatest proportion of their illegal monies from property crimes, almost equal amounts from prostitution and robberies, and the least amount from selling drugs. However, the average dollar return for a robbery was 2.6 times greater than the return for an average property crime, 3.7 times greater than the return on an average drug sale, and 6.0 times greater than for the average prostitution offense.

TABLE 6.18   Criminal Involvements of 20 Mexican-American Female Addicts
(Phoenix, 1977/1978): Crimes Committed Last 30 Days

Type of Crime	Percentage of Sample Committing This Type of Crime	Total Number of This Type of Crime Committed in 30 Days
Burglary	25.0	9
Shoplifting	30.0	38
Forgery	30.0	19
Theft from auto	15.0	4
Auto theft	5.0	1
Purse snatching	5.0	1
Picking pockets	0	0
Con games	0	0
Other "property" crimes	20.0	8
Assault and robbery	15.0	14
Armed robbery	20.0	4
Other "personal" crimes	0	0
Gambling	0	0
Prostitution	35.0	99
Other vice crimes	0	0
Drug sales	25.0	34

Any property crime	60.0%	Only property crime	20.0%
Any personal crime	30.0%	Only personal crime	10.0%
Any vice crime	35.0%	Only vice crime	15.0%
Any drug selling	25.0%	Only drug selling	15.0%

TABLE 6.19   Comparative Monetary Return for Different Types of Crimes
Committed During a 30-Day Period: 20 Mexican-American
Female Addicts

Type of Crime	Total Crimes Committed n	Total Crimes Committed %	Total Approximate Dollar Return*	Percentage of Total Dollar Return	Average Dollar Return per Crime
Property crimes	80	34.6	$3900	41.7	$ 48.75
Personal crimes	18	7.8	2250	24.1	125.00
Vice crimes	99	42.9	2050	21.9	20.70
Drug sales	34	14.7	1150	12.3	33.82
Total	231	100.0	$9350	100.0	$ 40.48

*The self-reported dollar amount for each crime was rounded to the nearest $50 prior to summing.

TABLE 6.20 Criminal Involvements of Various Age Cohorts of 20 Mexican-American Female Addicts

Age Cohort	Property		Personal		Vice		Drug Sales		Total	
	n	%	n	%	n	%	n	%	n	%
15–19 (3)	17	58.6	11	37.9	0	0	1	3.5	29	100.0
20–24 (10)	27	21.1	3	2.3	97	75.8	1	.8	128	100.0
25–29 (4)	6	54.6	4	36.4	0	0	1	9.1	11	100.0
30–34 (3)	30	47.6	0	0	2	3.2	31	49.2	63	100.0
Total (20)	80	34.6	18	7.8	99	42.9	34	14.7	231	100.0
15–19 (3)	17	21.3	11	61.1	0	0	1	2.9	29	12.6
20–24 (10)	27	33.8	3	16.7	97	98.0	1	2.9	128	55.4
25–29 (4)	6	7.5	4	22.2	0	0	1	2.9	11	4.8
30–34 (3)	30	37.5	0	0	2	2.0	31	91.2	63	27.3
Total (20)	80	100.0	18	100.0	99	100.0	34	100.0	231	100.0

(5) Although these Mexican-American female addicts were less likely to commit robberies than their male counterparts, the phenomenon requires a special note:

- Almost a third of these women had participated in at least one robbery during the 30-day study period, and the *average* number of robberies was 3.3.

- Ten percent reported robbery as the *only* type of crime they had committed during the study period.

- Of those who had committed at least one robbery, 50 percent reported the victim had been assaulted during the commission of the crime, and 66.7 percent derived *more* of their illegal income from robberies than from all other crimes they committed.

(6) The 20 Mexican-American female addicts ranged in age from 18 to 30, with an average age of 23.4 (median was 22). The types of crimes committed were related to age.

- The majority of the total crimes committed by women 15–19 were property crimes.

- The majority of the total crimes committed by women 20–24 were prostitutions.

- The majority of crimes committed by women 25–29 were property crimes.

- Women 30–34 split their criminal involvements equally between selling drugs and committing property crimes.

- The majority of the robberies were committed by a small number of the youngest addicts.

- Virtually all of the vice crimes were committed by young women in the age group 20–24.

- Virtually all of the drug sales were made by a small number of women in the 30–34 age group.

SUMMARY

These aggregate data from contemporary active addicts from Black and Mexican-American minority groups suggest such addicts will be committing an average of 26.2 crimes during the course of a month. However, the majority of these crimes will be vice crimes, notably procuring and prostitution and individual drug sales. At least in the four race/sex cohorts, the crimes were distributed as follows:

Property Crimes	587	26.3%
Crimes Against Persons	114	5.1%
Vice Crimes	733	32.9%
Drug Sales	795	35.7%
Total Crimes	2229	100.0%

With respect to specific race/sex cohorts, one might reasonably expect the following rank order of type of crimes committed during a 30-day period in support of one's drug use:

(1) Black males: vice crimes, drug sales, property crimes, and crimes against persons

(2) Black females: vice crimes, drug sales, property crimes, and crimes against persons

(3) Mexican-American males: drug sales, property crimes, vice crimes, and crimes against persons

(4) Mexican-American females: drug sales, vice crimes, property crimes, and crimes against persons

These aggregate data further suggest, not unexpectedly, that there will be considerable variation of criminal involvement among the various active minority group addicts, depending on their ages. The following expectations can be derived from these aggregate data:

(1) Addict criminals below age 25 will be committing significantly *fewer* crimes on the average than those who are older. For example, 42 addicts below age 25 committed an average of 12.9 crimes during a 30-day period, while 43 addicts age 25 and above committed an average of 39.1 crimes during the same period.

(2) Addict criminals below age 25 will be committing significantly more crimes against persons than those who are older. For example, of 114 crimes against persons committed by 85 addicts, 72, or 63.2 percent, were committed by the 42 addicts who were younger than 25. Stated differently, 21.1 percent of all crimes committed by addicts 15–19 and 10.0 percent of all crimes committed by addicts 20–24 were crimes against persons. This compares to all addicts 25–49 for whom only 2.5 percent of their crimes were crimes against persons.

(3) Drug selling will be more associated with the older addict criminals, those above age 30, than with the younger ones. In these study populations, drug sales accounted for 35.7 percent of the individual crimes, but persons age 30 and above accounted for 88.3 percent of all these sales.

(4) Within specific age cohorts, one might reasonably expect the following rank order of type of crimes committed during a 30-day period in support of one's drug use:

TABLE 6.21 Total Crimes Committed by Black and Mexican-American Active Addicts During a 30-Day Period

| | Blacks | | | | Mexican-Americans | | | | Total | |
| | Males | | Females | | Males | | Females | | | |
Type of Crime	n	%	n	%	n	%	n	%	n	%
Property crimes	150	22.2	209	28.2	148	25.6	80	34.6	587	26.3
Crimes against persons	49	7.2	17	2.3	30	5.2	18	7.8	114	5.1
Vice crimes	303	44.8	296	39.9	35	6.0	99	42.9	733	32.9
Drug sales	175	25.8	220	29.6	366	63.2	34	14.7	795	35.7
Total crimes	677	100.0	742	100.0	579	100.0	231	100.0	2229	100.0
Total Addict Criminals	25		15		25		20		85	
Mean Number of Crimes	27.1		49.5		23.2		11.6		26.2	

TABLE 6.22 Total Crimes Committed by Specific Age Cohorts Among Black and Mexican-American Active Addicts During a 30-Day Period

	Number of Crime in 30 Days														Total Number of Crimes	
	15–19		20–24		25–29		30–34		35–39		40–44		45–49			
Type of Crime	n	%	n	%	n	%	n	%	n	%	n	%	n	%	n	%
Property crimes	86	57.0	149	37.4	193	35.3	81	9.9	48	30.8	24	15.4	6	100.0	587	26.3
Crimes against persons	32	21.1	40	10.0	18	3.3	22	2.7	0	0	2	1.3	0	0	114	5.1
Vice crimes	3	2.0	202	50.8	280	51.2	210	25.8	8	5.1	30	19.2	0	0	733	32.9
Drug sales	30	19.9	7	1.8	56	10.2	502	61.6	100	64.1	100	64.1	0	0	795	35.7
Total crimes	151	100.0	398	100.0	547	100.0	815	100.0	156	100.0	156	100.0	6	100.0	2229	100.0
Total addict criminals	11		31		19		16		3		4		1		85	
Mean number of crimes	13.7		12.8		28.8		50.9		52.0		39.0		6.0		26.2	

TABLE 6.23 Comparative Monetary Return for Different Types of Crimes Committed by Various Race/Sex Addicts During a 30-Day Period

	Average Dollar Return per Crime				Total
	Blacks		Mexican-Americans		
	25	15	25	20	n=85
Type of crime	Males	Females	Males	Females	
Property crimes	$ 77.00	$ 39.00	$ 73.00	$ 49.00	$ 59.00
Crimes against persons	228.00	103.00	205.00	125.00	187.00
Vice crimes	12.00	14.00	44.00	21.00	15.00
Drug sales	36.00	11.00	20.00	34.00	22.00
Total crimes	$ 48.00	$ 22.00	$ 45.00	$ 40.00	$ 38.00

- 15–19: property crimes, crimes against persons, drug sales, and vice crimes
- 20–24: vice crimes, property crimes, crimes against persons, and drug sales
- 25–29: vice crimes, property crimes, drug sales, and crimes against persons
- 30–34: drug sales, vice crimes, property crimes, and crimes against persons
- 35+: drug sales, property crimes, vice crimes, and crimes against persons

These aggregate data further suggest, again not unexpectedly, that there will be considerable variation of monetary return for different crimes committed. Based on the experiences reported by these study cohorts, one can anticipate the following:

(1) The average *property crime* will net the addict criminal approximately $59.
(2) The average *crime against person* will net the addict criminal approximately $187.
(3) The average *vice crime* will net the addict criminal approximately $15.
(4) The average *drug sale* will net the addict "pusher" approximately $22.
(5) The average *crime* will net the addict criminal approximately $38.

Based on these average monetary returns, one should not be surprised that the addict criminal is turning more and more to crimes against persons that produce a monetary gain, i.e., armed robbery, muggings, and so forth.

Although property crimes (burglary, shoplifting, and so forth) are still the mainstay for the addicts seeking money in support of their drug use, crimes against persons now contribute a significant proportion to the total dollar return the addict criminal realizes from his or her criminal involvements. Consider the following:

(1) Among 25 Black male addicts, 35.6 percent of their *total* monthly illicit income came from property crimes and 34.2 percent came from committing crimes against persons.

(2) Among 15 Black female addicts, 49.8 percent of their total monthly illicit income came from property crimes and 10.8 percent came from committing crimes against persons.

(3) Among 25 Mexican-American male addicts, 41.7 percent of their total monthly illicit income came from property crimes and 23.7 percent came from committing crimes against persons.

(4) Among 20 Mexican-American female addicts, 41.7 percent of their total monthly illicit income came from property crimes and 24.1 percent came from committing crimes against persons.

As one would expect, the committing of crimes is the primary means addicts have of obtaining monies to be used in support of their drug use and other "living expenses":

(1) Among the 95 Mexican-American addicts incarcerated on felony charges in San Antonio, 59.0 percent reported at least half of their total criminal involvement had been in support of their drug use. Further, 54.8 percent reported at least 70 percent of their crimes were committed in order to purchase drugs.

(2) Among active Black addicts, the proportion of illegal to legal income is quite high. For example, 88.6 percent of the total monthly income for male addicts comes from committing crimes, as does 92.4 percent of the total monthly income for female addicts.

Finally, these data indicate a predilection among contemporary Black and Mexican-American active addicts (1) to become involved in the commission of crimes against persons in their quest for money, (2) to carry weapons with them while they are seeking money, and (3) to have few reservations about assaulting their victims during the commission of the crimes. Consider the following findings, which support such a contention:

(1) In *Philadelphia,* 38.6 percent of the active Black male addicts and 11.5 percent of the active Black female addicts had committed at least one assault/robbery or armed robbery during the previous month.

(2) In *Washington, D.C.,* 56.0 percent of the active Black male addicts and 33.3 percent of the active Black female addicts had committed at least one assault/robbery or armed robbery during the previous month. Of note, 20.0 percent of the males and 6.7 percent of the females committed robberies as their *only* type of crime.

(3) In *Phoenix,* 52.0 percent of the active Mexican-American male addicts and 30.0 percent of female addicts had committed at least one assault/robbery or armed robbery during the previous month. In addition, 20.0 percent of the males and 10.0 percent of the females had committed *only* robberies.

(4) Among incarcerated Mexican-American felons in *San Antonio*, those who were heroin abusers had more frequently committed armed robberies *and* more armed robberies than those felons who had not been heroin abusers.

(5) Among incarcerated Mexican-American felons in *San Antonio*, 50.5 percent of the heroin abusers had carried a weapon with them during the commission of crimes. This was double the proportion found in the population of nonusing incarcerated felons. Of the heroin abusers who carried weapons, 77.1 percent had been armed with a gun.

(6) Of the active Black male addicts in *Washington, D.C.* who committed robberies, 78.6 percent had assaulted their victims.

(7) Of the active Black female addicts in *Washington, D.C.* who committed robberies, 80.0 percent had assaulted their victims.

(8) Of the active Mexican-American male addicts in *Phoenix* who committed robberies, 61.5 percent had assaulted their victims.

(9) Of the active Mexican-American female addicts in *Phoenix* who committed robberies, 50.0 percent had assaulted their victims.

REFERENCES

BALL, J. C. (1970) "Two patterns of opiate addiction," pp. 81–94 in J. Ball and C. Chambers (eds.) The Epidemiology of Opiate Addiction in the United States. Springfield, IL: Charles C Thomas.

BALL, J. C. and M. P. LAU (1970) "The Chinese opiate addict in the United States," pp. 240–248 in J. Ball and C. Chambers (ed.) The Epidemiology of Opiate Addiction in the United States. Springfield, IL: Charles C Thomas.

CHAMBERS, C. D. (1974) "Narcotic addiction and crime: an empirical review," pp. 125–142 in J. Inciardi and C. Chambers (eds.) Drugs and the Criminal Justice System. Beverly Hills, CA: Sage.

CHAMBERS, C. D., W. R. CUSKEY, and A. D. MOFFETT (1970a) "Demographic factors in opiate addiction among Mexican-Americans." Public Health Reports 85 (June): 523–531.

CHAMBERS, C. D., R. K. HINESLEY, and M. MOLDESTAD (1970b) "Narcotic addiction in females: a race comparison." International Journal of Addictions 5 (Fall): 257–278.

CHAMBERS, C. D. and A. D. MOFFETT (1970) "Negro opiate addiction," pp. 178–201 in J. Ball and C. Chambers (eds.) The Epidemiology of Opiate Addiction in the United States. Springfield, IL: Charles C Thomas.

CUSHMAN, P. (1974) "Relationship between narcotic addiction and crime." Federal Probation 38,3: 38–43.

FILE, K. N., T. W. McCAHILL, and L. D. SAVITZ (1974) "Narcotic involvement and female criminality." Addictive Diseases: An International Journal 1, 2: 177–188.

GREENBERG, S. W. and F. ADLER (1974) "Crime and addiction: an empirical analysis of the literature 1920–1973." Contemporary Drug Problems 3, 2: 221–270.

INCIARDI, J. A. and C. D. CHAMBERS (1972) "Unreported criminal involvement of narcotic addicts." Journal of Drug Issues 2 (Spring): 57–64.

JAMES, J. (1976) "Prostitution and addiction: an interdisciplinary approach." Addictive Diseases: An International Journal 2, 4: 601–618.

PLAIR, W. and L. JACKSON (1970) Narcotic Drug Use and Crime: A Report on Interviews with 50 Addicts Under Treatment. Washington, DC: Department of Corrections.

PREBLE, E. A. and J. J. CASEY (1969) "Taking care of business—the heroin user's life on the street." International Journal of Addictions 4, 1: 1–24.

U.S. Bureau of Narcotics and Dangerous Drugs (1971) Drug Usage and Arrest Charges. Washington, DC: Department of Justice.

WEISSMAN, J. C., P. L. KATSAMPES, and T. A. GIACINTI (1974) "Opiate use and criminality among a jail population." Addictive Diseases: An International Journal 1, 3: 269–281.

WHITE, O. Z., C. D. CHAMBERS, and J. A. INCIARDI (forthcoming) "Mexican-American criminals: a comparison study of heroin using and non-using felons." Chemical Dependencies: Behavioral and Biomedical Issues.

7

DRUG ABUSE, CRIME, AND ECONOMICS
The Dismal Limits of Social Choice

FRED GOLDMAN

Drug abuse and crime are what we choose to make them. They are the products of criminal codes and the criminal justice system, media sensationalism, political expediency, and a host of social programs, just as they are products of the individual behaviors from which they must ultimately emerge, calculated, rational, pleasurable, or otherwise. As behaviors they are "complicated" and not well understood. Nor are they easily studied, since those that engage in them are submerged in various "deviant subcultures," exposing as little as possible to the membership from which the behavioral proscriptions originate.

Drug abuse in its most pathological form, addiction, "results from a complicated interplay of social, psychological, physiological, and pharmacological factors which must impinge on the individual addict at a critical time in his life cycle" (Isbell, 1962: 129). A recent compilation of theories of drug abuse (Lettieri et al., 1980) provides descriptions of forty-three contemporary theories generated from sixteen social science and biomedical disciplines. And attempts to explain the causes of crime, warns James Q. Wilson (1977: 58), "lead inevitably into the realm of the subjective and the familial," although most likely they lead to fewer than forty-three theories,

since "theories based on body type, mental abnormality, or mental illness
are rejected because the available data are inconsistent with them" (1977:
50)—something we are not spared in the theories of drug abuse. While drug
abuse and crime tend to have an affinity for one another, the complicated
interplay of contributing factors and intervening social conditions makes
nearly any explanation of how they are related seem "reasonable," albeit
"partial." But a single drug, heroin, brings them together in a rush of pharmacology and economics; and economics, which is given so little utility for
understanding either of these deviant behaviors, dominates as an explanation
of their association—an explanation in which opinion frequently substitutes
for evidence and untested hypotheses become well-known "facts."

"Of all drugs in the vast pharmacopia of mind-altering and addictive
drugs," the American Bar Association concludes (1972: 25), "there is only
one which is responsible for significant amounts of street crime—heroin."
This statement, the ABA immediately points out, is based on "informal
estimates," since "are no precise statistics that demonstrate exactly what
proportion of urban crime is committed by addicts." Therefore, they neglect
to add, there can be no precise statistics that demonstrate what proportion is
committed by addicts' nonaddicted brethren. What have we learned? Even
when specific research is not directly applicable to the addict/crime phenomenon, respected researchers' "craving" on the topic leads them to "commit" opinions. Having found "no evidence of a lasting impact of [nonaddict-
ive] drug use on delinquency levels," Johnston et al. (1978: 155) go on to
explain that they "cannot conclude that drug use does *not* lead to crime,
because one very important kind of user—the addict—is not sufficiently
represented in this sample," a reasonable statement given their empirical
analysis. Yet they continue, *it seems quite likely to us that many addicts
increase their level of crime to support their habits,*" a statement of opinion
that does not follow from the analyses (1978: 155; italics added).

If the relationship between heroin use and crime is "obvious," for scientist and citizen alike, the explanation rests with three principal variables: the
cost of heroin, its addictive properties, and the earning potential of those
who consume it. Indeed, not much by way of explanation is likely to separate the sophisticated scientist from the random citizen when it comes to an
understanding of why heroin use "inevitably" leads to crime. The logic is
simple. As the Canadian Government's Commission of Inquiry (1973: 321)
explains, an important factor

> is economic and associated with the illegality of heroin and its consequent
> high cost on the illicit market, and the demands made by extended tolerance
> and dependence. . . . There are very few legitimate ways in which most

individuals can afford to meet illicit market prices. Consequently, when tolerance pushes the cost of drug use above what the user can afford legitimately,
he is forced into a decision—either quit the drug and go through withdrawal,
or turn to criminal methods of acquiring the necessary money. While some
users refuse to become involved in criminal activities and consequently stop
using the drug, at least temporarily, many turn to petty crime, small robberies,
shoplifting and prostitution.

There is a caveat to the "inevitability hypothesis." The more affluent persons
with low-risk access to opiates—say, physicians, nurses, pharmacists, and,
perhaps, police—may be able to maintain otherwise exorbitant consumption of narcotics (Canadian Government's Commission of Inquiry, 1973).
This, of course, reinforces the importance of economic variables as a link
between the drug and crime.

Some implications of the inevitability hypothesis cannot be reassuring to
a citizenry that relies on public policy to discourage drug-related crime. It
should be emphasized that although the hypothesis appears to hold up,
alternative explanations of the drug-crime nexus may be more appropriate.
As an example, more than fifteen years ago, Chein et al. (1964: 64–65)
concluded that delinquency is not a consequence of drug use. Rather, "the
varieties of delinquency tend to change to those most functional for drug use;
the total amount of delinquency is independent of drug use." The shift
among delinquent activities is toward money-making crime: "Heroin is a
tranquilizer—perhaps the most effective tranquilizer known—but it comes
in expensive doses." Contemporary research into the temporal sequencing
of drug abuse and crime has continually confirmed this (Gandossy et al.,
1980; Greenberg and Adler, 1974). Are we faced with another type of
inevitability: For a given commitment of public resources, we must choose
the mix and frequencies of crimes we wish to face, discourage relatively
frequent property-related crime, and subject ourselves to the spectrum of the
relatively more violent nondrug crimes?

Also, the inevitability hypothesis has not been subjected to a "reasonable" test. Moreover, there is so much irrelevant evidence for and against it
that any comprehensive analysis of the literature is bound to arrive at a
"maybe" that tilts in the direction of the reviewer's own views or, at least,
recommends more research (Gandossy et al., 1980; Research Triangle Institute, 1976). More unsettling, however, is the implication of a causal link
between drug abuse and crime. As Wilson (1977: 58) put it, "if causal
theories explain why a criminal acts as he does, they must also explain why
he *must* act as he does, and therefore may make any reliance on deterrence
seem futile or irrelevant." Once regular (addictive?) drug use begins, is the

efficacy of a deterrent public policy in limbo, preempted by pharmacology and forcing us to deal with the consequences of "craving"?

O'Donnell (1967: 82) has written that the "drug subculture is perhaps the most utilitarian of deviant subcultures," and an image has emerged of those more deeply rooted in it as methodical, continually active "consumer/ workers" (Preble and Casey, 1969). Hustling, the most ubiquitous term of the subculture, is an activity based on calculation, and the sense of time and timing is budgeted and structured around drug use (Agar, 1973; Hofmann, 1975; O'Donnell, 1967). The likely outcomes of failure or success as consumer/worker are well understood at each level of drug involvement. But these characteristics and the domination of the behaviors of drug abusers place the active drug abuser in the vanguard of *homo economicus*. Perhaps this is the very market where public policies of a distinctly economic bent are most applicable. What follows is an analysis of the drug abuser qua consumer/worker, and the influence of economics in the drug-crime nexus. In keeping with the literature, this is my reading of the evidence—my opinion.

DRUG ABUSE, CRIME, AND ECONOMIC CHOICE

Drug abuse and crime are distinctly different activities, although for the individuals that engage in them, they may share many of the same determinants and purposes.[1] Perhaps Silberman (1978: 111) is correct, that "because their sense of self is so precarious, poor people invest considerable energy in a search for excitement," and this involves, among other things, the "use of alcohol and drugs, or one or another variety of criminal activity." Perhaps at a more pathological level, "addiction," Lukoff (1974) is correct, that drug addiction and crime are only an aspect of a more coherent pattern of deviance. Nevertheless, the starting point for an economic analysis of the relationship between drug abuse and crime, regardless of their degree of association or mutual determination, is to recognize that drug abuse and crime are distinctly different activities: Drug abuse is a consumption activity; the crimes of drug abusers are income-generating activities.[2]

At the most basic level, drug consumption is an act of choice, albeit one that is tempered by a variety of etiological factors. Moreover, to choose to consume is not a sufficient condition for consumption to occur. One must "possess" the drug, and possession is constrained by one's command over resources, one's ability to carry out those activities that will lead to possession of the drug, and the opportunity to exercise that ability. For most goods and services and most consumers, this loosely translates into having cash, a blank check, or a credit card; having the time to go shopping; and knowing where and when to shop. The process is sometimes a disappointing one, at least temporarily. "Desire, motivation, will, and desparation" are simply not capable of guaranteeing consumption, and, as Stephens and Smith (1976: 1) write about the process of shopping for heroin, "the addict is not always confident of success in his quest."

Drug consumption is drug abuse only where the activity is defined as such, and no such distinction (such as use/abuse, right/wrong, appropriate/ inappropriate) is assigned to the consumption process within the economic paradigm of consumer choice. The term *drug abuse* is a medicolegal label and an economic phenomenon only in the sense that the label itself serves to influence drug consumption—the selection of a particular drug and quantity to consume or possess, and the exchange process under which the drug market operates. Otherwise, the process of obtaining drugs is remarkably similar to the process of obtaining other consumer items. "Copping," as Stephens and Smith (1976: 14) found in their study of the purchase of heroin, is an activity where there is a "great amount of overlap between the consumer behavior patterns of the street addict and the legitimate consumer who shops for food, clothing, and other commodities. One is struck by the fact that street addicts utilize many of the same strategies in purchasing drugs as would a consumer in a more legitimate business transaction." Nevertheless, the legal proscriptions label the buyers and sellers of illicit drugs and alter what would otherwise be the course (and cost) of the market process.[3]

"Attached" to the labeling is a set of medicolegal conditions (such as misdemeanor, felony, psychosis) that influence what Moore (1977: 238) calls the "effective price" of consumption: The effective price of heroin is "an index of all the things that make heroin difficult, inconvenient, risky or otherwise 'costly' for individuals to consume [and includes, at least] dollar price, amount of pure heroin, toxicity of adulterants, the expected time necessary to find heroin, the threat of arrest, and the risk of victimization by criminals. . . . Among these components of the effective price, dollar cost is likely to be relatively unimportant." The responsiveness of consumption to changes in the effective price of drugs is currently an unexplored empirical question, although it is generally believed that the quantities "addicted" heroin users consume are unresponsive to changes in the money price of heroin. There is very little evidence (Silverman and Spruill, 1977) to support this. One may have expectations, a priori, concerning this relationship— perhaps "plausible" expectations based on, say, pharmacology or psychiatry. Yet, the relationships between effective price and consumption are determined in social settings and the otherwise "asocial" influence of pharmacology, biochemistry, personal drives, and the like, and are contaminated by this. This is the case for each of the individual components of effective price, including the dollar cost as well as the aggregate.

The ability of the drug user to respond (that is, to consume drugs) at any particular effective price is constrained by the resources available for expenditure. In this regard virtually all attention has been placed on the dollar expenditure on consumption. It is generally assumed that earnings will be at least equal to the dollar value of planned drug expenditures—planned since the earnings must precede the expenditure.[4] This is the heart of the inevitability hypothesis: Criminal activity is "caused by," or is a function of, planned expenditures.

Drug expenditures are dependent upon the quantity of the drug consumed and the price per unit. Pursuing Moore's concept of effective price, each quantity of drug has "attached to it" a dollar value of expenditures and a nonpecuniary expenditure—an ability successfully to negotiate "all the things that make heroin difficult, inconvenient, risky or otherwise 'costly.'" Income-generating activities may provide the dollar expenditures necessary for the purchase and consumption of drugs. More than this is necessary, however, and the ability to assume risk, accommodate inconveniences—in short, successfully transact in the market for drugs—is, as Moore suggests, likely to be relatively more important than the dollar cost. Although the term *market* is vague in this context, its spatial character is suggested by Gould et al. (1974: 44): "There is a setting in which practically every sure-enough dope fiend carries out his love affair with heroin—the streets. . . . They are the dope fiend's territory, where he cops dope, hustles, hangs out, eats, plays, hides out, and sometimes sleeps." (Does the "dope fiend" and "hustling in the streets" represent a popular imagery of drug abusers, but one that is greater in image than its share of abusers in reality?)

Command over the resources necessary to survive in the streets and the continual "expenditure" of these resources form a requisite part of the activity of consumption. Moreover, just as the dollar expenditures for consumption have to be obtained or "earned," nonpecuniary resources have to be available. The literature is replete with descriptions of the failure of those for whom such resources are the limitation of their consumption—"the burnouts, the mature-outs." The literature suggests that this resource is time-bound, principally a function of chronological age—not yet available for "the young" and no longer available for "the old" (and "old" seems to come quickly in the streets). The successful "dope fiends" (i.e., consumers whose actual expenditures are, regularly at least, equal to planned expenditures) are continually able to "take care of business."

Variation in drug use etiologies notwithstanding, a substantial body of evidence has accumulated indicating that "full-blown addiction" is something one develops into over time, that any drug use is a learned behavior, that typically one is initiated into the use of drugs by one's peers and friends, and that transition into drug use, particularly use of heroin, generally means entering into "deviant subcultures" and learning the behaviors and attitudes appropriate to them (Agar, 1973; Chein et al., 1964; Gandossy et al., 1980; O'Donnell, 1966). Heroin is rarely the first drug used. When it is finally used, "considerable" time passes before one enters into the state of "addiction," if ever. Although the reported sequencing of drug use, at times deterministically called "stepping-stone" theories, varies by the sample under study, alcohol and tobacco are usually the legal precursors to illicit drugs,[5] marijuana the first illicit drug, and then, perhaps, an amphetamine, barbiturate, or psychedelic will precede any heroin use (O'Donnell et al., 1976). There may be short-cut pairings in the sequence (say, alcohol to opiates) and the simultaneous use of two or more drugs (polydrug use), but nevertheless there is a transition.

The most important transition period for the drug-crime nexus is the period from first use of heroin to what is variously reported as regular use, daily use, or onset of addiction. Patterns of stable, long-term heroin use have been known for some time. Known variously as chippers, weekenders, occasional users, recreational users, dippers and dabbers, and the like, these are persons for whom the pharmacological cycle of escalation—euphoria, tolerance, increased dosage, and so forth—does not always occur. Moreover, heroin use is far from a universally pleasurable experience. As Zinberg (1974: 157) suggests, "We have surely overestimated the seductive power of heroin. We have also given it more credit for pleasure production than it deserves." For many persons the initiation period is short-lived and followed by abstinence and drug switching (O'Donnell et al., 1976). But what of the persons for whom there is simply a lag between the first use of opiates and the onset of addiction? The literature suggests that nearly one or more years elapses, on average, before addiction sets in.[6] Is there, early on, a desire to expand consumption but inadequate earnings power: Does economics dominate pharmacology? Of course, it really does not require a couple of years for persons to shift their consumption patterns toward daily or "heavy" use. The physicians Winick (1961) studied took only two months to make the transition.

With the exception of drug selling and prostitution, income-generating activity would have to be sufficiently skilled to provide regular, ongoing returns that would net the monies required to sustain heavy use. The skills of the hustler are learned; experiential skills and related criminal activity require contacts and information. Perhaps more important, in a sector where "labor market activities" are not infused with society's schema of property rights and legal recourse, one requires an ability to maintain preservation of self and property commensurate with the returns obtained. One grows into this.

Similarly, drug use is learned and, stepping-stone theories aside, familiarity with drugs, their administration, and their source is a basic prerequisite for heavy use. In short, one does not simply and immediately become a large-scale successful criminal or consumer of opiates. The literature is quite clear on this point: One learns and advances to each of these over time. And in these early stages, the principal explanation for the association between drug abuse and crime (i.e., crime unrelated to drugs) is likely to be found in the subculture attachment. Neither pharmacological properties of opiates nor the cost of drugs is a viable explanation for the early association.

Three points about these comments are warranted. First, they are, politely, hypotheses and not fact. They are "tendencies" that are inferred from the literature and much of what has been reported is consistent with these statements. Second, nearly every sentence should be preceded by "on average." Drug treatment programs, correctional facilities, hospitals, and the streets have their number of exceptions—say, the 11-year-old with a "heavy Jones." They are the exception. There is variability in any of the statistics that would describe these phenomena, as Robins (1979) indicates for "addict careers." Finally, and related to this, given variability in the transition period from heroin use to "addiction," what are its determinants? If it is "addiction" and not simply occasional use, which is believed to be the impetus to crime, can we spread out, forestall, or, perhaps, reduce the likelihood of heavy use? Or is Robins (1978: 195, italics added) correct in positing her own "inevitability" hypothesis that narcotic use "has a *natural course* characterized by moving from regular use, to daily compulsive use, to withdrawal and abstention, to the relapse that renews the cycle [although] the cycles' natural periodicity is still unknown." Is this a "natural course" in which pharmacology dominates economics?

THE ECONOMICS OF SOCIAL PHARMACOLOGY

The economic components of drug expenditures are the quantities consumed per time period and the price per unit paid for the quantity. These, multiplied by one another, are identically equal to expenditures or what is loosely termed the "habit." And it is the habit that takes us most of the way into the drug/crime nexus and prepares us for the invariability hypothesis. *Habit* in this context has two meanings: It is some dollar figure, drug expenditures, but it is also indicative of consumer psychology. It implies a level of drug use that the drug user simply cannot do without. The addicted user "craves" that level and, for the addict, the consequences of not satisfying the craving are dire. With a few more assumptions, principally about the legal earnings potential of those who reach a state of addiction, we will have constructed a persuasive inevitability hypothesis connecting drug addiction with crime.

Those who are not addicted sift through the hypothesis into a more complex set of multiple associations, intervening variables, reverse causality, and so forth. Some of these drug users are heroin users waiting their turn, when abstention or occasional use will become regular use and the onset of addiction will lead to a habit large enough to qualify for the "inevitable" link to crime. It is all part of the "natural" cycle (Robins, 1978). There are, of course, some narcotics users for whom the cycle will never occur. Following a period of occasional use, they will abstain from further consumption; others will simply remain occasional users (O'Donnell et al., 1976; Zinberg, 1979). For those caught up in the "natural cycle" of narcotics use, it would appear that there "must" be, at some point, a time when it leads to a "natural cycle" of crime. Our interest should center, therefore, on "addicts," a stock of persons continually growing larger from the influx of new and old faces, and smaller with their exit into the involuntary abstention and/or replacement-drug programs, the voluntary abstention of maturity or burn-out, or the coroner's office. The reasoning and plausibility of it all is so straightforward that it is surprising to see how easily it dissolves in a muddle of economics and social pharmacology.

The economic connection between drug abuse and crime originates with the "habit," drug expenditures per period of time. But it is the quantity component of expenditures that is of initial importance, since only this is "responsible" for the development of tolerance, which requires a larger quantity, and subsequent tolerance (Hofmann, 1975). Clearly, if the user consumes an approximately constant quantity of narcotics over time, but a quantity that is *below* some "addiction threshold," then increases in habit size (i.e., drug expenditures) due to an increase in drug prices should not lead him to join the legions who qualify for the inevitability hypothesis. Two aspects of the quantity component are thus crucial to linking narcotics use to crime: One is the threshold of use (that is, *quantity* and *frequency* of consumption) at which a "pharmacological dependence" or "addiction behavior" sets in,[7] and the other is the quantities of narcotic drugs actually consumed per time period.

Consider the latter. It is unsettling to find out that at present "we know remarkably little about how much heroin addicts actually do consume or would consume if heroin [were less expensive]" (Robins, 1979: 327). In fact, reviewing this literature nearly thirty years ago, Meyer (1952: 14) indicated that establishing the quantity of drugs consumed by addicts is difficult since "in many cases addicts may not know the actual content of their dosage due to the variable dilution of drugs sold on the illegal market." Besides, addicts exaggerate their daily dosage. Habit is status; habit helps qualify the addict for entry into drug treatment programs. Even so, the studies generally show a wide range in the daily dosage. The impact of dosage, however, depends on its purity.

Unfortunately, the purity of narcotics is not easy to gauge since drug sellers try to disguise it. Quinine, for example, is used as an adulterant and its bitter taste makes it difficult to assess the heroin content (Sapira, 1968). Even the packaging system is difficult to describe, and since heroin is cut as it goes through the distribution system, the quality and quantity of heroin at any given price varies widely and is often a function of whether the dealer is also a drug user, especially at lower levels in the distribution system (Agar, 1973; Holahan, 1972; Moore, 1977; Preble and Casey, 1969; Smith, 1973). Not only do "dealers sometimes give a short count by removing a small amount from each unit [but they] are not overly precise when they divide the heroin for packaging" (Agar, 1973: 51).

It would appear that there is some uncertainty in what it will take to satisfy the craving of the moment and that users would be regularly accustomed to accepting the outcome of a gamble in the market. For example, while a variety of caveats would have to accompany any statement concerning which users would have received which packets, Leveson and Weiss (1976: 119) report that "of 132 street packages of heroin recently sampled in New York City, 12 contained no heroin at all, while the remainder were diluted with quinine so that heroin concentration ranged from 1 percent to 77 percent." Writing of heroin seizures, Smith (1973) reports large samples exceeding 30 percent purity and small seizures varying from 3 to 10 percent. Heroin purity varies everywhere within lower levels of the distribution system (Brown and Silverman, 1974; Moore, 1977; Stephens and Smith, 1976). In fact, recognition of this among the consuming population helps employ "touts," whose function is to provide information on price, quality, and location of heroin (Hughes et al., 1971; Stephens and Smith, 1976).

It would also appear, therefore, that price changes due to fluctuations in the supply of narcotics are likely to take the form of a change in the contents of the "bag." And price per unit, remember, is also a determinant of "habit," i.e., drug expenditures. Quality-adjusted price per gram of heroin does fluctuate over time and across geographical areas (Agar, 1973; Brown and Silverman, 1974; Silverman and Spruill, 1977). Agar (1973: 54) writes that "a $5 bag bought in Harlem will bring $7 in Greenwich Village and from $8 to $10 in other white Manhattan neighborhoods. Fifty miles away in Kingston, New York, the price is $15 to $25." However, the important point Agar makes is that this is a price per bag and not the quality-adjusted price per gram. The grams and purity are locked up in the bag and remain as much a mystery to the user as they do to the researchers.

Consequently, the dollar size of a habit may not be very sensitive to price increases. The sensitivity of drug expenditures per user will depend on that user's "sensitivity" to the bag, since price per bag is relatively invariant on the street. (The "nickel bag" has been around for a long time.) But sensitivity itself depends not only on the contents measured as quality-adjusted quantity, which the user can judge only as "up" or "down," but also on placebo effects, social settings, drug experience, and a host of interdependent factors (Hofmann, 1975; Platt and Labate, 1976). In fact, it is plausible to expect that the response to increasing prices over time is the purchase of increasingly diluted bags and, in the absence of countervening consumer behavior, a systematic withdrawal from the pharmacological effects of the drug. Who should count as an addict? asks Robins (1977: 26). "Should men and women be counted as addicts if they administer heroin daily, even if the quality of the drug they are getting is so poor that they have no withdrawal symptoms when they abstain?" Heroin use may be costly and the proceeds of a great deal of crime may support it, but the functioning of the market places the economic component of the inevitability hypothesis in jeopardy of rejection. What of the dependency brought on by surpassing some threshold of consumption?

It is now commonplace to point out the ambiguities and inadequacies of the terms *addiction* and *addict* (Hofmann, 1975; Robins, 1977; Stimmel, 1975).[8] The addict is a social being and not simply the product of a dose-response chemical impact that can produce systematic biophysiological reactions in an experimental laboratory setting. "The idea 'I need to have opiates' is certainly influenced by the phenomenon of (physical) dependence," write Chein et al. (1964: 248), "but, indeed, is poorly correlated with the intensity of this biological phenomenon." Thus, the euphoria, craving, desperation, and the like, which help form the bridge between consumption activities and income-generating activities, are as much the captive of psychological phenomena as they are the biophysiological "addictive" properties of particular drugs. The importance of these properties dissolves still further with recognition that even they are a function of social conditions, the "setting" or "total environment" in which drugs are consumed (Canadian Government's Commission of Inquiry, 1973; Hofmann, 1975; Platt and Labate, 1976; Robins, 1978). In fact, the setting "may completely obscure the typical pharmacological response to a drug" (Canadian Government's Commission of Inquiry, 1973: 285). If we grant primacy to the state of psychological dependence on heroin, and there is no reason to restrict it to a particular drug, then the "certainty" of a consumer's response to "addictive" properties is . . . uncertain!

Both the economic and pharmacological links between the consumption of heroin and income-generating activities appear too weak to support the inevitability hypothesis. This does not mean that drug use does not "result in" or "lead to" crime, or that economics and pharmacology play no role in such a relationship. It does suggest that "inevitability" may be too strong a term and that pharmaeconomic determinism is for those who believe the world is flat.

As consumers, drug abusers generally have considerable experience with drugs. "If their favorite—heroin, morphine, demerol, methadone, barbiturate, or amphetamine—was not available to them," writes Zinberg (1974: 156), "they could or would use another." Some narcotics users simply regulate their habit on their own. Referring to increases in habit size due either to dosage (quantity) or to price increases, Silberman (1978: 179) writes that "most long-term heroin addicts are able to cut down their heroin intake when the cost of a daily habit gets too high for them to manage." Whether "most" addicts can do this is not known, but the wide-scale introduction of methadone treatment has made methadone the "most important drug for assuring the plausibility of personal self-regulation and self-regulating narcotics markets" (Inciardi, 1977; see also Agar and Stephens, 1975). As a reasonable substitute for heroin, its widespread availability on the street would seem to be a countercyclical device for dealing with heroin shortages. Street methadone is relatively inexpensive and of uniformly good quality. Most important, a principal source of street methadone is the treatment facilities from which the drug is diverted. Should an individual experience "unmanageable increases in habit size" because of increased dosage, the quantity side of drug expenditures, the consumption of methadone can be used to buffer both the economics and pharmacology, and similarly when a decrease in the supply of heroin increases habit size because of the increased price of heroin. Moreover, in the latter situation, due to, say, concerted law enforcement, movement into drug treatment programs is likely to expand the availability of illicit methadone. In fact, entry into methadone treatment, as well as arrest when entry is "too much hassle," are part of the scenarios of the self-regulation of heroin consumption (Baridon, 1976; Silberman, 1978) and the street version of "social security" (Preble and Miller, 1977).

The conventional view that drug abuse is linked to crime—in fact, leads to crime—is a tenuous one where it solely relies on a pharmaeconomic determinism of heroin consumption. The likelihood of the relationship cannot be ruled out, however, for heroin or any other drug. There may very well be a systematic relationship between a propensity to consume and a propensity to earn, and a role for pharmacology, albeit less decisive. "To reduce their tension and control their fear, many criminals drink and use drugs before going out on a job," writes Silberman (1978: 81), but the net impact is uncertain, since "whereas liquor and drugs fortify the nerves, they also muddy the judgment." Drugs help generate work time in legal and illegal markets, and they decrease work time; and for any given amount of time, they may enhance or reduce productivity (Alderman and Davis, 1976; Dupont and Basen, 1980; McGlothlin, 1979; United Nations, 1972). This varies by drug and work activity, and no simple statement of expectations will suffice for an empirical evaluation of the net effect of a particular drug on a particular activity. Linkages may be particularly complex. The use of antihypertensive drugs to control elevated blood pressures, thus reducing risk of adverse cardiovascular events (Hypertension Detection and Follow-Up Program, 1980), is likely to reduce absenteeism on the job (Alderman and Davis, 1976). Healthier people provide more hours of work. Yet a study of a work-site treatment program indicated that there was more absenteeism among those who were treated (i.e., had controlled) blood pressures. The ad hoc explanation for this involved "labeling the sick!" (Haynes, 1978).

The Canadian Commission (1973: 402) reports that "of all drugs used medically or non-medically, alcohol has the strongest and most consistent relationship to crime." Alcohol is not only implicated in antisocial behavior more than any other drug, but it is "generally the drug most often linked with serious crime" (Tinklenberg, 1975: 74). Moreover, Vaillant (1966) points out that, like their narcotic-addicted counterparts, delinquent alcoholics commit a relatively large number of property crimes, even though alcoholism is a relatively inexpensive habit. "Inevitably," one must conclude that nonalcohol drugs lead to less crime than alcohol (McGlothlin, 1979). Amphetamine abuse is also related to criminal activity, primarily of an agressive and violent nature (United Nations, 1972). In fact, why should we expect the pharmacological impact of opiates to be so simply directed in its drive toward crime, leading to property crime and not violent crime (McGlothlin, 1979) which, for some categories of property crime, are systematically associated? How do we add up and compare these crimes of pharmacology?

THE ECONOMICS OF MAKING A BUCK

Now we can introduce crime, the antisocial product of drug abusers' income-generating activities. The theories and speculation about the earnings activities of drug abusers are less developed as a literature than the literature on drug consumption. With the exception of opiates and, in particular, heroin, the sources of expenditures for the consumption of drugs have not been an issue for explicit study. Drug consumption patterns that exclude opiates are assumed to be either less costly or not "addicting"; that is, the cost can be regulated and, in the absence of an inevitability hypothesis, drug abuse and crime relapse to the worlds of individualized theories. It is as if drug dependencies could be rank ordered, with nonopiates placed below the dependency of heroin addiction; and as if the low rank meant they had no bearing on behavior or "motivation." It is as if expenditures on drugs could be put in rank order where habitual costs below some subjective level of "exorbitant" had no bearing on behavior, even though the consumers may have virtually no legal earnings potential (say, 15-year-old, inner-city high school dropouts). Nevertheless, all drug use must be financed and the options for accomplishing this are limited.

Drug expenditures and, for that matter, all expenditures for consumer goods and services are purchased with earnings, legal or illegal; with transfer payments such as public assistance and monies obtained from family and friends; with nonearned or nonlabor income such as dividends and interest; with debt or borrowing in "credit markets"; with liquidated wealth. Drugs can also be obtained directly (i.e., without purchase or money outlay) as "income-in-kind" for a service; directly via, say, skimming bags, ripping off drug sellers, or simply by consuming part of a drug stock otherwise sold; directly through bartering goods from legal or illegal markets; or as a gift. These methods of obtaining drugs do not exhaust the possibilities, nor do they neatly fit into a particular taxonomy. For example, a person may be temporarily unemployed and qualify for public assistance, and thus obtain an income *transfer*. Another person may have as his particular hustle (he "works" at this) remaining qualified for public assistance, perhaps under several different names, and thus obtains income transfers.[9] Are they both simply transfers—that is, unearned—or is the latter case an example of earnings, albeit unethical and, perhaps, illegal? While all means of obtaining drugs may be of interest, the principal concern in the drug/crime nexus is the area of earnings, the return to the supply of legal and illegal labor.

There is no reason to believe that drug abusers are not distributed across the full range of earnings-generating activities (i.e., the full range of legal and criminal occupations) and across the full range of transfer programs. How drug abusers are distributed across these activities, how they shift across them over time, and the amount of labor supplied to each of them is as much of an empirical mystery as their drug-consuming behavior. Occupational choice is neither permanent nor "predetermined" by biosocial factors, although such factors may influence choice. Experience in an occupation, for example, may improve the relative attraction of continuing in it. Given occupational choice, the supply of labor time (and effort per time unit) is not "predetermined," although it may be influenced by factors such as institutional constraints (e.g., union or company policy), general economic conditions of unemployment/employment likelihoods, or required settings (e.g., on late nights or weekends shoplifters cannot easily work; prostitutes can; see Plate, 1975; Stephens and Smith, 1976). And the return to labor is a function of many factors ranging from skill and ability to luck to market conditions. Finally, occupational choice, labor supply, and the return to labor are not independent of one another. It is also reasonable to expect that configurations of occupational choice, labor supply, and its return are influenced by consumption patterns, and the reverse. This is what Waldorf (1973: 48) means when he writes that "if a job cannot offer immediate money to purchase drugs, then the addict is liable to toss it over for more immediate profitable pursuits." Many jobs may be tossed over, or toss over "addicts"; many jobs may be stable. But these outcomes occur in preaddiction as well as addiction periods (Zinberg, 1979; Nurco, 1979; Robins, 1979). As another example, argued below, the principal link in the drug/crime nexus is drug selling/drug consumption: Persons who consume "a lot" of drugs have an incentive to sell them, and the reverse.[10] Is it the access to or availability of goods, low transactions costs of obtaining them, familiarity with the goods, low cost information, and the like that generate a relative affinity between consumption and earnings activities? One point is clear: There is a lot to explain in the choice of occupations, even when they are only dichotomized as legal and criminal, and in the determinants of earnings—the labor supplied and the return to it. It is unlikely that the consumption of a particular drug does any more than share in the explanation. Moreover, the activity of an occupation is likely to have by-products or unintended consequences. For example, accidents and injury to oneself and others will vary across occupations; so will a variety of health-related effects. Luft (1978) demonstrates this convincingly and shows that although "poverty affects health," it is the reverse, the adverse impact of job-related disability, that affects poverty and is primarily responsible for the poverty/health nexus. Drug abusers/criminals have no shortage of "early disability" (Jones and Vischi, 1979). How these are perceived or realized will probably create decisions about income-generating activities.

"Poverty in the midst of a generally wealthy society," Posner writes in his text, *Economic Analysis of Law* (1977: 350), "is likely to increase the incidence of crime: the foregone income of a legitimate alternative occupation is low for someone who has little earning capacity in legitimate occupations, while the proximity of wealth increases the expected return from crime, or, stated another way, the cost of honesty." Similarly, Ehrlich (1974) interprets racial differences in crime rates as indicative of differentials for blacks and whites in rates of returns to labor in legal and illegal markets: If blacks are discriminated against in legal markets while both blacks and whites have equal opportunity in illegal markets, then to the extent that returns to labor are a determinant of occupational choice and labor supply, one would expect black labor to be supplied in relatively greater amounts in illegal markets. Undertaking criminal activities is, in these views, a response to opportunities, incentives (and disincentives) as reflected in social class, race, and, no doubt, sex, age, health differences, and so forth, in the population. Although these differences are not likely to explain all of the variation in crime—criminal activities of an income-generating type—they, too, are caught up in the drug/crime nexus. How particular individuals respond to their opportunities may vary, but they do respond: "Crime and welfare are now basic components of the urban labor market," writes manpower specialist Eli Ginzberg (1978: 137); they operate "as alternative or supplementary sources of income for a large segment of the population." Some use drugs, too!

O'Donnell et al. (1976) reported that in a nationwide sample of young men, 5 percent of those currently working 30 hours or more per week had used heroin at least one time, as had 18 percent of those currently unemployed. Although the limited sample of heroin users precluded an analysis of concurrent heroin use and employment, there is substantial evidence that "many" drug abusers are legally employed, and that they work during all phases of their drug involvement. The National Commission on Marijuana and Drug Abuse (1973), after an extensive review of the literature on drug use and criminal activity, reports that 41 to 66 percent of the various study populations were employed immediately prior to arrest, incarceration, or treatment. Based on a study of the incidence of heroin use in the general population of New York State, the New York State Narcotic Addiction Control Commission estimated that 53 percent of the regular users of heroin were employed, 34 percent were in school, and 13 percent were unemployed. Nor is it known how many of the unemployed were actively seeking employment.[11]

Inadequacies in both the "quantity and quality of jobs," according to the task force on Work in America (1973: 28, 89), has led to "costs of such job-related pathologies as political alienation, violent aggression against others, alcoholism and drug abuse," and, they later add, delinquency. Labeled as a "psychiatric disorder," drug abuse on the job is linked to "job insecurity, unpleasant working conditions or hazardous work. Although little quantitative research has been done to support this statement, DuPont and Basen (1980: 139) provide extensive documentation of drug abuse in industry and conclude that "studies suggest that the stereotype of the heroin addict as a person who is highly unstable and unable to hold a job must be revised." It is reasonable to assume that if drug abuse in the work place were a rare event or even an event followed by considerable "visibility, dysfunction and exit," so that the screening (and removal) process was a simple one, "industry" would be less inclined to devote resources to the problem.[12] Although there are a variety of reasons companies may initiate drug abuse control programs, their existence is testimony to the presence of the working drug abusers. As for heroin, in particular, in a study of "a United Auto Workers local affiliated with a plant employing 3400 people, 15 percent of the workers were estimated to be addicted to heroin" (Work in America, 1973: 86).

The most in-depth study of the drug/legal work nexus reported to date, and the one that prompted DuPont and Basen's conclusions, is Caplovitz's (1976) *The Working Addict*. Through interviews with persons who had worked at full-time jobs but were currently in drug treatment programs, Caplovitz found that 61 percent of his sample of "addicts" had become addicts after they entered the labor force. They were able to hold full-time jobs because "they apparently assimilated work habits to the point that they were able to maintain them even after they became addicts," and even though most of the working addicts had a "fairly heavy habit." (1976: 66–71) Caplovitz also found that "almost all these addicts resorted to crime to supplement their income in supporting their habit. "But," he explains, "if crime were the sole source or primary source of funds for drugs, we should find no relationship between [legal] income and cost of habit. That this relationship is found indicates that working addicts made use of the [legal] income and not just crime to support their habit." As for the nature of their crime, 74 percent of the working addicts committed income-generating criminal acts while employed; 32 percent of the 74 percent stole from their employers; and 64 percent of the 74 percent stole outside of work through various hustling activities (Caplovitz, 1976: 130). The nature of the crime "outside of work" is obscured by the finding that persons dealing in drugs (buying and selling) are more likely to be involved in "hustling" on and off the job; those who steal on the job steal off the job. But the overwhelming point is that, at least for the Caplovitz sample, remaining on the job with or without stealing implies that significant gains are not realized from off-the-job stealing. Perhaps they are not "perceived" as possible and, therefore, not attempted. Perhaps these are risk-adverse addicts who steal or deal only under low-risk conditions and, therefore, have few opportunities or considerable competition. Perhaps they were not "addicted" and "treatment" was being used as a form of paid vacation. They would not even have to take their methadone; it could be sold on the streets and the proceeds added to the public assistance for which certified methadone treatment patients qualify (Preble and Miller, 1977). After all, in Detroit about 30 percent of the persons enrolled in methadone programs were clinically tested and found methadone-free (Stoloff et al., 1975). There may be any number of plausible hypotheses to explain the behaviors Caplovitz reports. Nevertheless, for this group criminal labor off the job was like working overtime, and there was a certain "compatibility" between legal and illegal labor markets. Their crime (illegal earnings) does not appear any more desperate and excessive than does their legal market work.

This should give us pause to consider further the information gathered from treatment programs—the institutional framework meant to bail out those whose drug consumption is "out of control." A study (Gearing, 1974) of the first 1230 persons admitted to a New York City methadone mainte-nance treatment program between 1964 and 1968 shows 33 percent of the study population was employed just *prior* to admission to the program, the period the literature suggests is one of "social dysfunction." Of the employed group, 40 percent maintained positions in unskilled jobs. This should be considered in light of the admissions criteria requiring at least five years of addiction to heroin and a previous record of arrests and incarceration— certainly not conducive to maintaining employment. Lukoff (1974) reports the source of income in the early 1970s for clients in a program located in a ghetto community with an extremely high rate of heroin addiction. Admis-sion was limited to those at least 21 years of age who had been addicted to heroin for at least 2 years. Primary sources of income for the "typical" patients were legitimate jobs (18 percent), welfare (19 percent), spouse, kin, or other (14 percent), and illegal sources (48 percent). The "typical" patient was black (77.4 percent) with less than a high school education. Finally, from a national study (Neman and Demaree, 1976) of outpatients admitted to treatment during 1972–1975 and reporting to the DARP system, one can get a sense of the extent of legal employment among persons for whom "intensive" consumption of narcotic drugs should "invariably" have led to property crime: males during the sixty days prior to admission to treatment. The data show that nearly 30 percent of the males available for employment worked at a legitimate job for more than one-half of the sixty-day period.[13] The average (mean) value of work was 51.4 days, a figure worth consider-ing, since the typical sixty-day period has only 43 working days if weekends are excluded. The majority (56 percent) reported "no occupation," and another 23 percent were listed as "unskilled" or "semi-skilled." As Neman and Demaree (1976: 361) point out, "the category of support (for all consumption, not just drugs) most frequently reported for males preceding entry into treatment was legitimate jobs, including over 25 percent of the male patients," while 20.1 percent reported illegal activities as the major source of support (for 11.4 percent this was a minor source); 15.4 percent were supported by public assistance; and 22.2 percent were supported by family and friends.

Rates of legitimate employment should be viewed in the context of legal market opportunities. That is, we need some indication of the labor force experiences of a nonabusing counterpart to those whose apparent "dismal" legal sector participation indicates, so it is assumed, their predisposition to criminal activity. There is little information about this for local markets, although we can gain some insight by examining national statistics and periodic studies of labor market conditions likely to prevail for "typical" persons residing in areas of greatest illicit drug use.[14] Overall unemployment[15] in the civilian labor force in 1966 was 3.8 percent; by 1969 it was 3.5 percent and had not been this low since 1953, when it was 2.9 percent (Employment and Earnings, 1975: 20). However, in an attempt to analyze the situation of workers in urban slums, the U.S. Department of Labor developed an indicator of subemployment that was then incorporated into intensive surveys by the Department of Labor in ten slum areas in 1966 (Ginsberg, 1975: 94–95):

> With the traditional concept (which provided a nationwide average of 3.7 percent unemployment for January 1967), joblessness in these urban slums averaged about 10%, nearly three times the national figure. But using the subemployment measure, the situation appeared to be much worse. Subemployment was from two to six times as great as official unemployment, ranging from 24% in Boston to 47% in San Antonio.

Although the special Labor Department surveys have not been repeated, a study of the employment profiles of 51 inner cities reported that from 1970 to 1971, when national unemployment averaged from 5 to 6 percent, subemployment in these inner cities averaged about 30 percent (Ginsberg, 1975: 96).

Drug abuse is not confined to urban slums, although it may be disproportionately concentrated in such areas, especially the abuse of narcotic drugs. The National Urban League (1976, 1977) provides quarterly estimates of a Hidden Unemployment Index, which incorporates the "discouraged" workers (i.e., those who "want a job now," but are no longer actively seeking work) and part-time workers who want full-time jobs and adds these to the number officially unemployed. This is similar to the most comprehensive economic hardship indicator developed recently by the U.S. Bureau of

Labor Statistics[16] and it provides national estimates of a closer approxima-
tion to the nonabusing reference group. National Urban League (1976,
1977) quarterly estimates of unemployment for 1976 indicate that "unofficial" unemployment is nearly twice the official rate, and the rates for blacks
are nearly twice those for whites, whether official or "unofficial." In the four
quarters of 1976, hidden unemployment for teenage blacks ranged from
52.3 to 63.8 percent; hidden unemployment for all blacks ranged from 22.4
to 25.5 percent (National Urban League, 1976, 1977). In these markets, it
would appear that drug abusers—in particular, black drug abusers—do
quite well in securing legal employment.

The principal interest in the drug/crime nexus is the criminal activity of
the drug user, not the legal market activities. However, an integrating feature
of both legal and illegal activities of drug abusers appears to be the character
of the process by which the activities take place—hustling. Criminal earnings are generated in a loosely defined "street market," and in order to
participate in it successfully, one must be a "hustler." Hustling, as Waldorf
(1973: 50) puts it, "means any activity that utilizes guile or deceit to gain
money. [It] may be either legal or illegal, but most often it is illegal." Gould
et al. (1974: 42) describe the chief ingredients for heroin addicts: "Hustling
requires spending a lot of time on the streets, talking with other hustlers,
being in the right place at the right time, and being ready for anything. But a
good dope fiend is doing all these things anyway. So becoming a good dope
fiend is the same thing as becoming a good hustler." And herein lies another
important integrating link, this one between drug consumption and criminal
activities: drug abuse, the consumption activity, and drug selling, the
earnings-generating activity, are very strongly related to one another.

The "pure heroin" habit sizes of user populations have been cited by
Holahan (1972: 289) as small, 20 mg/day; medium, 50 mg/day; and dealer,
180 mg/day. O'Conner et al. (1972: 88) refer to the drug costs of the heroin
users they interviewed as "$10 twice a week (heroin users) to $250 a day
(dealer's habit)." If hustling is the key word in heroin addicts' occupational
choice, drug selling is the premier hustle, and the bulk of heroin addicts use
drug selling and related distribution system income-generating activities to
support heroin consumption. Waldorf (1973: 50) writes that one in three
persons in his "addict sample" supported drug use by selling drugs; another
48 percent sold drugs as partial support of their habit. Thus, 80 percent were
attached to and earning monies in the drug distribution system. Among the
postaddiction utilization of income sources for Baridon's (1976: 45) addict
sample, more than 60 percent sold drugs (44 percent sold them "frequently"
or "very frequently"), although most of the sample worked at legitimate jobs
"providing considerable income to many." Hughes et al. (1971) observed a

"heroin copping community" where 34 percent of the 125 addicts were primarily engaged in drug distribution. They write that "it is erroneous to equate the huge habits of dealers with direct economic loss to the innocent public. Furthermore, workers (28 percent of the heroin copping community), who reported less frequent use and less expensive habits, paid for their drugs largely through their own legitimate income." Moore (1977) estimated that addicts derive 45 percent of their funds to purchase heroin from working within the heroin distribution system. Of the remaining 55 percent, more than a third is obtained from legal sources and "victimless" crimes. Ruth's (1972) study of the histories of 65 New York City drug addicts supports Moore's estimates: 50 percent of the illegal funds "earned" by drug addicts resulted from selling drugs, and only .6 percent came from muggings.

Selling heroin and other narcotics is one way of maintaining a continuous supply and a method of financing consumption. If there is a positive and increasingly intense relationship between the quantity of heroin consumed and the user's state of drug dependence and if there is a similar relationship between drug dependence and the propensity to engage in income-generating criminal activites, the heroin use/property crime relationship will be reduced to the extent that heavy heroin users self-select into drug-dealing occupations. Therefore, "if other factors remain the same, the total social cost of heroin addiction will be less if the percentage of consumed heroin earned from pushing is increased" (Holahan, 1972: 289).

It may be that persons who consume sizable quantities of heroin engage in drug dealing. It may be that persons who sell heroin also consume large quantities of it because of the relatively lower price, higher purity, availability, and so on. An important point is, however, the extent to which the distribution system "removes" the financial onus from the heavy users and leaves a body of users for whom there is no compelling reason to expect that the "desperation" of drug needs will lead to revenue-raising crime. Drug selling has accounted for 30–50 percent of the main support of habit in a variety of studies; scarcity may lead to temporary (or long-term) unemployment as a drug dealer. Perhaps the seller is the key to the drug/crime nexus. Since sellers have the largest habits, on the average, and are more likely than nonsellers to be drug-dependent because of habit size, movement from sales to "unemployment" (due, say, to law enforcement activity) may be instrumental in establishing a strong crime-heroin relationship. Even this possibility receives little support from Baridon's (1976) study, however, since 93 percent of those frequently dealing drugs "took a cure" rather than "hustled more" when habit costs became "unmanageable."

Participation in criminal activities may be relatively attractive for drug abusers and nonabusers. There is a ready potential for obtaining cash, a general lack of discrimination, flexible hours, rewards to skills not other-wise marketable, little penalty for the lack of a formal education, and on and on. Thus, hustling in illegal markets is a labor supply phenomenon that is rational as a choice, given actual or perceived alternatives. As Silberman (1978: 89–90) puts it, "to youngsters growing up in lower class neighbor-hoods, crime is available as an occupational choice, much as law, medicine or business management is for [middle-class youth]." The drug-dependent consumer, however, is not likely to be a leading criminal and earn the monies of his or her nondependent criminal counterpart (Plate, 1975). Besides "muddied judgment," preoccupation with consumption activities precludes income-generating activities. The drug addict's "time budget is structured around his drug use" (O'Donnell, 1967: 82), and "seeking drugs becomes an all-consuming activity" (Waldorf, 1973: 48). Thus, as Zinberg (1974: 162) points out, the addict does not like to travel or "even take the time for the fattest pickings." Whether the manner in which such persons go about earning income is rational or irrational is unimportant;[17] it is more important that they are unlikely to earn "a lot" of income on a regular, ongoing basis.

Summing up the literature on this point, Moore (1977: 91) writes that "heroin users appear as people who struggle to make $10,000 in the periods during which they are not institutionalized. If the incomes were much higher than this, it would be hard to explain why more ghetto residents are not addicts, since the users' incomes would be substantially above the mean. . . . Property offenses finance a much smaller proportion of the total heroin consumption than is usually assumed." Perhaps this explains why piecing together the literature on income sources leads to the conclusion that the "big habits" are financed from drug sales and the "small habits" are financed from a variety of legal and illegal activities that drug abusers shift into in propor-tions not dissimilar to those of their nonabusing brethren. The transition through occupations and labor supply and earnings would very likely be similar for both abusing and nonabusing groups, if the abusing group did not have access to the financial rewards of drug treatment programs as an added income/consumption choice.

Does drug abuse lead to crime? McGlothlin et al. (1978: 311) argue that "when the individual spends large amounts of money for heroin, does not deal, and has no source of legitimate income, then criminality is a necessary condition for addiction to exist." Whether there are many such persons spending large amounts of money for heroin and supporting it from criminal activity, and how narrowly we want to restrict the terms of the relationship, will, in large part, determine whether drug abuse leads to crime. Drug abuse and crime are what we choose to make them. The more restricted the set of opportunities an individual faces, the greater the likelihood one of the re-

maining activities will be chosen. We do not need heroin to reach the dism\
limits of social choice, but with heroin we seem to get there a little faster:

> "When the weather is bad, there's no dope in town, and hustling has been bad, then . . . everybody just goes to sleep and hopes tomorrow will be better" [Gould et al., 1974: 47].

NOTES

1. One of the reasons why the drug/crime literature is generally ambiguous or misleading is the loose manner in which terms are used. Although it may not always be possible, I hope to avoid that tradition. I shall use the term *drug abuse* to mean any use of all nonalcohol, illicit drugs. *Drug addict or* addiction are narrower terms and will refer to the regular and dependent use of narcotics as is "generally employed" in the literature. *Crime* and *property crime* will be used interchangeably and will refer to crimes in which the primary "motivation" is to obtain monies. Otherwise, the term *violent crime* will be used. Any exceptions to this scheme will be clarified in the text. Still pretty loose, eh?

2. "A consensus seems to exist among medical, law enforcement and research authorities, as well as drug users themselves, that few if any crimes of violence result directly from the use of the opiate narcotics" (Canadian Government's Commission of Inquiry, 1973: 321).

3. For discussion of the "shopping qua copping" areas and activities, also see Agar (1973), Hughes et al. (1971), and Moore (1977). For a review of the impact of "labeling," see Williams (1976).

4. There are credit markets which permit consumption activity to precede the earnings process. Credit markets are not likely to be germane here.

5. Since the sale of alcohol is restricted by age, the legal age varying by state but usually at least 18 years, the findings of O'Donnell et al. (1976)—that by age 17, 69 percent to 87 percent of male birth cohorts (for the years from 1944 to 1954) had used alcohol—"suggest" a substantial "likelihood" that "some" alcohol use was illicit.

6. There is voluminous literature on this point that can be derived from reports of persons in drug treatment. For example, McGlothlin et al. (1978) report the mean age of first narcotic use and mean age at first daily narcotic use for males in two admission cohorts to the California Civil Addict Program. In both a 1962–1964 admissions cohort and a 1970 admissiosns cohort, approximately two years elapsed between first narcotic use and first daily narcotic use. Gerstein et al. (1979) report a one and one-half year lapse between age of first heroin use and age at first addiction for a sample of women entering the County of San Diego/University of California Narcotic Treatment Program between 1970 and 1974.

7. This will vary by individual, the purity of the drug and other variables (Platt and Labate, 1976; Stimmel, 1975).

8. Even the utility of the "addict" as an image lacks consistency. In 1962, according to the U.S. Supreme Court, the addict was once "one of the walking dead." A few years later, with the publication of Preble and Casey's (1969) "Taking Care of Business," the walk turned into a run as the addict image switched gears to "ripping and running" (Agar, 1973) in the street scene's version of the workaholic (Goldman, 1980).

9. Casey and Preble (1974) refer to monies earned in illegal markets as "involuntary transfers." However, obtaining these monies requires "work," the supply of criminal labor. One expects a return for labor. Hence, the transfers are better viewed as criminal salary. Divide this by the time spent earning it to get the criminal wage rate.

10. There is nothing unusual in this. For example, persons who have considerable interest in the stock market and purchase stocks have an incentive to develop a "Wall Street" occupation. Persons who work in Wall Street occupations (say, stockbrokers or analysts) have an incentive to buy stock and bonds.

11. A problem with the statistics reported on the labor force activities of drug consumers is that the conventions chosen by the researchers generally do not follow the reporting conventions of the Bureau of Labor Statistics, the principal surveyor or labor force activities of the U.S. population. Consequently, comparisons with the population at large are "problematical."

12. Unless, of course, the rare event generated substantial costs.

13. These figures are derived from Neman and Demaree (1976) by eliminating from their distribution the categories which contain persons unavailable for work and, consequently, not in the "labor force."

14. Even these statistics are difficult to interpret as the experiences of a nonabusing counterpart. We do not know how drug abuse has influenced them. We only assume that these figures are not likely to be "significantly influenced" by the persons in drug treatment programs or undetected drug abusers in the population.

15. "The definition of unemployment has been the subject of continuing controversy over the years," according to Julius Shiskin (1976), Commissioner of Labor Statistics. Some of the controversy is explained in Shiskin's Bureau of Labor Statistics Report.

16. Formally known as U-7, the Bureau of Labor Statistics indicator adds full-time job seekers, plus discouraged workers, plus one-half of those working part-time for economic reasons as a percentage of the labor force minus one-half of those working part-time for economic reasons. See Julius Shiskin (1976: 4). As an example of measures of hidden unemployment, discouraged workers, according to National Urban League usage, includes all persons not in the labor force who "want a job now." The Bureau of Labor Statistics includes only the group who "think they cannot get a job."

17. Compare Zinberg (1974: 161), "Generally speaking, addict stealing is uncontrolled and irrational," with Smith and Stephens (1976: 170), "The classic stereotype of the half-crazed and desperate dope fiend madly rushing about committing irrational criminal acts received no support in the study data."

REFERENCES

AGAR, M. H. (1973) Ripping and Running: A Formal Ethnography of Urban Heroin Addicts. New York: Academic Press.
————— and R. C. STEPHENS (1975) "The methadone street scene: the addict's view." Psychiatry 38.
ALDERMAN, M. H. and T. K. DAVIS (1976) "Hypertension control at the worksite." Journal of Occupational Medicine 18.
American Bar Association (1972) New Perspectives on Urban Crime. Chicago: Author.
BARIDON, P. C. (1976) Addiction, Crime, and Social Policy. Lexington, MA: D. C. Heath.
BROWN, G. F. and L. P. SILVERMAN (1974) "The retail price of heroin: estimation and applications. Journal of the American Statistical Association 69.
Canadian Government's Commission of Inquiry (1973) Interim Report: The Non-Medical Use of Drugs. New York: Penguin.
CAPLOVITZ, D. (1976) The Working Addict. New York: City University Graduate School and University Center.

CHEIN, I., D. L. GERARD, R. S. LEE, and E. ROSENFELD (1964) The Road to H: Narcotics, Delinquency and Social Policy. New York: Basic Books.

DuPONT, R. L. and M. M. BASEN (1980) "Control of alcohol and drug abuse in industry." Public Health Reports 95 (March/April).

EHRLICH, I. (1974) "Participation in illegitimate activities: an economic analysis," in G. S. Becker and W. M. Landes (eds.) Essays in the Economics of Crime and Punishment. New York: Columbia University Press.

Employment and Earnings (1975) U.S. Bureau of Labor Statistics, Volume 21. Washington, DC: Government Printing Office.

GANDOSSY, R. P., J. R. WILLIAMS, J. COHEN, and H. J. HARWOOD (1980) Drugs and Crime: A Survey and Analysis of the Literature. Washington, DC: National Institute of Justice.

GEARING, F. R. (1974) "Methadone maintenance treatment five years later—where are they now?" in M. Greene and R. Dupont (eds.) The Epidemiology of Drug Abuse, American Journal of Public Health 64 (December).

GERSTEIN, D. R., L. L. JUDD, and S. A. ROVNER (1979) "Career dynamics of female heroin addicts." American Journal of Drug and Alcohol Abuse 6.

GINSBURG, H. (1975) Unemployment, Subemployment, and Public Policy. New York: New York University Center for Studies in Income Maintenance Policy.

GINZBERG, E. (1978) Statement before the House Committee on the Judiciary Subcommittee on Crime, 95th Congress. Washington, DC: Government Printing Office.

GOLDMAN, F. (1980) "Social epidemiology and social policy during the 'heroin years,' 1960–1975," in E. Josephson and O. Ochs (eds.) Drug Policy and Social Research. Washington, DC: Hemisphere.

GOULD, L. C., A. L. WALKER, L. E. CRANE, and C. W. LIDZ (1974) Connections: Notes from the Heroin World. New Haven, CT: Yale University Press.

GREENBERG, S. W. and F. ADLER (1974) "Crime and addiction: an empirical analysis of the literature, 1920–1973." Contemporary Drug Problems 3.

HAYNES, R. B. (1978) "Increased absenteeism from work after detection and labelling of hypertensive patients." New England Journal of Medicine 299 (October).

HOFMANN, F. G. (1975) A Handbook on Drug and Alcohol Abuse: The Biomedical Aspects. New York: Oxford University Press.

HOLAHAN, J. F. (1972) "The economics of heroin," in P. M. Wald and P. B. Hutt (eds.) Dealing with Drug Abuse. New York: Praeger.

HUGHES, P. H., G. A. CRAWFORD, N. W. BARKER, S. SCHUMANN, and J. H. JAFFE (1971) "The social structure of a heroin copping community." American Journal of Psychiatry 128.

Hypertension Detection and Follow-Up Program (1979) "Five-year findings of the HDFP, parts I and II." Journal of the American Medical Association 242 (December).

INCIARDI, J. A. (1977) Methadone Diversion: Experiences and Issues. Rockville, MD: National Institute on Drug Abuse.

ISBELL, H. (1962) Statement in Proceedings, White House Conference on Narcotic and Drug Abuse. Washington, DC: Government Printing Office.

JOHNSTON, L. D., P. M. O'MALLEY, and L. K. EVELAND (1978) "Drugs and delinquency: a search for causal connections," in D. B. Kandel (ed.) Longitudinal Research on Drug Use. New York: John Wiley.

JONES, K. R. and T. R. VISCHI (1979) "Impact of alcohol, drug abuse and mental health treatment on medical care utilization." Medical Care 17 (December).

LETTIERI, D. J., M. SAYERS, and H. W. PEARSON [eds.] (1980) Theories on Drug Abuse: Selected Contemporary Perspectives. Rockville, MD: National Institute on Drug Abuse.

LEVESON, I. and J. H. WEISS (1976) Analysis of Urban Health Problems. New York: Spectrum.

LUFT, H. (1978) Poverty and Health. Cambridge, MA: Ballinger.

LUKOFF, I. F. (1974) "Issues in the evaluation of heroin treatment," in E. Josephson and E. E. Carroll (eds.) Drug Use: Epidemiological and Sociological Approaches. New York: John Wiley.

McGLOTHLIN, W. H. (1979) "Drugs and crime," in R. L. DuPont et al. (eds.) Handbook on Drug Abuse. Rockville, MD: National Institute on Drug Abuse.

———— D. M. ANGLIN, and B. D. WILSON (1978) "Narcotic addiction and crime." Criminology 16.

MARTIN, W. R. (1980) "Diagnosis of drug dependence," in S. Einstein (ed.) Drugs in Relation to the Drug User. New York: Pergamon.

MEYER, A. S. (1952) Social and Psychological Factors in Opiate Addiction. New York: Columbia University/Bureau of Applied Social Research.

MOORE, M. S. (1977) Buy and Bust. Lexington, MA: D. C. Heath.

National Commission on Marijuana and Drug Abuse (1973) Drug Use in America: The Problem in Perspective: Second Report. Washington, DC: Government Printing Office.

National Urban League (1977) Quarterly Economic Report on the Black Worker, Reports 7, 8.

———— (1976) Quarterly Economic Report on the Black Worker, Report 6.

NEMAN, J. F. and R. G. DEMAREE (1976) "Behavioral criteria for assessments of outcome during treatment for drug users in the DARP: 1972–1975 admissions," in S. B. Sells and D. D. Simpson (eds.) Studies in the Effectiveness of Treatments for Drug Abuse, Volume V. Cambridge, MA: Ballinger.

New York State Narcotic Addiction Control Commission (1971) An Assessment of Drug Use in the General Population. New York: Author.

NURCO, D. N. (1979) "Etiological aspects of drug abuse," in R. L. DuPont et al. (eds.) Handbook on Drug Abuse. Rockville, MD: National Institute on Drug Abuse.

O'CONNOR, G., L. WURMSER, T. C. BROWN, and J. SMITH (1972) "The economics of heroin addiction: a new interpretation of the facts," in D. E. Smith and G. R. Gay (eds.) It's So Good, Don't Even Try It Once. Englewood Cliffs, NJ: Prentice-Hall.

O'DONNELL, J. A. (1967) "The rise and decline of a subculture." Social Problems 15.

———— (1966) "Narcotic addiction and crime." Social Problems 13.

————, H. L. VOSS, R. R. CLAYTON, G. T. SLATIN, and R. G. W. ROOM (1976) Young Men and Drugs—A Nationwide Survey. Rockville, MD: National Institute on Drug Abuse.

PLATE, T. (1975) Crime Pays. New York: Simon & Schuster.

PLATT, J. J. and C. LABATE (1976) Heroin Addiction. New York: John Wiley.

POSNER, R. A. (1977) Economic Analysis of Law. Boston: Little, Brown.

PREBLE, E. and J. J. CASEY (1969) "Taking care of business—the heroin user's life on the street." International Journal of the Addictions 4.

PREBLE, E. and T. MILLER (1977) "Methadone, wine and welfare," in R. S. Weppner (ed.) Street Ethnology: Selected Studies of Crime and Drug Use in Natural Settings. Beverly Hills, CA: Sage.

Research Triangle Institute (1976) Drug Use and Crime. Springfield, VA: National Technical Information Service.

ROBINS, L. N. (1979) "Addict careers," in R. L. DuPont et al. (eds.) Handbook on Drug Abuse. Rockville, MD: National Institute on Drug Abuse.

——— (1978) "The interaction of setting and predisposition in explaining novel behavior: drug initiations before, in, and after Vietnam," in D. B. Kandel (ed.) Longitudinal Research on Drug Use. Washington, DC: Hemisphere.

——— (1977) "Estimating addiction rates and locating target populations: how decomposition into stages helps," in J. D. Rittenhouse (ed.) The Epidemiology of Heroin and Other Narcotics. Rockville, MD: National Institute on Drug Abuse.

RUTH, H. (1972) "The street level economics of heroin addiction in New York City." (unpublished)

SAPIRA, J. D. (1968) "The narcotic addict as a medical patient." American Journal of Medicine 45.

SHISKIN, J. (1976) "Labor Force and Unemployment." U.S. Bureau of Labor Statistics Report 486.

SILBERMAN, C. E. (1978) Criminal Violence, Criminal Justice. New York: Random House.

SILVERMAN, L. P. and N. L. SPRUILL (1977) "Urban crime and the price of heroin." Journal of Urban Economics 4.

SMITH, J. P. (1973) "Substances in illicit drugs," in R. H. Blum et al. (eds.) Drug Dealers—Taking Action. San Francisco: Jossey-Bass.

STEPHENS, R. C. and R. B. SMITH (1976) "Copping and Caveat Emptor: The Street Addict as Consumer. New York: Bureau of Social Sciences Research, New York State Office of Drug Abuse Services.

STIMMEL, B. (1975) Heroin Dependency. New York: Stratton Intercontinental Medical Book Corporation.

STOLOFF, P., D. B. LEVINE, and N. L. SPRUILL (1975) The Effect of Drug Treatment on Property Crime in Detroit. Arlington, VA: Public Research Institute.

TINKLENBERG, J. R. (1975) "Assessing the effects of drug use on antisocial behavior." Annals of the American Academy of Political and Social Science 417 (January).

United Nations (1972) "Drug abuse and criminality." Bulletin on Narcotics 24 (October–December).

VAILLANT, G. E. (1966) "A 12-year follow-up of New York addicts: some social and psychiatric characteristics." Articles of General Psychiatry 15.

WALDORF, D. (1973) Careers in Dope. Englewood Cliffs, NJ: Prentice-Hall.

WILLIAMS, J. R. (1976) Effects of Labelling the "Drug Abuser." Rockville, MD: National Institute on Drug Abuse.

WILSON, J. Q. (1977) Thinking about Crime. New York: Vintage.

WINICK, C. (1961) "Physician narcotic addicts." Social Problems (Fall).

Work in America (1973) Report of a Special Task Force to the Secretary of Health, Education, and Welfare. Cambridge, MA: MIT Press.

ZINBERG, N. E. (1979) "Nonaddictive opiate use," in R. L. DuPont et al. (eds.) Handbook on Drug Abuse. Rockville, MD: National Institute on Drug Abuse.

8

DRUG TREATMENT AND CRIMINALITY
Methodological and Theoretical Considerations

CHARLES E. FAUPEL

INTRODUCTION

The history of treatment for opiate addiction in the United States is characterized by a great deal of experimentation and inconclusive results. Prior to the twentieth century, addiction was viewed largely in terms of moral depravity, although by the 1890s the medical profession began to realize the physiological basis of opiate addiction. During the period of the 1890s and following, the primary debate among medical people was whether abrupt, rapid, or gradual withdrawal was the most effective form of treatment (Terry and Pellens, 1970).

Treatment efforts were confounded by the introduction of the opiate derivative heroin in 1898. Heroin came to be considered a cure for morphine addiction, and it was only later that the addictive qualities of heroin were recognized. Doctors continued to prescribe maintenance dosages of opiates to addicts until 1914 when the Harrison Act was passed, which in effect banned the practice of opiate maintenance.[1] The freedom of the physician

AUTHOR'S NOTE: The author wishes to express his appreciation to Janet Bruno and Mel Jones for their many thoughtful criticisms and comments on drafts of this chapter.

was thus greatly restricted, and Glasscote et al. (1972) note that many physicians were jailed for violation of the Harrison Act.

Opiate addiction then became a criminal offense, and the addict suffered legal stigmatization as well as physiological dependence. As a result of the criminalization of opiate use, the addict was forced to turn to illegal markets for his supply. This underground market in turn resulted in a dramatic increase in the cost of the opiate habit (by now, primarily heroin), and in many cases the addict was forced to rely on still further criminal activity to support his or her habit. Increasing numbers of addicts thus found their way into the criminal justice system.

For a short period, from 1920 to 1924, local health departments began to supply maintenance dosages of opiates in response to this situation. Interestingly, the Treasury Department initially endorsed this measure, but eventually abuses of these programs led the government sweepingly to shut down *all* maintenance programs. In 1924 the final program was closed, out of a total of 44 once in operation (Glasscote et al., 1972).

Thus forced to turn again to illegal supplies, and consequently to adopt a criminal lifestyle, the addict was not uncommonly destined to a federal penitentiary. It was principally in response to this dramatic increase of heroin addicts in federal prisons that the U.S. government established two "narcotics farms," officially called U.S. Public Health Service Hospitals. The first, located in Lexington, Kentucky, opened its doors in 1935. Three years later, in 1938, the second hospital opened in Fort Worth, Texas. Treatment at these hospitals consisted of withdrawing the addict from heroin by administering gradually decreasing dosages of morphine for ten days, after which the addict was considered free of narcotics. (Methadone replaced morphine after it was introduced in the 1940s.) In addition, the addict was provided with vocational and psychiatric care.[2]

A new concept in treatment was introduced in 1958. Charles Dederich, an ex-alcoholic, founded a total therapeutic community in California which came to be called Synanon.[3] The philosophy of Synanon and other subsequently established therapeutic communities was simple, but probably more profound than any other treatment philosophy to the present time. Briefly, protagonists held that in order to modify behavioral patterns formed and reinforced over a lifetime, a 24-hour community environment that encourages a "constructive" rather than a "destructive" lifestyle is required. In addition to abstinence from drugs and antisocial behavior, this involved the development of interpersonal and vocational skills.

Several years after Dederich established the Synanon program, the first outpatient methadone clinic was opened in 1965, by Drs. Vincent Dole and Marie Nyswander. Similar to the federal hospitals, this program and those which followed sought to reduce physical dependence through gradually decreasing dosages of methadone, a synthetic narcotic developed in the early 1940s.

The 1960s witnessed a rapid increase in the prevalence of locally based treatment facilities. Some idea of the rapidity of increase is suggested by a national survey conducted by the Institute of Behavioral Research at Texas Christian University in 1968. The Institute attempted to locate every organization that conducted a program specifically oriented to drug treatment. A total of 183 such programs were located, and included facilities operated by federal, state, and local governments, as well as programs run by private groups. Of those programs responding, 77 percent had been in operation less than five years (since 1963), and only two (the U.S. Public Health Service Hospitals) had been in operation for more than twenty years (Jaffe, 1979).

Not only did the *number* of treatment centers increase, but there emerged in the 1960s a diversity of treatment modalities, including variations of standard detoxification procedures, outpatient drug-free treatment, and prison-based programs, in addition to elaborations of methadone and residential treatment.[4] The dominant treatment modalities, however, have been methadone maintenance and therapeutic communities. Furthermore, programs that do not strictly qualify as methadone maintenance or residential treatment typically incorporate elements of the process and philosophy of either or both of these modalities. For these reasons, this chapter limits its focus to these two dominant treatment forms. Before discussing the relevant findings with regard to the effectiveness of these modalities, it will be helpful to describe briefly the treatment process employed by each.

METHADONE MAINTENANCE

In the early 1940s the synthetic narcotic methadone was developed in Germany, and it was not long before the value of methadone as a withdrawal drug began to be recognized. Producing similar physiological effects as heroin and morphine, the drug was relatively popular among addicts. Furthermore, methadone had the added benefit of producing a longer-lasting effect—from 24 to 36 hours. It was reasoned that the addict could maintain his habit with less drug consumption for a period of time until (ideally) he eventually withdrew from opiate use altogether.

In 1965 the first outpatient methadone clinic was established in New York City by Drs. Vincent Dole and Marie Nyswander. Since this time, virtually dozens of clinics have been established in New York. Moreover, New York hosts some of the largest methadone treatment programs in the country. Because of this, the New York programs have been more extensively studied

and evaluated than others; furthermore, descriptions of methadone treatment are typically "New York style" programs. Due to smaller caseloads,
differing philosophies, and other factors, methadone clinics in other cities
throughout the country may vary from the description presented here.

The addict seeking treatment in these clinics is first interviewed by an
attending physician who determines the patient's tolerance level. Small
dosages are administered initially (usually 10–40 mg. daily, depending on
the program), with gradually increasing dosages over a period of several
days until a "maintenance dose" is reached, whereby the patient is relieved
from his craving for narcotics for the 24- to 36-hour effective period of the
drug.

Initially, urine samples are taken on a frequent basis to ensure that the
patient remains clean from heroin.[5] After the patient has been enrolled in the
clinic for a period of time, samples are usually taken less frequently (e.g.,
once per month) unless he or she has been found to be using heroin, at which
time the case is likely to be reviewed and appropriate adjustments made.
Since federal regulations only insist on *sampling* urine, the disposition of
violators will vary from clinic to clinic. After the client has been stabilized,
the supply of methadone will be gradually decreased, with the ultimate aim,
theoretically, of reducing methadone consumption to zero.

The popularity of methadone maintenance is evidenced by the fact that in
1978 approximately 75,000 heroin addicts were receiving daily dosages of
legal methadone (Lowinson and Millman, 1979).

THERAPEUTIC COMMUNITIES

The founding of Synanon in 1958 marked the beginning of a novel
approach to drug treatment. It was a mode of treatment that later came to be
called the therapeutic community. Following the example of Synanon, Daytop Village was established in New York in 1963. Other centers were later
established in most of the metropolitan areas of the country. Currently there
are over 300 such programs in the United States, which range in size from
35–500 beds (DeLeon and Rosenthal, 1979).

The therapeutic community is a total, 24-hour environment. Treatment
includes confrontation and encounter therapy, educational opportunities,
development of employable skills, aid in job placement, and other supportive services. The program is a relatively long-term one, often involving up to
18 months and more from entry to graduation, depending on the progress of
the individual client. An important feature of most programs is the "reentry"
phase, whereby after demonstrating a readiness to begin functioning in the
outside world, the resident is encouraged to find employment while still

maintaining contact with the program. Initially the recovering addict maintains a resident status within the program while working during the day; after a period of time an "outpatient" or "aftercare" status is achieved and contact with the program is made only on a periodic basis until the resident finally "graduates" from the program.

Therapeutic communities have changed considerably since the founding of Synanon in 1958. For example, increasing emphasis is being placed on the "reentry" phases of treatment, preparing the resident to function in conventional society. Also, reliance on encounter therapy now plays a more marginal role than was the case in the early years, with a greater reliance on professional counseling. This often involves the utilization of supportive community services in the treatment process. These and other changes distinguish current residential treatment from the classic Synanon model. The basic philosophy behind residential treatment, however, has not changed significantly. These programs still seek to remove the addict physically, socially, and emotionally from his or her former environment, and to build primary relationships and skills that will nurture conventional values and lifestyles.[6]

HOW EFFECTIVE IS TREATMENT?

A survey of the literature addressing the effectiveness of drug treatment in reducing criminality reveals three general trends: (1) a rather lopsided focus on methadone maintenance as a treatment modality; (2) methodological limitations resulting in inadequate data for establishing of pre- and posttreatment criminality; and (3) a paucity of theoretical accountability for the effectiveness of treatment. This last point deserves more attention than we shall be able to give here, and a more extensive theoretical model awaits future publication. We shall, however, attempt to lay the groundwork for such a model at the conclusion of this chapter. Presently, however, a brief discussion of what has already been done in the evaluation of treatment effectiveness should serve to highlight the three trends noted above.

Austin and Lettieri (1976, 1977) have compiled annotative bibliographies of research articles and monographs dealing with the nature of the relationship between drugs and crime and the criminal justice system. The research included in these bibliographies comprises virtually all of the major works to that time. Given that no new major research breakthroughs have occurred in the area of drug treatment since that time, the works included here can be considered representative of our knowledge of the effectiveness of treatment. In addition to these works, George Nash (1976) has presented the findings of several studies on the effectiveness of treatment, some of which have not been published and thus were not included in the Austin and Lettieri volumes. Because these studies are significant both in terms of their findings and in the quality of their methodology, they have been included for consideration here as well.

STUDIES ON THE EFFECTIVENESS OF METHADONE TREATMENT

Of a total of 48 empirical studies that deal specifically with posttreatment criminal behavior, 28 focus either on methadone maintenance alone, or on multitreatment modalities that include methadone maintenance as a primary part of the treatment process (e.g., the Lexington U.S. Public Health Hospital). In addition to these, three other studies include methadone maintenance along with therapeutic communities as part of their treatment sample. Hence, of a total of 48 empirical studies considered in the three source anthologies, 31 (64.6%) focus on methadone maintenance as a primary treatment modality, either as the sole treatment modality or in combination with other styles of treatment.

The 31 studies addressing the effectiveness of methadone maintenance have drawn mixed conclusions. While most report at least moderate success with regard to reduced criminality, it is difficult to interpret these findings because of variation in methodologies. Three specific problem areas inherent in the methodologies of these studies present difficulties in assessing the reported success of methadone treatment.

Criteria for Establishing Criminality

Nearly all of the studies assessing the effectiveness of methadone maintenance rely on official records for establishing a reduction in criminality. Arrest statistics are most often used, although other forms of official statistics are used as well. Gearing (1974), for example, relies on arrest rates and reports 201 arrests per 100 man years prior to admission to various New York methadone programs. This contrasts with 1.24 arrests per 100 man years following admission, representing a 99.9 percent reduction in criminality. Dole et al. (1968), on the other hand, use *conviction* rates as the basis for establishing treatment effectiveness, and report nearly a 90 percent reduction in criminality, with 52 convictions per 100 man years prior to treatment, compared to 5.8 convictions per 100 man years in the year following admission. These smaller conviction rates are hardly surprising, due to the attrition of cases from the criminal justice system between arrest and conviction; how much of a percentage differential in the pre- and posttreatment rates for which attrition accounts is more difficult to establish, and makes comparisons difficult.

Still another criterion for establishing pre- and postadmission criminality is used by Patch et al. (1973a, 1973b) in a study of methadone clients in Boston. Here, the number of *charges* against a client before and after admission to treatment are compared, revealing an overall average reduction in crime of 41 percent for three programs. The use of criminal charges, while ostensibly reflecting more realistically the amount of criminality, is deceiving and limits the comparability of the findings presented here with those of other studies. It has become almost standard practice for police to drum up several charges for a single offense in order to provide more room for plea-bargaining. Hence, the use of charges as a basis for criminality may distort the extent and nature of criminal behavior.

Other studies report arrest rates as indicators of crime, but rely on self-reports to counselors of such arrests (e.g., Cuskey et al., 1973). The obvious difficulty of such a technique is that arrestees are not likely to admit to their treatment counselor high rates of arrests, particularly those arrests following admission to treatment.[7]

Not only does the variation in the criteria for establishing criminality make the interpretation of reported treatment effectiveness difficult, but the reliance on official records as indicators of criminality has itself been called into question (e.g., Beattie, 1960; Wheeler, 1967; Inciardi, 1978). The fact that the two studies that rely on self-reports of criminal behavior (Soloway, 1974; Brotman and Freedman, 1968) report no or only limited reduction in criminality gives substance to the criticism that official statistics do not reflect the actual extent of criminal behavior. More important, the two studies mentioned above would suggest that the use of official statistics may tend to depress the rate of *posttreatment* criminality due to selective law enforcement, lower visibility of a "maintained" addict, or other extraneous factors. It is argued, therefore, that a more realistic assessment of criminality is likely to be obtained through the self-reporting of criminal behavior to *outside independent investigators,* at least in conjunction with official statistics. While difficulties in this reporting technique have also been noted, it does not suffer from the same sort of systematic bias inherent in the use of official statistics. Using self-reports in conjunction with official statistics may further serve to alleviate extreme cases of over- and underreporting of criminality.

Uncertain Time Comparisons

Several of the methadone effectiveness studies are methodologically weak, due to protracted time periods employed for pre- and/or posttreatment comparisons. In some cases the data itself are limited to the year prior to and the year after admission to treatment. Bowden (1976) and Maddux and

McDonald (1973) both use one-year pre- and postadmission arrest rates. Curiously, these studies report relatively low pre- and postadmission differentials (a 24 percent and a 20 percent reduction respectively). In other studies, longer periods are used, but no controls are introduced for length of time in treatment or for length of pretreatment addiction. In these studies, pretreatment arrest rates are usually calculated from a few months to several years. Cushman (1974), for example, reports an 89 percent reduction in arrest rates after admission to treatment; however, pretreatment statistics include all arrests since addiction, with no temporal controls to determine how many of these arrests actually occurred just prior to admission. Similarly, patients in the sample were in treatment up to 6.5 years, and, again, no data are provided concerning when the posttreatment arrests occurred.[8]

It is reasonable to assume that the arrest rate will be much higher in the year immediately preceding admission to treatment, due to court referrals of chronic offenders or simply by virtue of the fact that addicts are more likely to seek treatment voluntarily after successive encounters with the law. This assumption has been empirically demonstrated. Hayim (1973) and Lukoff and Quatrone (1973) compare arrest rates in the year immediately prior to treatment with those during the total period of addiction, and observe a sharp rise in criminal arrests during the baseline year. *Furthermore, when comparing postadmission arrests with pretreatment rates since addiction, the authors observe a higher rate during treatment.*

Finally, lacking in most studies are posttermination arrest records. One study that does include such follow-ups (Nash, 1973) finds that methadone maintenance had very little effect on posttermination criminal behavior, particularly when compared to the effectiveness of residential treatment. Other studies control for length of time in treatment (e.g., the Dole et al. and Gearing studies), usually observing a negative relationship between duration of treatment and number of arrests. This offers little indication, however, of the effectiveness of treatment beyond the treatment period itself. Lacking in these studies is a follow-up of treatment clients *after they have terminated treatment.* It would seem that such follow-up measures should be a critical part of a research design if treatment objectives include long-range rehabilitation of the addict. Because of this oversight, it is not possible in most cases to evaluate the effectiveness of methadone maintenance in terms of long-range consequences.

Lack of Comparison Data

A final limitation characterizing nearly all of the methadone treatment studies is their failure to include control data on nontreatment drug users. Again, it is reasonable to assume that repeated experience with arrest will lead a select portion of addicts to seek treatment, thereby resulting in a sampling bias with regard to the addict population as a whole. Studies that have undertaken such comparisons (Bloom and Capel, 1973; Brill and Lieberman, 1969) do not observe large differences between nontreatment addicts and postadmission methadone divertees with regard to criminal behavior. The differences are even less pronounced when controlling for variables such as age.

This particular criticism is not meant to imply that methadone treatment is not effective for at least some of its clients. Rather, it suggests that because of inherent biases in the selection of cases for observation, many studies tend to overestimate the overall effectiveness of methadone maintenance.

STUDIES ON THE EFFECTIVENESS OF THERAPEUTIC COMMUNITIES

Receiving much less attention in the literature is residential drug-free treatment (therapeutic communities). In contrast to the 31 studies addressing methadone treatment, only five of the 48 studies focused on the effectiveness of therapeutic communities.[9] Indeed, one of the major works, which evaluates 24 therapeutic communities and is included in Nash's review, was never published (System Sciences Inc., 1973). Nash (1976: 247) attempts to explain this omission:

> The fact that this study—the largest study of the impact of residential therapeutic communities on criminality—had such positive findings, but was never published or released, is probably a comment on the politics of drug abuse treatment. Results from similar studies of residential drug-free treatment were not released. For a variety of reasons, the policy decision to increase methadone maintenance treatment opportunities had already been made. Research findings on the impact of methadone maintenance treatment were used and widely cited publicly as justification for the increase in funding.

Whatever the reason, therapeutic communities have certainly not suffered from overexposure in the professional literature. Two of the five studies focus solely on residential treatment (DeLeon et al., 1972; System Sciences Inc., 1973), while the remaining three consider other treatment modalities as well (Mandell et al., 1973; Cuskey et al., 1973; Nash, 1973).

The studies generally observe a strong positive relationship between residential treatment and reduced criminality. System Sciences Inc. (1973) reports a 59 percent decline in arrests after four to six months of treatment, and an 81 percent reduction after ten to twelve months in the program. Similarly, in his original sample of six programs, Nash (1973) observes a 53 percent reduction in arrest rates, with 101 arrests per 100 man years prior to treatment compared to 47 arrests per 100 man years after entering treatment. The remaining three studies also demonstrate a significant but less pronounced reduction in criminality. The smallest reduction is reported by Mandell et al. (1973), with a 24.4 percent pre- and posttreatment differential.

The studies evaluating residential treatment, while more consistent in reporting positive results than methadone studies, suffer from similar methodological limitations. As in the methadone studies, measures of criminality are primarily obtained from official records. While two of the studies rely on self-reports (Cuskey et al., 1973; Mandell et al., 1973), these are self-reports of arrests and do not reflect the actual extent of criminal behavior.

Also like the methadone studies, the residential studies vary in the time frame they employ to establish baseline arrest rates. One study, for example, uses as baseline data arrest rates within the two months prior to treatment (Mandell et al., 1973). System Sciences Inc. (1973), on the other hand, measures arrests from two years prior to treatment for comparison with posttreatment arrests. Cuskey et al. (1973) and Nash (1973) both base their pretreatment arrest rates on the number of arrests both prior to and following addiction. Finally, DeLeon et al. (1972) rely on the one-year period prior to entry into treatment for comparison with posttreatment arrests.

There is a similar variation in the posttreatment time period used. The Mandell et al. (1973) study records only self-reported arrests for the two-month period prior to interview; the System Sciences Inc. (1973) study of twelve treatment programs in New York City uses official arrest data for the two-year period after entering treatment; and the DeLeon et al. (1972) study of Phoenix House dropouts reports arrest histories of these individuals for one year after *leaving* the program.[10]

Importantly, the use of postadmission arrests as indicators of reduced crime is particularly suspect with regard to residential treatment programs. Therapeutic communities provide little opportunity for drug use or criminal behavior since they provide total, 24-hour care. Postadmission arrest rates are thus likely to be greatly deflated. Finally, the criticism that studies of methadone effectiveness fail to include comparison data of nontreatment users also applies to the studies focusing on residential treatment. None of the five studies reviewed here compares posttreatment arrest rates with the arrest rate of a purposively drawn street sample.

These criticisms are not to imply that the treatment process does not play an important role in the abatement of criminal behavior as part of an overall alteration in lifestyle. The DeLeon et al. (1972) study in particular, with its separate analysis of posttermination dropouts, provides strong preliminary evidence that the treatment effort is successful even after termination from the program. Similarly, Nash (1973) followed up his subjects for two years from admission, which for most subjects included a considerable period after their termination from the program. Again, the results are encouraging when compared to the methadone programs in the same study.

Even more important, however, is the *consistency* with which positive results are reported. All of the five studies reviewed report findings that consistently suggest residential communities are comparatively more effective than nonresidential programs in reducing criminality, at least in the longer view. While there are obvious limitations that call into question the actual degree of effectiveness, these limitations are also found in the methadone studies, whose findings fluctuate from extremely high pre- and postadmission differentials (see Gearing, 1974; Dole et al., 1968) to a *negative* impact (Hayim, 1973; Lukoff and Quatrone, 1973). In contrast, the percentage reduction in the therapeutic communities ranges from a low of 24.4 percent to a high of 81 percent. Even this range in reduction may be inflated by the methodological bias inherent in the Mandell et al. (1973) study, which reported the lower reduction.[11] It is argued that while no *single* study of therapeutic communities boasts as high a criminal reduction as do the Gearing and Dole et al. studies, the consistent, positive results place residential treatment in a favorable position as an effective treatment modality.

Admittedly, there is some variation in effectiveness reported among residential community centers. It would appear, however, that these variations are as much due to actual differences in the quality of individual treatment programs as they are to methodological differences in the studies. That is, we could *expect* to find more variation among residential communities than among methadone programs, since the treatment process in the residential community revolves around one-to-one and group counseling. Success in these programs is thus largely dependent on the skills of counselors, which are certain to vary from program to program. Methadone treatment, on the other hand, relies more heavily on the mitigating effect of the drug itself, which should result in more consistent levels of effectiveness across programs. It is suggested, therefore, that the variation found between studies of therapeutic communities is more reflective of the actual variation in treatment effectiveness, which, ostensibly at least, lends more credibility to the results obtained in these studies.

It is no longer enough, however, simply to assert that one form of treatment is better than another; indeed, this is not the purpose of the present discussion. We must begin to ask some important and theoretically relevant questions: What accounts for effective treatment? What factors external to the treatment process affect treatment outcome and why? More important for this discussion, what are the dynamics operative in the treatment process itself that may account for changed behavior? Except for occasional demographic controls introduced into the analyses of some of the studies, these and similar questions have been largely unexplored. Sociologists have yet to develop an adequate theoretical basis for their empirical findings.

The following section is suggestive of the sociological and social-psychological mechanisms operative in the therapeutic community as change agents in the spiral of heroin addiction and concomitant criminal behavior. By concentrating on the therapeutic community we do not mean to argue that this treatment modality is superior to any other. Accepting the limitations and shortcomings of the therapeutic community and of those studies evaluating it, we intend to interpret the program goals and processes in a sociologically relevant framework. It is hoped that this will provide a groundwork for future theoretical development.

WHY IS TREATMENT EFFECTIVE?

Addiction is a complex and dynamic phenomenon that has social, psychological, and legal implications in addition to manifest physical symptoms. Possibly no other treatment modality has recognized the *social* nature of heroin addiction as explicitly as has the therapeutic community. Indeed, a major thrust of treatment in most residential programs is oriented to the social dimensions of heroin addiction. Most broadly, residential treatment attempts to remove addicts from their environments, "resocialize" them, and prepare them for reentry into conventional society.

> The above [social influence] theoretical frame has been useful in providing an operational concept from which the therapeutic techniques are derived, tested and used. Based on this perspective, the clinical process assumes the following: In most cases, individual abusers should be initially removed from their immediate environments which may be contributory to continued abuse behavior, and best reside within a controlled therapeutic setting with the capability for dramatically reducing negative environmental influences. During this residential period, personality and interpersonal dynamics underlying abuse can be improved through a regimen of varied therapeutic activities, thereby lessening and eventually eliminating drug taking behaviors. Following this period as a means of testing the individual's growth derived from the residential experience, the individual in a scheduled, supportive and supervised manner, re-enters the outside community [Biase et al., 1980: 2–3].

It seems appropriate, therefore, that we seize upon the opportunity provided by the therapeutic community to propose a socially based theoretical framework for interpreting treatment dynamics and outcome.

The ultimate goal of treatment in a residential community is to foster a commitment on the part of the addict to a "conventional" lifestyle. Such a lifestyle potentially encompasses several dimensions: Legitimate employment, abstention from drug use, and refrainment from criminal behavior are probably the three most commonly recognized indicators of conventionality. Since the focus of the present discussion is the effectiveness of treatment in the reduction of criminality, we can, if we wish, operationally define the conventional lifestyle as abstaining from criminal behavior; it is important to recognize, however, that this indicator represents but a slice of a broad, dynamic transformation process.

Within the treatment context, the transformation process can best be conceptualized at two levels: First, we can speak of those "commitment" mechanisms employed by the treatment program in effecting the transformation; second, these mechanisms are transferred to the motivational structure of the individual through concomitant social-psychological processes. Let us then begin to lay a conceptual framework for residential treatment as a social process.

MECHANISMS OF COMMITMENT

The dynamics of commitment have received considerable attention in the sociology of religion (see Gerlach and Hine, 1968; Glock, 1962; Hine, 1970; Lofland and Stark, 1965; Payne and Elifson, 1976). These dynamics are not limited to religious phenomena, however (see Ginzberg et al., 1951), and appear to be operative in the transformation processes sought in residential treatment as well.

Possibly no one has so clearly conceptualized this process as has Kanter (1968, 1972) in an extended study of commitment processes operative in utopian communities. Kanter (1968: 504) distinguishes two broad processes at work in the "successful" communities, "one a dissociative process which would operate to free the personality system from other commitments, and one an associative process, operating to attach the personality to the current object of commitment." Elsewhere, Gerlach and Hine (1968) and Hine (1970) have employed the term *bridge-burning* to refer to essentially the same processes.

In her later work, Kanter (1972) distinguishes several specific mechanisms that serve to initiate and reinforce the processes of association and dissociation. While the therapeutic community cannot be directly compared with Kanter's utopian communities, some of the mechanisms Kanter finds operative in these communities apply to the therapeutic community as well.

Sacrifice

"The process of sacrifice asks members to give up something as a price of membership" (Kanter, 1972: 76). Addicts admitted to the therapeutic community are immediately made to realize that sacrifices will be expected of them in the program. Some programs even require an initial monetary sacrifice before an addict will be admitted. Even more important, because the therapeutic community is a total environment, the addict must initially relinquish the satisfaction of marital and family relationships. In addition, total celibacy is required until the addict earns the right to weekend "passes," during which time such behavior is not monitored. Because of these and similar sacrifices, many addicts who knock on the doors of residential communities opt not to take advantage of the services offered them. Those that do, find that these sacrifices constitute only part of the commitment process entailed in their treatment experience.

Renunciation

The addict is not only required to make initial sacrifices upon entry into treatment, but is encouraged and expected to renounce his or her past life-style and the interpersonal relationships associated with it. Drug use of any sort (legal or illegal) is prohibited except when medically necessary. Associations with known addicts are severely sanctioned. Indeed, even nostalgic reflection on the "good old days" and "how good it felt to be high" are strongly discouraged.

A number of techniques are employed by residential communities to encourage such renunciation of the street life. Added workloads may be assigned as a punitive measure; weekend passes are frequently denied. In the early years of residential treatment, the "haircut" was conferred upon a wayward resident by his peers. Yablonsky (1965: 241) emphasizes the role of the haircut.

> This form of verbal attack employs ridicule, hyperbole, and direct verbal onslaught. . . . An important goal of the "haircut" method is to change the criminal-tough guy pose. The self-image held by newcomers is viciously attacked and punctured in the "haircut."

Because of the abusive potential of the haircut, most programs have done away with this technique, at least in its more severe forms. This is not to say, however, that the erring resident is not chastised by his peers for inappropriate behavior or espousing wrong (street) values. One addict, for example, who is a participant in a current research project being conducted by the author, points to the differences between the therapeutic community and her experience in the Lexington hospital:

> [At Lexington] we used to sit around at night and just bullshit about all this stuff—for hours! It just seemed to never end 'cause it was so exciting. . . . It's called like 'war stories.' Everybody told them. That's the difference between there and 'East Coast House.' In the 'East Coast House' you couldn't even talk about, 'Hey, I used to do this.' If you did, you got instantly yelled at. You didn't do any of those kinds of things. They stripped you of all that.

In the past, techniques oriented to the renunciation of the addict/criminal lifestyle have been possibly the most central—and most visible— mechanisms employed by the therapeutic community. While such techniques still occupy an important part of residential treatment, increasing emphasis is being placed on preparing the resident for reentry into the wider society through mechanisms of "association."

Communion

Whereas sacrifice and renunciation serve to *dissociate* addicts from their past life styles, "communion" works toward attaching them to a conventional way of life. It is not enough simply to burn bridges with the past; new relationships must be provided to take the place of old acquaintances. This is what Kanter refers to as "communion." In the residential community, communion is sought at two levels: attachment to the group itself, and, eventually, attachment to the wider conventional society. Yablonsky (1965: 264) describes the way the program itself becomes an object of attachment for the addict:

> Synanon helps many people who formerly failed to get past the difficult early phase of abstinence by providing a community of understanding *ex-addicts*. The newcomer in Synanon has people with whom he can communicate and who understand him during this period of transition from drugs to a "clean" constructive life.

Attachment to the group is not an end in itself, however. Ultimately, the goal of treatment is successfully to place the addict in conventional society. "Reentry" processes are being increasingly emphasized in residential treatment. One of the more innovative programs, for example, is the "Miniversity" program recently begun as a demonstration project by Daytop Village (New York). In conjunction with the City University of New York, the Miniversity provides the residents of Daytop Village the opportunity to earn matriculated undergraduate credits toward the undergraduate degree, which will, in turn, more adequately prepare them for a role in conventional society. In addition to programs like this, the therapeutic community is structured in such a way that the addict is confined to the program on a 24-hour basis until he or she demonstrates a strong attachment to the program and its goals. He is then given the opportunity to venture out into the community during the day to seek employment, develop employable skills, and generally adjust to life outside the program. Gradually, addicts progress to an "aftercare" status, during which time they live in the community full-time and report to the program on a periodic basis. Only after an addict successfully moves through all of these phases does he or she "graduate" from the program. Through such a phasing structure, with the opportunities provided therein, the program facilitates the "communion" of the addict with conventional society.[12]

SOCIAL-PSYCHOLOGICAL CONCOMITANTS

An individual is not, of course, bounced like a billiard ball from a life-style of addiction and crime to one of conventionality. The mechanisms employed by the therapeutic community are designed to trigger a motivational response on the part of the addict. This transfer to the motivational structure is mediated through certain social-psychological processes. These processes often occur simultaneously, and are distinguished here only for conceptual purposes.

Investment

The mechanisms of sacrifice and renunciation constitute for the addict an investment in the goals of the program. The addict not only invests his or her time and possibly money, but makes "subjective" investments as well, including emotional energy, street status, and, more generally, the security of a way of life that has been cultivated over a period of years. Becker (1960) depicts these investments as "side-bets" and suggests that when an individual makes such side-bets, he or she is committed to a line of activity that will net a payoff. This notion has also been applied to occupational choice by Ginzberg et al. (1951: 194):

> Early decisions exercise a very real influence on later options. . . . As they [students] proceed, they increasingly commit themselves; they attempt to accomplish certain goals in the hope of preparing themselves for a certain type of life. . . . Because of his investment in educational preparation for work, an individual hesitates to disrupt his plan.

So it is with the addict who is required to make sacrifices and renounce old ways. The burning of bridges exacts a certain social and psychological cost on the reforming addict. The more it costs (that is, the greater the investment), the more is at stake in the addict's transformation.

Cognitive Dissonance

Though it is not necessarily the case, heavy investment is likely to result in a state of "cognitive dissonance" for the addict. Cognitive dissonance is a concept developed by Festinger (1957) to describe the cognitive state of an actor when there is a disparity between his actions and his belief system, attitudes, or, more generally, self-concept. In an attempt to reduce this dissonant state, Festinger suggests, the actor will usually alter his attitudes to bring them into conformity with his behavioral patterns. Kanter (1968: 505) affirms this notion when she writes:

> The more it "costs" a person to do something, the more "valuable" he will have to consider it in order to justify the "expense" and remain internally consistent.

The theory of cognitive dissonance would thus suggest that all of those bridge-burning acts (or "nonacts," such as the abstinence from drugs and crime) will bring pressure on the addict to shift his values in the direction of conventional normative standards. Not only does the addict thereby reduce the dissonance, but this transformation of values is a necessary prelude to the "payoff" he can expect in the form of acceptance by conventional society.

Restabilization

We are employing this term to refer to the development and integration of the altered self-concept. Kanter (1972: 103) uses the term *mortification* to refer to essentially the same process:

> Mortification processes provide a new identity for the person that is based on the power and meaningfulness of group membership; they reduce his sense of a separate, private, unconnected ego. Self-esteem comes to depend on commitment to the norms of the group and evaluation of its demands as just and morally necessary.

We have opted for the term *restabilization,* for it is descriptive of the emergent consistency between behavior (and other objective circumstances), attitudes, and self-concept. Crucial to this restabilization process is the continual reinforcement by the group of the emerging self-concept based on conventional values. It is here where the associative mechanisms of communion employed by the treatment program are of critical importance.

The hoped-for consequence of the processes described above is the resocialization of the individual from an addict/criminal to a law-abiding, nondrug user. While certainly the treatment process is far more intricate and complex than the above discussion has been able to capture, our purpose here has been to propose a conceptual framework for a socially based explanation of treatment effectiveness. It is hoped that this framework will facilitate future developments in this area.

SUGGESTIONS FOR RESEARCH

By way of summary, it seems clear that treatment efforts are not totally unfruitful in the reduction of criminality. Because of the profound shortcomings of the studies regarding both modalities, however, the data should not be considered definitive, and the *extent* of treatment effectiveness should not be overestimated.

The following suggestions for future research are oriented toward increasing our understanding and knowledge of treatment effectiveness, particularly as it is manifest in reduced criminal activity:

(1) Self-report data should be obtained by outside, independent investigators and used in conjunction with official data presently being employed. This should provide (a) a more accurate picture of the extent of criminality before and after treatment; (b) more accurate comparisons of effectiveness between various treatment modalities; and (c) greater insight into the *nature* of criminal activity actually being engaged in as compared to that which is most salient to the criminal justice system.

(2) Longer pre- and posttreatment time periods should be employed in the evaluation of treatment effectiveness. Preferably, (a) pretreatment criminality should be measured prior to addiction, since the onset of addiction, and one year prior to treatment, and (b) posttreatment criminality should be measured for a period of three or more years following *termination* of treatment.

(3) Comparison samples composed of individuals with similar demographic, drug use, and criminality characteristics should be drawn from both street and other treatment populations.

(4) The time has come for theoretical exploration into the effectiveness of drug treatment. It is hoped that the discussion presented here will stimulate further work in the area. Conceptual and theoretical elaboration is required; indicators need to be developed of such concepts as "sacrifice," "renunciation," "investment," and the like. In addition, outside factors, exogenous to the treatment process itself, should be delineated and taken into account. Finally, we would strongly urge the development of competing theoretical perspectives.

NOTES

1. It should be noted that the Harrison Act did not explicitly make the prescription of opiates illegal. It was a substance control act that prohibited the dispensing of opiates for all but medical

purposes. Lindesmith (1968) argues, for example, that maintenance prescriptions should be defined as a medical procedure.

2. The federal hospitals admitted both voluntary and court-ordered patients. Because the hospitals were originally opened to treat prisoner addicts, voluntary patients were admitted only after all prison referrals were made. Hence, over half the patients at any given census were prison referrals; however, because of the shorter treatment time for voluntary patients, the hospitals have treated substantially more walk-in patients over their nearly 40-year history. Interestingly, Glasscote et al. (1972) report that more than two-thirds of the voluntary patients have left prematurely, against medical advice. Without follow-up care, the effectiveness of these hospitals has been questionable. In 1973, the Lexington hospital was converted into a minimum-security prison, leaving the Fort Worth center as the only official federal treatment program.

3. The word *synanon* originated with one of the early residents of the program. Attempting to say two words in the same breath—symposium and seminar—he managed to come out with "synanon." From this point forward, the organization was known as "Synanon (capital S) and the group seminars referred to as synanons (small s). See Yablonsky (1965: vii–viii).

4. See Cole and Watterson (1976) for classification rationale.

5. Several addicts with whom I have talked have indicated that such samples are not effective, and have devised many ways of circumventing these tests. Hence, even urine samples rely on the forthrightness of the patient if they are to be effective.

6. This description of the treatment process was compiled primarily from interviews with residents and treatment personnel of one therapeutic community in an eastern city. This program is in the mainstream of contemporary therapeutic communities, however, and reflects the dominant trends in residential treatment.

7. It is interesting, however, that the Cuskey et al. study fails to demonstrate reduced criminality in the posttreatment period.

8. A number of other studies suffer from similar limitations. For example, the Schut et al. (1975) study lacks both pre- and postadmission controls. Dole et al. (1968) control only for posttreatment arrests, comparing those in treatment for one year with those in the program longer than one year. Similarly, Gearing (1974) compares time periods only after admission to treatment, with no distinction between immediate pretreatment arrests and all other postaddiction police encounters.

9. There was an additional TC program reported (Lynn and Nash, 1975). However, this was a prison-based program, and due to its unique character it is not discussed here as a therapeutic community.

10. This study also reports arrests for those still in treatment; however, it includes separate analyses for dropouts and active residents, providing important comparisons between pretreatment, and posttermination criminality.

11. See Nash (1976) for a methodological critique of this study.

12. In this respect, the contemporary therapeutic community diverges somewhat from Kanter's understanding of communion. Whereas Kanter's utopian community seeks to attain communion with the group *exclusive of the rest of society,* the ultimate goal of residential treatment is to form this bond *with the wider society,* but exclusive of the drug subculture. Kanter's model is, nevertheless applicable here. As indicated, to accomplish communion with the conventional society, the communal bond must first be established with the group itself in much the same manner as Kanter describes. Furthermore, even though communion is sought with the wider society (in contrast to Kanter), this is still accomplished in conjunction with the dissociative mechanisms operating to separate the addict from his or her past.

REFERENCES

AUSTIN, G. A. and D. J. LETTIERI (1977) Drug Users and the Criminal Justice System. Washington DC: Government Printing Office.

—— (1976) Drugs and Crime: The Relationship of Drug Use and Concomitant Criminal Behavior. Washington DC: Government Printing Office.

BEATTIE, R. H. (1960) "Criminal statistics in the United States—1960." Journal of Criminal Law, Criminology, and Police Science 51: 49–65.

BECKER, H. S. (1960) "Notes on the concept of commitment." American Journal of Sociology 66: 32–40.

BIASE, D. V., M. ISAAC, L. SYROW, and H. GUDITIS (1980) "Daytop Miniversity: advancement in drug free therapeutic community treatment: a summary of the progress of women participants." Presented at the Second Annual Women in Crisis Conference, Washington, D.C., June 6.

COLE, S. G. and O. WATTERSON (1976) "A treatment typology for drug abuse in the DARP: 1971–1972 Admissions," in S. B. Sells and D. D. Simpson (eds.) The Effectiveness of Drug Abuse Treatment, Volume 3: Further Studies of Drug Users, Treatment Typologies, and Assessment of Outcomes During Treatment in the DARP. Cambridge, MA: Ballinger.

DeLEON, G. and M. S. ROSENTHAL (1979) "Therapeutic communities," pp. 39–47 in R. L. DuPont et al. (eds.) Handbook on Drug Abuse. Washington, DC: Government Printing Office.

FESTINGER, L. (1957) A Theory of Cognitive Dissonance. Evanston, IL: Row, Peterson.

GERLACH, L. P. and V. H. HINE (1968) "Five factors crucial to the growth and spread of a modern religious movement." Journal for the Scientific Study of Religion 7: 23–40.

GINZBERG, E., S. W. GINSBURG, S. AXELRAD, and J. L. HERMA (1951) Occupational Choice: An Approach to a General Theory, New York: Columbia University Press.

GLASER, D. (1966) "Some notes on measurement of outcome in treating addiction," pp. 375–377 in Rehabilitating the Narcotic Addict. Fort Worth, TX: Institute on New Developments in the Rehabilitation.

GLASSCOTE, R., J. N. SUSSEX, J. H. JAFFE, J. BALL, and L. BRILL (1972) The Treatment of Drug Abuse: Programs, Problems, Prospects. Washington DC: American Psychiatric Association.

GLOCK, C. Y. (1962) "On the study of religious commitment." Religious Education (supplement to the July/August issue): 598–610.

HINE, V. H. (1970) "Bridge burners: commitment and participation in a religious movement." Sociological Analysis 31: 61–66.

INCIARDI, J. A. (1978) "The Uniform Crime Reports: some considerations on their shortcomings and utility." Public Data Use 6: 3–16.

JAFFE, J. H. (1979) "The swinging pendulum: the treatment of drug users in America," pp. 3–16 in R. L. Dupont et al. (eds.) Handbook on Drug Abuse. Rockville, MD: National Institute on Drug Abuse.

KANTER, R. M. (1972) Commitment and Community: Communes and Utopias in Sociological Perspective. Cambridge, MA: Harvard University Press.

—— (1968) "Commitment and social organization: a study of commitment mechanisms in utopian communities." American Sociological Review 33: 499–517.

KLEBER, H. D. and F. SLOBETZ (1979) "Out-patient drug free treatment," pp. 31–38 in R. L. Dupont et al., (eds.) Handbook on Drug Abuse. Rockville, MD: National Institute on Drug Abuse.

LINDESMITH, A. R. (1968) Addiction and Opiates. Chicago: AVC.

LOFLAND, J. and R. STARK (1965) "Becoming a world-saver: a theory of conversion to a deviant perspective." American Sociological Review 30: 862–875.

LOWINSON, J. H. and R. B. MILLMAN (1979) "Clinical aspects of methadone maintenance treatment," pp. 49–56 in R. L. Dupont et al., (eds.) Handbook on Drug Abuse. Rockville, MD: National Institute on Drug Abuse.

McGLOTHLIN, W. G., M. D. ANGLIN, and B. D. WILSON (1977) An Evaluation of the California Civil Addict, DHEW (ADM) 78–558. Washington, DC: Government Printing Office.

NASH, G. (1976) "An analysis of twelve studies of the impact of drug abuse treatment upon criminality," pp. 231–271 in Drug Use and Crime: Report of the Panel on Drug Use and Criminal Behavior. Springfield, VA: National Technical Information Service.

PAYNE, B. P. and K. W. ELIFSON (1976) "Commitment: a comment on the use of the concept." Review of Religious Research 17: 209–215.

TERRY, C. E. and M. PELLENS (1970) The Opium Problem. Montclair, NJ: Patterson-Smith. (Originally published in 1928 by the Bureau of Social Hygiene, Inc., New York.)

WHEELER, S. (1967) "Criminal statistics: a reformation of the problem." Journal of Criminal Law, Criminology, and Police Science 58: 317–324.

YABLONSKY, L. (1965) Synanon: The Tunnel Back. New York: Penguin.

BIBLIOGRAPHY OF EMPIRICAL STUDIES

Key to indicators:

*Studies that focus on methadone maintenance as their sole treatment modality.
**Studies that focus on "multimodal" programs that involve a primary reliance on methadone maintenance.
†Studies that focus on therapeutic communities as their sole treatment modality.
††Studies including both methadone maintenance and therapeutic communities.
Studies without indicators focus on programs that include neither methadone maintenance nor therapeutic communities, or for which these modalities play only a minor role.

ADAMS, S. and V. McARTHUR (1969) "Performance of narcotic involved prison releasees under three kinds of community experience." Research Report 16, Department of Corrections, Washington D.C.

*ALEXANDER, M. and C. McCASLIN (1974) "Criminality in heroin addicts before, during, and after methadone treatment." American Journal of Public Health 64 (December supplement): 51–56.

BERECOCHEA, J. E. and G. E. SING (1972) "The effectiveness of a halfway house for civilly committed narcotics addicts." International Journal of the Addictions 7: 123–132.

*BLOOM, W. A. and W. C. CAPEL (1973) "An exploratory study of the relation of heroin addiction to crime in New Orleans," pp. 123–132 in Proceedings of the Fifth National Conference on Methadone Treatment, Volume 1. New York: National Association for the Prevention of Addiction to Narcotics.

*BOWDEN, C. L. (1976) "Arrests before and during methadone maintenance." Presented at the Third National Drug Abuse Conference.

BRILL, L. and L. LIEBERMAN (1969) Authority and Addiction. Boston: Little, Brown.

BROTMAN, R. and A. FREEDMAN (1968) A Community Mental Health Approach to Drug Addiction. Washington, DC: Government Printing Office.

California Bureau of Criminal Statistics (1976) Drug Diversion 1000 P.C. in California, 1974. Sacramento: Bureau of Criminal Statistics.

——— (n.d.) Follow-up Study of Persons First Released from California Rehabilitation Center During 1963–1966. Sacramento: Bureau of Criminal Statistics.

*CUSHMAN, P. (1974) "Narcotic addiction and crime." Rhode Island Journal of Medicine 57: 197–204.

††CUSKEY, W.R., J. IPSEN, and T. PREMDUMAR (1973) "An inquiry into the nature of changes in behavior among drug users in treatment," pp. 198–357 in National Commission on Marijuana and Drug Abuse, Drug Abuse in America: Problems in Perspective. Washington DC: Government Printing Office.

†DELEON, G., S. HOLLAND, and M.S. ROSENTHAL (1972) "Phoenix House: criminal activity of dropouts." Journal of the American Medical Association 222: 686–689.

*DOLE, V.P., M.E. NYSWANDER, and A. WARNER (1968) "Successful treatment of 750 criminal addicts." Journal of the American Medical Association 206: 2708–2711.

*DOLE, V.P., J.W. ROBINSON, J. ORRACA, E. TOWNS, P. SEARCY, and E. CAINE (1969) "Methadone treatment of randomly selected criminal addicts." New England Journal of Medicine 280: 1372–1375.

**DUPONT, R.L. (1972) "Heroin addiction treatment and crime reduction." American Journal of Psychiatry 128: 856–860.

** ——— and M.H. GREENE (1973) "The dynamics of a heroin addiction epidemic." Science 181: 716–722.

DUVALL, H.J., B.Z. LOCKE, and L. BRILL (1963) "Follow-up study of narcotic drug addicts five years after hospitalization." Public Health Reports 783: 185–193.

*EDWARDS, E.D. and N.S. GOLDNER (1975) "Criminality and addiction: decline of client criminality in a methadone treatment program," in E. Senay et al. (eds.) Developments in the Field of Drug Abuse. Cambridge, MA: Schenkman.

FISHER, S. (1965) "The rehabilitative effectiveness of a community correctional residence for narcotic users." Journal of Criminal Law, Criminology, and Police Science 56: 190–196.

*GEARING, F.R. (1974) "Methadone maintenance treatment five years later—where are they now?" American Journal of Public Health 64 (December supplement): 44–50.

* ——— (1972) "A road back from heroin addiction," pp. 157–158 in Proceedings of the Fourth National Conference on Methadone Treatment. New York: National Association for Prevention of Addiction to Narcotics.

*HAYIM, G.J. (1973) "Changes in the criminal behavior of heroin addicts under treatment in the Addiction Research and Treatment Corporation: interim report of the first year of treatment," pp. 1–62 in G.J. Hayim et al. (eds.) Heroin Use in a Methadone Maintenance Program. Washington DC: U.S. Department of Justice, National Institute of Law Enforcement and Criminal Justice.

*JOSEPH, H.A. and V.P. DOLE (1970) "Methadone patients on probation and parole." Federal Probation 34: 42–48.

KAPLAN, H.B. and J. MEYEROWITZ (1969) "Evaluation of a half-way house: integrated community approach in the rehabilitation of narcotic addicts." International Journal of the Addictions 4: 65–76.

KRAMER, J.C., R.A. BASS, and J.E. BERECOCHEA (1968) "Civil commitment for addicts: the California program." American Journal of Psychiatry 125: 816–824.

**LANGENAUER, B. and C. BOWDEN (1971) "A follow-up study of narcotic addicts in the NARA program." American Journal of Psychiatry 128: 41–46.

*LUKOFF, I. and D. QUATRONE (1973) "Heroin use and crime in a methadone maintenance program: a two year follow-up of the Addiction and Research Corporation Program: a preliminary report," pp. 63–112 in G. J. Hayim et al. (eds.) Heroin Use in a Methadone Maintenance Program. Washington DC: U.S. Department of Justice, National Institute of Law Enforcement and Criminal Justice.

LYNN, R. and G. NASH (1975) "A study of seven prison based drug abuse programs." Drug Abuse Treatment Information Project, Montclair State College, Montclair, N.J.

*MADDUX, J. F. and L. K. McDONALD (1973) "Status of 100 San Antonio addicts one year after admission to methadone maintenance." Drug Forum 2: 239–252.

††MANDELL, W., P. G. GOLDSCHMIDT, and P. GROVER (1973) Inter-Drug—An Evaluation of Treatment Programs for Drug Abuse, Volumes 2 and 4. Baltimore: The Johns Hopkins University School of Hygiene and Public Health.

Massachusetts Department of Corrections (1971) "An evaluation of the special narcotics addiction program at the Massachusetts Correctional Institution, Walpole." Massachusetts Department of Corrections.

McGLOTHLIN, W. (1976) "California civil commitment: a decade later." Journal of Drug Issues 6: 368–379.

MILLER, D. E., A. N. HIMELSON, and G. GEIS (1967) "Community's response to substance misuse: the East Los Angeles Halfway House for Felon Addicts." International Journal of the Addictions 2: 305–311.

††NASH, G. (1973) "The impact of drug abuse treatment upon criminality: a look at 19 programs." Montclair State College, Upper Montclair, N.J.

*NEWMAN, R. G. and S. BASHKOW (1973) "Arrest histories before and after admission to an ambulatory detoxification program," pp. 101–108 in Proceedings of the Fifth National Conference on Methadone Treatment, Volume 1. New York: National Association for the Prevention of Addiction to Narcotics.

*_____ , and M. GATES (1973) "Arrest histories before and after admission to a methadone maintenance treatment program." Contemporary Drug Problems 2: 417–424.

*PATCH, V. D., A. E. RAYNES, and A. FISCH (1973) "Methadone maintenance and crime reduction in Boston—variables compounded." Presented at the annual meeting of the American Psychiatric Association.

*PATCH, V. D., A. FISCH, M. E. LEVINE, G. J. McKENNA and A. E. RAYNES (1973a) "Heroin addicts and violent crime," pp. 386–390 in Proceedings of the Fifth National Conference on Methadone Treatment, Volume 1. New York: National Association for the Prevention of Addiction to Narcotics.

*_____ (1973b) "Urban versus suburban addict crime," pp. 393–396 in Proceedings of the Fifth National Conference on Methadone Treatment, Volume 1. New York: National Association for the Prevention of Addiction to Narcotics.

*SCHUT, J., R. A. STEER, and F. I. GONZALEZ (1975) "Types of arrest for methadone maintenance patients before, during, and after treatment." British Journal of the Addictions 70: 80–93.

*SECHREST, D. K. and T. E. DUNCKLEY (1975) "Criminal activity, wages earned, and drug use after two years of methadone treatment." Addictive Diseases 1: 491–512.

SING, G. E. (1969) California Civil Addict Program: Research Report 37. Sacramento: California Department of Corrections.

**SOBOL, N. L., W. F. WEILAND, R. JACOBSEN, T. M. WOCHOK, R. C. WOLFE, and L. D. SAVITZ (1973) "The Philadelphia TASC program (Treatment Alternatives to Street Crime)," pp. 928–942 in Proceedings of the Fifth National Conference on Methadone Treatment, Volume 2. New York: National Association for the Prevention of Addiction to Narcotics.

*SOLOWAY, I. H. (1974) "Methadone and the culture of addiction." Journal of Psychadelic Drugs 6: 91–99.

†System Sciences Inc. (1973) "A comparative analysis of 24 therapeutic communities in New York City funded by the Addiction Service Agency of the City of New York." Bethesda, Md: System Sciences Inc. (mimeograph)

**VAILLANT, G. E. (1965) "A twelve-year follow-up of New York narcotic addicts: I. The relation of treatment to outcome." American Journal of Psychiatry 122: 727–737.

**_____ (1973) "A 20 year follow-up of New York narcotic addicts." Archives of General Psychiatry 29: 237–241.

*WEILAND, W. F. and J. L. NOVACK (1973) "A comparison of criminal justice and non-criminal justice related patients in a methadone treatment program," pp. 116–122 in Proceedings of the Fifth National Conference on Methadone Treatment, Volume 1. New York: National Association for the Prevention of Addiction to Narcotics.

9

SAMPLE BIAS IN DRUGS/CRIME RESEARCH
An Empirical Study

ANNE E. POTTIEGER

Sample bias is a major potential problem in research on any kind of deviant behavior. This is due to both the statistical and the sociocultural nature of deviance. Statistically, deviance is commonly nonnormative behavior in a frequency-distribution as well as a cultural sense; the more empirically rare a particular type of deviant behavior is within a total population, the more impractical random sampling of the entire population becomes as an approach to obtaining a random sample of persons engaged in that type of deviance. Socioculturally, on the other hand, deviance is a behavior pattern that tends to provoke efforts to control or eradicate it, so that individuals engaged in deviant behavior commonly do so in secret. The more dire are the consequences for them of being identified as deviant by the appropriate social control agents, the more difficult it becomes for a researcher to identify the universe of deviant persons with sufficient accuracy to permit drawing a random sample from only that universe of deviants. In the particular case of research on the drugs/crime nexus, both these problems are extreme. The rarity of persons engaged in both crime and drug use within the total U.S. population makes a national sample impractical, and yet the severe consequences of being identified as either criminally involved or illicit-drug-involved prohibit description of only that part of the total population which is drugs/crime-involved.

The most overwhelmingly common response to this dual problem for drugs/crime studies has been to confine research samples to those criminally-involved drug users who have already come to the attention of criminal justice or treatment agencies. Sample bias of this type, in fact, is so pervasive in drugs/crime research that it is generally treated as not only inevitable but too commonplace to merit discussion. Not much commentary is needed in reporting on a sample restricted to incarcerated addicts, for example, when the bulk of the extant literature consists of reports on similarly captive samples. And, after all, what can the researcher say? Both the reasons for this kind of sample restriction and its undesirability are widely recognized among drugs/crime researchers; more general crime/criminal justice research suggests that reliance on officially recognized samples introduces systematic biases into crime-related research; but the nature of such biases—particularly in regard to the crime/*drugs* relationship—is essentially unknown.

The problem of bias in captive drugs/crime research samples is discussed in this chapter in three steps. First, the possibility that captive samples are not, in fact, biased is considered and rejected. Second, given the apparent necessity of the assumption that captive drugs/crime samples are biased, the possibility of using the extant research literature to determine the nature of such biases is evaluated, with the conclusion that such an approach would not work. Finally, the bulk of this chapter is devoted to a direct empirical comparison of drugs/crime data from captive and on-the-street samples, using interview data from a 1977–1978 study done in two cities. While the noncaptive samples from this study are *not* random samples, it will be argued that they are sufficiently close to random samples that comparing them to institutionalized samples—especially given controls for city, type of institutionalization, gender, age, and ethnicity—is of value in determining the nature of captive sample biases in research on drug use and crime.

THE ARGUMENT THAT CAPTIVE
SAMPLES ARE UNBIASED

The traditional justification given for limiting drugs/crime research samples to officially recognized offenders is that such persons are, after all, a subsample of drugs/crime-involved people; that they are accessible to the researcher; and that data from a subsample are obviously preferable to no data. In and of itself, this justification is adequate as long as no attempt is made to generalize the research findings to noncaptive populations.

But this traditional reasoning has occasionally been extended to the argument that captive samples are representative of all crime/drugs-involved persons. The extention has been made by means of a two-part, semiempirical argument, that (1) it is the compulsive user of an addicting and illegal drug who is of greatest concern in the drugs/crime nexus, and (2) such a person will necessarily come to official attention within a relatively short period of time—Winick (1962), for instance, suggests two years. Although limited specifically to the *heroin*/crime connection, this is an interesting argument, since it asserts that a major factor prohibiting random sampling of heroin users—namely, the strenuous efforts of social control agencies against them—is precisely what makes random sampling unneccessary for research on them.

The empirical evidence tends to indicate that, on the whole, the argument is just too simple. For example, heroin addicts are asserted to be the main drugs/crime problem, because heroin is expensive and yet addiction compels users to obtain it; crime is one of the few options for obtaining large amounts of money readily, and yet the addiction-compelled need to commit crime on a regular basis will increase the likelihood of apprehension. This is fine as far as it goes, but it neglects the complications introduced by the availability of alternative drugs, particularly methadone, which can satisfy the need for heroin without requiring a heroin-sized financial outlay (for a review of pertinent research, see Gandossy et al., 1980: 93–108). Similarly, one can readily document the great amounts of law enforcement time and money dedicated to narcotics offenses and street crime. But it is even easier to show that great numbers of property crimes are never reported, that many reported crimes never result in arrest, and that a vast number of addict offenses are victimless crimes such as drug sales and prostitution. Hence, self-report studies of addict crime show incredibly small arrest risks for most categories of offenses (see Chambers, 1974; Inciardi, 1979). Finally, it should also be noted that both nonaddicting substances (such as the amphetamines) and legally manufactured addictive substances (such as the barbiturates)—as well as alcohol, which is moderately addictive but completely legal and quite inexpensive—have been linked to the commission of both violent crimes and property offenses (see Eckerman et al., 1976; Gandossy et al., 1980).

Further, even if one were interested in only heroin users, and even if one could assume that the great majority of heroin users come to official attention within two years, the conclusion that a captive sample of heroin users is representative of all heroin users is still problematic. Police discretion, court overloads, availability of treatment slots, local political climate, legally irrelevant as well as relevant characteristics of the offender, and a host of other circumstances result in nonuniform—that is, biased—handling of offenders once they have come to official attention, even within legal jurisdictions, let alone for purposes of comparison between them. In addition, official records on offenders handled by either criminal justice or treatment agencies are commonly incomplete, inaccurate, and inconsistent between jurisdictions (Gandossy et al., 1980: 10–13, 15–16), adding further sources of potential bias to data gathered on captive drugs/crime samples.

In short, the argument that captive samples are unbiased data sources for research on (all) drugs/crime-involved persons is one that must be rejected. Both the complexity of the relationship between crime and drug use and the nonuniformity of official handling of drugs/crime offenders mean that criminally involved drug users are not all equally likely to end up in a captive sample—that is, that captive drugs/crime samples are biased drugs/crime samples.

USING EXTANT RESEARCH TO DEFINE CAPTIVE SAMPLE BIASES

But specifically what does it mean to say that captive drugs/crime offenders are not representative of all drugs/crime offenders? Surely *some* captive offenders are highly similar to *some* noncaptive offenders. Perhaps captive offenders are representative of a substantial proportion of noncaptive offenders. Might there be some way, then, of methodologically compensating for the biases in captive samples so that research on them—or at least some of them—can be interpreted more broadly?

The answers to such questions require definition of the nature of captive sample biases: a statement of what factors in captive samples are how strongly different in what direction from those factors as found in noncaptive samples. For such a purpose, the kind of indirect evidence discussed thus far would be problematic, because of the large number of interrelated variables involved. Some kind of direct empirical comparison of captive and noncaptive samples would be much simpler analytically and hence less subject to logical errors.

On the face of it, a captive-noncaptive comparison seems possible just from the extant research literature. There have been, after all, an increasing number of drugs/crime studies done with addicts on the street; there are many studies using arrested, incarcerated, or treatment samples. Why not simply review this literature and compare the findings from the two different kinds of samples?

The simplest aspect of the answer is that such a comparison is prohibited by the problem of measurement comparability. Not only instrumentation but even the kind of information gathered in particular drugs/crime studies varies widely (see Elinson and Nurco, 1975; Rittenhouse, 1978). This variation is compounded by the circumstance that many on-the-street studies are specifically ethnographies emphasizing qualitative description of group structure and dynamics, while most captive-sample studies employ a methodology having much heavier emphasis on quantified individual-level variables. Relatedly, many captive-sample studies rely on arrest data, while on-the-street studies generally obtain self-reported crime data. In short, although measurement comparability is a general problem of major import in evaluating the drugs/crime literature for *any* purpose, it is particularly acute in the case of captive-noncaptive comparison.

A more complex difficulty in using the extant literature this way is the issue of controls for multiple sample dimensions. Officially recognized and on-the-street samples are highly likely to differ on more sampling dimensions than simply that of apprehension versus nonapprehension. The most obvious examples are time period, geographic particulars, and subcultural context. To take an extreme instance, if one found major differences between results of a 1964 street survey of black addicts in New York City and a 1980 jail study of Cuban addicts in Miami, would it be due to the sixteen-year difference? ethnic/subcultural differences? city police department differences? the happenstance of a major Cuban immigration into Miami just prior to the study? differential treatment/criminal justice relationships in the two cities? or the captive-versus-street samples? The only way to tell if it really is the last of these that accounts for the differences is to control for at least the obvious other sampling factors. But such controls are problematic in at least two ways. First, on-the-street studies tend to focus on relatively homogeneous, and hence limited, subpopulations for which there are likely to be no comparable officially recognized samples. Second, studies of specifically drugs-*crime* as opposed to drugs-*arrest* relationships tend to have such small samples that breaking them down into subsamples would yield too few cases for analysis.

It should be specifically noted here that, again, part of the problem under discussion is due to the complexity of the drugs-crime relationship and the relatively primitive state of our understanding of it. We are fairly certain that a large number of factors are implicated in the relationship as intervening or confounding variables—age, ethnicity, gender; historical and community circumstances; criminal justice and treatment agency activities and structures; crime opportunities and drug availabilities—but these factors also appear to interact and hence operate differently in different combinations. It is these combinational impacts that are currently only poorly understood.

This last comment introduces another level of complication to the discussion. Suppose that in the same community, at the same time, using the same instrument, one found a street sample in which the male-female addict distribution was 60–40, and a jail sample in which it was 90–10? Obviously, the jail sample is not representative in regard to gender, but what about analysis of other differences? If other variables are strongly related to gender, then jail-street differences in them may not be jail-street so much as male-female differences. A similar argument could of course be advanced in terms of ethnicity or age group. Obviously, then, simultaneous controls for all these kinds of subsample characteristics would readily reduce most drugs/crime study samples into such tiny subcategories that analysis would be highly suspect, not to mention very complex. Further, it would in almost all instances be so complex as to be impossible as a strategy for analyzing the existing literature, in that only rarely are published results reported in this fashion.

In summary, both measurement comparability problems and the need for multiple controls present severe difficulties for any attempt to define the specific biases of captive drugs/crime samples by means of a literature review. When these difficulties are considered together, the task appears likely to require an extreme effort for a probably suspect analytic result.

A MULTIPLE SUBSAMPLE STUDY

The ideal approach to defining captive sample biases, of course, would be several very large multiple subsample studies that would gather data on the same drugs and crime topics, using the same instrument, for randomly drawn samples of both captive and active offenders. But if it were possible to draw random noncaptive samples, the need to define the biases of captive samples would not be nearly so acute. The study discussed in the rest of this chapter is therefore less than ideal, but since it is also considerably more feasible than the ideal it has actually been carried out.

From July 1977 through October 1978, as part of a larger study funded by the National Institute on Drug Abuse, interviews were conducted with 942 heroin users in Miami, Florida, and San Antonio, Texas.[1] The highly structured, pretested interview schedule focused specifically on drug use and criminal behavior, and it generally required less than an hour to administer. The majority of the respondents were active heroin users interviewed "on the street," while the remainder were users from the same communities who were interviewed in jails and treatment centers.

The active offenders were located by means of a multiple-starting-point "snowball" method. The principal investigator had extensive contacts within the local drug subcultures in both cities, and these contacts were used as starting points for the interviews. During or after each interview, at the point when rapport seemed highest, the interviewer asked to be directed to other current users. These persons were in turn located and interviewed, and the process was repeated until the social network surrounding each respondent was exhausted. Confidentiality was guaranteed to the respondents, names or other identifying information were not recorded, and respondents were paid a fee for participating. While the resulting samples of active users were thus *not* random samples, the use of numerous starting points in each locale eliminated much potential bias. In addition, the method had the further advantage of restricting the sample to persons currently active in the street subculture and sufficiently involved in it to be known to other participants—eliminating, that is, former users and persons only peripherally involved.

The same interview schedule was used with captive respondents, except that the questions about current criminal activities and drug use were asked for the time periods prior to institutionalization rather than prior to the interview. Because of the small numbers involved, all heroin users in the drug treatment centers or county jails at the time interviewing took place were included in the samples, so that any particular subsample size was a function of interviewing time spent at that location. Finally, it should be noted that the primary focus of the study as a whole was unapprehended

TABLE 9.1 Age and Ethnicity of All Heroin Users Interviewed, by City, Gender, and Interview Location (percentages)

| | Miami | | | | | | San Antonio | | | |
| | Males | | | Females | | | Males | | Females | |
(n)	Strt (323)	Jail (23)	Trtm (41)	Strt (153)	Jail (17)	Trtm (16)	Strt (198)	Jail (120)	Strt (22)	Jail (29)
15–17	0.6	0.0	0.0	2.6	0.0	0.0	9.1	0.8	9.1	0.0
18–24	20.1	65.2	39.0	35.3	64.7	37.5	55.6	45.0	68.2	62.1
25–34	64.7	34.8	61.0	52.9	35.3	56.3	28.8	39.2	18.2	31.0
35–49	13.6	0.0	0.0	8.5	0.0	0.0	4.5	14.2	4.5	6.9
50+	0.9	0.0	0.0	0.7	0.0	0.0	2.0	0.8	0.0	0.0
White	55.4	30.4	39.0	54.2	17.6	50.0	6.6	11.7	27.3	27.6
Black	31.9	65.2	58.5	27.5	82.4	43.8	5.1	20.0	31.8	27.6
Mx-Am	0.0	0.0	0.0	1.3	0.0	0.0	86.9	67.5	36.4	37.9
Cuban	6.5	4.3	2.4	10.5	0.0	0.0	0.0	0.0	0.0	0.0
P.Ric	4.3	0.0	0.0	3.9	0.0	0.0	0.5	0.8	0.0	0.0
Oth.H	1.6	0.0	0.0	0.6	0.0	0.0	0.0	0.0	0.0	3.4
Other	0.3	0.0	0.0	2.0	0.0	0.0	1.0	0.0	4.5	3.4

NOTE: Columns may not add to 100.0% due to rounding. Abbreviations for ethnicity are: Mx-Am, Mexican-American; P. Ric, Puerto Rican; Oth.H, other Hispanic; Other, all other ethnic identifications and missing data.

crime among active heroin users. For this reason, the jail and treatment samples were considerably smaller than the samples of active users in the free community.

Among the total 942 heroin users interviewed, definite variations were found between active and captive samples in terms of ethnicity and age. The nonrandom sampling method used (which included extra effort to include women in the jail and treatment samples) forbids attaching a great deal of substantive significance to these differences, but they are reported in Table 9.1 by city and gender.

SUBSAMPLES FOR ANALYSIS

For present purposes, the primary significance of the figures in Table 9.1 is their indication that small subsample sizes would make it difficult to employ simultaneous controls for multiple sampling dimensions, as discussed in the preceding section, and still use the entire 942 interviews. Even with this rather large sample size, subcategories in some instances would be too small for analysis once the sample were broken down simultaneously by city, gender, type of interview location, ethnicity, and age group. The control method employed was therefore the one resulting in the largest possible number of cases for analysis. Three pair of active-versus-captive comparison groups were selected, all of them male and all between the ages of 22 and 32: San Antonio Mexican-Americans on the street versus in jail, Miami blacks on the street versus in treatment, and Miami whites on the street versus in treatment. Only the male samples were large enough to withstand breakdown into ethnicity-age groups, and the age range of 22 to 32 was chosen to maximize subsample size in the Miami captive samples, while keeping the range small enough to be meaningful.

The 22–32 age range included 85 percent of the 40 black or white men in the Miami treatment samples. It also included 72 percent of the black or white active male heroin users interviewed in Miami—a substantial percentage. However, as Table 9.1 indicates, many of the active San Antonio respondents were considerably younger than those in Miami. The most dramatic breakpoint is one not reported on the table: 32 percent of both the active males and the active females were in the 15–19 age category, compared to 3 percent of the active males and 7 percent of the active females in Miami. Thus, markedly fewer of the San Antonio respondents were included in the present analysis—about 44 percent and 46 percent of the active and incarcerated Mexican-American men. However, the resulting San Antonio comparison-pair subsample sizes were more than adequate (better, in fact, than those in Miami), and it seemed desirable to use the same age range in both cities.

ANALYTIC METHOD

Given this choice of active-captive comparison groups, the remaining analysis planning task was to select a method for examining differences between them. Twenty variables were chosen for this purpose, in order to have at least a minimum number of specifics with which to define differences between the active and captive samples.

Seven of the selected variables pertain to the respondents' drug use histories and criminal histories. Four of these are simple age variables: age at first alcohol high, age at first drug use (with "drug" in this and all subsequent uses meaning "drug other than alcohol"), age at first heroin use on a continuous basis (i.e., at least several times a week over a period of at least several months), and age at first crime. A fifth age variable is the age at which the respondent had first engaged in *both* drug use and crime (hence, the later of the two ages if they were not identical). A historical sequence variable was also used: age-at-first-crime minus age-at-first-drug-use, limited to a range of -5 (crime five or more years before drug use) through $+5$ (drug use five or more years before crime). These last two variables, then, both deal with the historical nexus between drug use and crime. The seventh historical variable employed is the number of drug types the respondent had ever tried, out of a list of twenty types.[2]

The other thirteen variables indicate current drug use and crime. Six are measures of current use frequency, on a seven-point scale,[3] of selected drug-type combinations: heroin/illegal methadone, alcohol, other depressants/analgesics, cocaine, other stimulants, and hallucinogens/solvent-inhalants. An additional drug use variable is the number of drug types the respondent was currently using, out of the previously mentioned list of twenty types. Five other variables pertain to criminal offenses during the last twelve months: number of robberies, assaults of any type (including murder and rape), theft-related offenses of any type, drug sales, and weapon uses during the commission of an offense. Both the drug use frequencies and the offense counts are combination variables, employed as a compromise between the complexity of the original 20 drug types and 24 offense types, on the one hand, and, on the other, the oversimplification that would be entailed in using only one or two indicators for each. Finally, the other current drugs/crime variable came directly from a question asking respondents to estimate what percentage of their criminal activity was for the support of their drug use.

With these 20 variables to be compared across three active-captive sub-sample pairs, a decision had to be made about statistics. Strictly speaking, statistical analysis is of course not appropriate for this kind of data because the samples were not randomly drawn. But statistics were computed anyway, with two justifications: (1) the sampling procedure employed can be defended as one likely to have results very similar to those of a random sampling plan, which in any case does not seem feasible for use with active heroin users; and (2) the subsample sizes involved are small enough that statistical guidance regarding probabilities of significance seems highly desirable.

The particular statistics chosen were used because they are for ordinal-scale, nonparametric data. Most of the variables are highly skewed in distribution, and a few are bimodal as well. Such data require nonparametric statistics (i.e., statistics that do not assume normal, or bell-curve, distributions). The skew in the distributions also means, however, that even those variables with an interval-level scale (e.g., number of robberies) are much more adequately described in terms of medians and other relational position (i.e., ordinal) measures than in terms of means and other interval-level measures. Therefore, all variables were treated as ordinal-scale data.

Two statistics were used. For the primary analysis, the Kolmogorov-Smirnov two-sample test was used to look for differences between each pair of active and captive subsamples on each of the variables. This test is a conceptually simple one which is sensitive to *any* kind of difference in the frequency distributions of two samples. It is based on the rationale that if two samples are drawn from the same population, then the cumulative frequency distributions of those samples should be similar because each would show only random deviations from the population distribution. The probability that two samples are from the same population depends on the size of the maximum difference between the cumulative frequencies, considering the size of the samples; the smaller the samples, the larger the difference must be to reject the null hypothesis at a given level of significance. For this analysis, two-tailed probabilities were computed in order to test for differences in either direction (for example, captive respondents committing either more or fewer robberies than active respondents).[4]

Finally, for secondary information, Spearman correlation coefficients were computed for each of the six subsamples taken separately. The main purpose of these correlations was to look for differences between active and captive subsamples in the way drug and crime variables were related to each other.[5]

RESULTS OF AN OVERALL TEST
FOR DIFFERENCES

Table 9.2 is a peculiar kind of summary of the overall results of the Kolmogorov-Smirnov tests for differences between active and captive subsamples. This highly condensed summary gives probability figures for 60 tests—the 20 variables compared in three active-versus-captive subsample pairings. These probabilities, it should be recalled, represent the chances in each of 60 tests that the active and captive subsamples in each pair were drawn from the same population. Ordinarily, the use made of such figures is

TABLE 9.2 Kolmogorov-Smirnov 2-Tailed Probabilities That Active (A) and Captive (T=treatment; J=jail) Samples Are from the Same Population: Three Selected Comparisons of Male Heroin Users Age 22–32*

| | Miami | | | | San Antonio | |
| | White A/T | | Black A/T | | Mx-Am A/J | |
(Total n's)**	(133A, 14T)		(71A, 21T)		(76A, 37T)	
Age at first alcohol high	.213	d	.001	DDD	.351	
Age at first drug use	.674		.183	d	.232	d
Age at first continuous heroin use	.037	DD	.944	S	.916	S
Number of types ever used	.518		.006	DDD	.088	D
Age at first crime	.851	S	.999	SSS	.003	DDD
Age first doing both	.399		.778	s	.246	d
Age-1st-C minus Age-1st-D	.161	d	.018	DD	.001	DDD
Heroin/illegal methadone	.252	d	.999	SSS	.933	S
Cocaine	.045	DD	.006	DDD	.999	SSS
Other stimulants	.999	SSS	.465		.001	DDD
Alcohol	.142	D	.835	S	.189	d
Other depressants/analgesics	.001	DDD	.726		.001	DDD
Hallucinogens/solvent-inhalants	.999	SSS	.999	SSS	.022	DD
Number of types using now	.048	DD	.930	S	.002	DDD
Robberies	.933	S	.873	S	.230	d
Assaults	.245	d	.858	S	.999	SSS
Theft-related offenses	.777	s	.030	DD	.077	DD
Drug sales	.888	S	.082	D	.137	D
Weapon uses with crime	.417		.897	S	.006	DDD
% of crime to support drug use	.016	DD	.156	d	.001	DDD

*See text for explanation of "S" and "D" notations.
**Ns for particular tests may be lower due to missing data. Where this occurs, a larger difference must exist for the same probability level to be attained.

simply to see whether the probabilities are low enough (for example, .05 or less) to reject the null hypothesis of no differences. But it is also possible to name a level for *accepting* the null hypothesis (for example, the parallel figure to the previous example would be .95 or more).

The letters in Table 9.2 beside each probability figure represent this type of interpretation, made for the sake of an overall comparison of the active and captive subsamples. "Significant" *differences* are noted as differences at the .01 (DDD), .05 (DD), .15 (D), and .25 (d) levels; "significant" *similarities* are indicated analogously—.99 (SSS), .95 (SS), .85 (S), and .75 (s). Working with such generous significance levels as .25 on both ends of the scale, we could expect half the tests (.25 plus .25) to show up as "significant" just by chance alone. But counting up all of the instances in which significance is indicated at any of these levels, we find 52 of the 60 tests have probabilities of either .25 and less or .75 and more—that is, 87 percent of the tests rather than only 50 percent. Looking at just the probabilities indicating similarity (those of .75 and above), we could expect 15 such figures (25 percent of 60 tests) by chance—but we find slightly more: 20, or 33 percent of the tests. Looking only at the probabilities indicating differences, however, we find 33 tests at .25 or less—55 percent of the tests performed, rather than the 25 percent to be expected by chance.

If significance levels of .15 and .85 are employed, we would expect nine "significant" tests on each end by chance (15 percent of 60 tests), but we find 17 significant similarities (28 percent of the tests) and 25 significant differences (42 percent). Finally, if the totally respectable significance levels of .01 and .99 are used, we could expect to find perhaps one significant test at each end (1 percent of 60 tests = 0.6). But there are seven similarities and eleven differences significant at this level—12 percent and 18 percent respectively, rather than 1 percent each.

In short, when the overall test summary in Table 9.2 is considered, these active and captive samples of heroin users do indeed display a number of strong similarities. After all, it would be rather astonishing if they did not. But they also show an even larger number of significant differences.

The matter of defining what these differences and similarities are is more complex. Table 9.2 suggests that this kind of analysis might best be approached by looking at the three active/captive pairings separately. Not only are the tests on some variables significant for one pairing while insignificant for another, but there are even cases in which one pairing shows a significant similarity while another shows a significant difference on the same variable. The following sections therefore address each active/captive pairing by itself before we return to an overall perspective on the problem.

THE MIAMI WHITE SUBSAMPLES

Given the small n for the Miami white treatment subsample—only 14 cases—it is not surprising that the probabilities reported in Table 9.2 for this pairing tend to be the least extreme. It is more surprising that it shows as many significant tests as it does. Two similarities and five differences are even significant at the .95/.05 level (compared to one each—5 percent of 20 tests—which would be expected by chance alone).

The most obvious topic area of importance for these particular subsamples is current drug use. The active and treatment subsamples are clearly identical in regard to the use of stimulants other than cocaine, and hallucinogens or solvent-inhalants; probabilities of no difference are .999 in both cases. The frequency distributions indicate that for both drug categories, the nature of the similarity is that the great majority of men in both subsamples—77 to 86 percent—reported no current use of these substances. However, differences between the subsamples are indicated for all the rest of the current drug use variables. Because the Kolmogorov-Smirnov probabilities of no difference are based on the size of the maximum difference between the cumulative frequencies of the two samples, the *nature* of the difference can be summarized by noting the cumulative percentage for each sample at the point of greatest difference. For the remaining current drug use variables, these value points, the active and treatment cumulative percentages for them, and the probabilities of no difference are shown in Table 9.3. These figures suggest that for the Miami white subsamples, the men in treatment are in treatment because they are more deeply involved in serious drug use, both physiologically and financially, than their peers on the street. Specifically, they appear likelier to be heroin *addicts;* they are clearly more likely to be strongly involved with depressants other than heroin at the same time; they are significantly more likely to be using the most expensive street drugs (heroin and particularly cocaine) frequently; and overall, they are more likely to be using quite a number of substances concurrently.

The same explanation receives further support from the question about the percentage of criminal activity which is for the support of drug use. The

TABLE 9.3

Value Points	Active Percentages	Treatment Percentages	Probabilities
Heroin/illegal methadone daily	57.1%	85.7%	p = .25
Alcohol several times a week or more	53.4%	85.7%	p = .14
Other depressants/analgesics daily	21.1%	78.6%	p = .001
Cocaine several times a week or more	25.6%	64.3%	p = .05
Using four or fewer drug types	38.3%	0.0%	p = .05

significant difference (p = .02) reported in Table 9.2 is indicated by the cumulative frequencies to be specifically a difference at the extreme end of the scale. While 20.5 percent of the 122 active men for whom data were available reported that *all* of their criminal activity was for the support of drug use, this response was given by 64.3 percent of the men in the treatment sample.[6] It should be noted that crimes to support drug use were also the norm among the active men, since 87.7 percent of them reported that at least half of their crimes were of this type. But as one would expect from looking at how many men in each sample used heroin or cocaine on a daily basis, the men in treatment had been devoting significantly *more* of their criminal activity to getting money for drugs.

This does *not* mean, however, that men in the treatment sample were necessarily committing more crimes. Table 9.2 indicates that the samples were fairly similar in regard to number of robberies, theft-related offenses, and drug sales committed—all three of the money-making crime types examined. On the other hand, a difference may or may not exist in regard to violence-related offenses. For the tests on assaults, robberies, and use of a weapon while committing crime, only the probability figure for assaults (.245) indicates a possibly significant difference. But the frequency distributions show an interesting consistency: In all three offense categories, the point of largest difference between the samples is at the none-versus-any split, and in all three cases men in the treatment sample were more likely to have committed at least one such offense. Specifically, the active/treatment percentages admitting to assault were 21.8/50.0, to robbery 35.3/50.0, and to weapon use during crime 33.8/57.1. What might be considered significant as opposed to lesser involvement showed the same kinds of differences, although generally smaller ones (see Table 9.4). Because of the small size of the treatment sample, the figures in Table 9.4 must be interpreted with caution. But they have been noted here because they are consistent in suggesting greater involvement in violence among the men in treatment than for the active men, and because this kind of difference is also consistent with the previously discussed data on drug use. That is, the men in treatment have a significantly greater need than their peers on the street for money to get drugs; more willingness to engage in violent crime and the insurance provided by use of a weapon seem consistent with this need.

TABLE 9.4

Offense Categories	Active Percentages	Treatment Percentages
Three or more assaults	4.5%	19.0%
Ten or more robberies	13.5%	21.4%
More than one or two weapon uses	27.8%	50.0%
Twenty-five or more weapon uses	14.3%	28.8%

Another way of examining the drugs/crime relationships in these samples is to look at correlations between the six drug-use-frequency variables and the five offense-type counts. For the active men, only one of these thirty correlations is as high as .32 (a positive relationship—more use, more offenses—between cocaine and weapon uses). But for the men in treatment, thirteen are this high. The correlations between use of heroin/illegal methadone and robberies, theft-related offenses, and weapon uses are all around .40, compared to .16 to .21 for the active men. Positive relationships are even stronger for cocaine/robberies (.69) and cocaine/drug sales (.59), compared to .29 and .25 for the active sample. But there are also a number of negative correlations: the more "other depressants/analgesics" use, the fewer robberies (−.43), assaults (−.56), and theft-related offenses (−.51); the more hallucinogen/solvent-inhalant use, the fewer robberies (−.38), assaults (−.38), theft-related offenses (−.51), and drug sales (−.54); and finally, the more use of stimulants other than cocaine, the fewer drug sales (−.46). All thirteen of these correlations for the men in treatment are significant at the .10 level, and those of over .45 are significant at a .05 level. The corresponding figures for heroin/methadone and cocaine use among the *active* men are, as noted, only about half as large; in the case of the other drug types, the active sample correlations are between +.09 and −.13, indicating little if any relationship.

These correlation figures seem to indicate at least two things. First, they suggest a number of specific drugs/crime connections among the men in treatment: expensive drugs/money-making crimes, cheaper drugs/fewer money-making crimes, and perhaps a special access to cocaine for men engaged in drug sales. But second and more to the point for the purpose at hand, these figures indicate different kinds of drugs/crime relationships for active and captive samples. Both cocaine and heroin/illegal methadone use are positively correlated with robberies, thefts, drug sales, and weapons use for the active men, but much more weakly (in the .15 to .30 range) than is the case for men in treatment; and for use of other drugs, there are no correlations, positive or negative, greater than ±.16 with any of the offense types. Altogether, then, it seems that the drugs/crime nexus takes a much more diverse appearance among the active men, while the men in treatment seem to belong to a much more limited range of types.

Finally, the historical variables appear to support the general idea that for the Miami white subsamples, the central differences between the men in treatment and those on the street are (1) serious drug use and (2) the drugs/crime relationship. Specifically, Table 9.2 indicates similarity in age at first crime (p = .851), and no difference for age at first drug use (p = .674), number of drugs ever used (p = .518), or age at which respondents were first engaged in both drugs and crime (p = .399). A possible difference does appear for age at first alcohol high, since the probability of no difference is only .213; interestingly, the nature of this difference is that the men in treatment tended to have their first alcohol high at a later age than the active men, as indicated by 13.6 and 15.3 as the active and treatment medians. But a clearly significant difference occurs for age at first continuous heroin use. Looking at data not included in Table 9.2, frequency distributions indicate that the men in treatment first tried heroin at a median age of 17.2 and that this first use was also the beginning of continuous use for them. But the men still active did not begin until a median age of 19.6 and took almost a year to begin continuous use (median 20.5). For both variables, the point of maximum difference in cumulative frequencies is at age 17: By this age, 57.1 percent of the men in treatment had begun both first and first continuous heroin use, while only 23.3 percent of the active men had at least tried heroin and only 17.4 percent had begun continuous use. The respective probabilities of no difference are .110 and .037, with only the latter being included among the probabilities reported on Table 9.2.

The difference in historical drugs/crime nexus is indicated by the remaining variable, for which Table 9.2 shows the second most probable difference among the historical items. This is the sequence variable, which ranges from −5 through +5, representing crime five or more years before drug use through drug use five or more years before crime. The point of maximum difference in cumulative frequencies occurs at −2: 25.6 percent of the active men but 57.1 percent of the men in treatment had begun crime two or more years before beginning drug use, a difference approaching significance (p = .161). Broken into three ranges, −5 to −2, −1 to +1, and +2 to +5, the treatment sample percentage distribution is 57.1/21.4/21.4, compared to 25.6/37.2/37.2 for the active sample. But why would the men now more involved in drug use have more typically begun crime before drug use? This study does not permit direct checking of it, but a hypothesis might be suggested regarding some kind of greater individual-level (psychological?) inclination toward "deviance"/"reckless behavior"/"risk-taking" and the like. In evidence, it can be argued that first drug use for adolescents most typically is undertaken in a group, while first crime is *more* likely to occur as the impulsive behavior of an individual acting alone. Similarly, the differences found in the current drugs/crime variables also support the general idea of more risk-taking by men now in treatment: more simultaneous involvement with multiple depressants, more drug types in general being used, and even a slight but consistent tendency toward more violence-related offenses. In any case, (1) there is a significant difference on the sequence variable, and (2) its *methodological* significance is similar to that for the current drug use/crime correlations discussed earlier. That is, the treatment sample seems to include a more limited *range* of cases. Rather than being relatively equally distributed along the sequence range, as is the case for active men, the men in treatment are more bunched together at the negative end of the scale. Again, this suggests—at least—a more diverse set of drugs/crime relationships among the men still active on the street.

To summarize the differences between the white Miami subsamples, it might be said that the apparently key factor is logical to the point of matching a commonsense expectation. That is, the men in treatment for drug use could be expected to differ from those on the street by being more deeply involved in serious drug use—and this is in fact what the differences indicate. Their use of heroin began earlier, now they are probably using heroin/illegal methadone more heavily, they are definitely using additional depressants more heavily, they are using more drugs concurrently, and they are also using cocaine more frequently. Further, there seems to be a more definite pattern of relationship between their drug use and their criminal activity, since the number of the money-making crimes varies significantly with their use of drugs, according to how expensive those drugs are. Finally, this in turn leads to a second kind of general conclusion about differences between the active and treatment samples. This is a methodological conclusion that the heroin users on the street are much less readily characterized as a group than are the users in treatment. Because the purpose of this discussion is analysis of the differences between active and captive samples, the more complex analysis of the drugs/crime nexus among active users has not been carried out here. If it were, however, it would clearly entail subdivision of the active sample into many more subcategories than would be required for the treatment sample.

THE MIAMI BLACK SUBSAMPLES

The black as well as the white subsamples in Miami are an active-versus-treatment comparison. Given the conclusions from the white subsamples, this implies that we should begin by looking at the "obvious" area of differences: severity of drug involvement. But as Table 9.2 indicates, the black active and treatment samples are identical in regard to heroin/illegal methadone use ($p = .999$), similar or at least not significantly different in use of other depressants (p of .835 for alcohol and .726 for other depressants/analgesics), identical on hallucinogens/solvent-inhalants ($p = .999$), quite close on number of drugs being used ($p = .930$), and with no difference indicated for use of stimulants other than cocaine ($p = .465$). Only for use of cocaine does a difference appear ($p = .006$). The frequency distributions indicate that the point of maximum difference in cocaine use is at the "several times a week or more" level, with 33.8 percent of the active men compared to 76.2 percent of the men in treatment reporting use at this frequency. But even the difference for daily use would show statistical significance, since only 15.5 percent of the active men but 52.4 percent of those in treatment reported using cocaine daily.

It might be noted that use of the depressants is a major difference between the white and black subsamples in Miami. While 80 to 81 percent of both the active and treatment samples of black men were using heroin/illegal methadone daily, a similar percentage appeared only in the white treatment sample. For other depressants/analgesics, on the other hand, black men in both samples were unlikely to be using heavily, while the white men in treatment were.

Turning to the data on current crime, it will be recalled that the tests for the white samples showed no difference on theft-related offenses and drug sales, and a small but consistent tendency for more violence-related offenses in the treatment sample. Neither holds for the black sample comparisons. All three of the violent offense categories—robberies, assaults, and weapon uses—appear similar in the black active and treatment samples, with .87, .86, and .90 being the respective probabilities of no difference. But the black samples do clearly differ from each other on the other offense types. For drug sales, the point of greatest difference in cumulative frequencies falls at 15 sales: 88.6 percent of the active men, compared to 57.1 percent of the men in treatment, reported more than 15 drug sales for the last twelve months. For theft-related offenses, the maximum difference is at 34: 78.9 percent of the active men but 42.9 percent of those in treatment had committed more than 34 such offenses. In both cases, then, the men in treatment—more cocaine use and not—had engaged in *fewer* money-making crimes than the active men. Medians provide another way of summarizing this difference. The active men had committed a median of 89.9 theft-related offenses in the last twelve months, compared to 27.0 for the men in treatment; for drug sales, the active sample median is 140.5, compared to 49.3 in the treatment sample.

Obviously, these two subsamples are different from each other in regard to current drug use and crime, but the difference is not the same as in the white active/treatment comparison. Yet, results from the question on percentage of crime for the support of drug use resemble the results with the white samples. Specifically, the point of maximum difference is again at the extreme end of the scale, with 55.6 percent of the 18 men in treatment for whom estimates were available reporting that *all* of their crime was for drug use, compared to 25.7 percent of the 70 active men giving estimates. The probability of no difference for this variable is therefore .156—ordinarily, a fairly good indication of a difference for samples of this size. But 9.5 percent of the total 21 men in treatment gave no answer. If they had said "less than 100 percent of it," the probability figure would move even further away from significance. In addition, while 28.9 percent of the 133 active *white* men gave estimates between 75 and 99 percent, this was true of 45.1 percent of the 71 active *black* men—indicating, as does the higher probability figure, that the difference is not nearly so clear-cut between the black active and treatment samples as between the white active and treatment samples.

When drug/crime correlations are examined for the black samples, again a generally similar pattern to that for the whites emerges. As for the active whites, the active black sample shows only a few, unimpressive positive correlations, only one of which (.29 for heroin/illegal methadone with weapon uses) is significant at the .05 level. For the treatment sample, there are six coefficients larger than this one (that is, ±.30 or stronger), although in this smaller sample still only two are large enough to be significant at the .05 level (− .43 between hallucinogen/solvent-inhalant use frequency and number of theft-related offenses, and + .40 for cocaine and theft-related offenses). As with the white samples, the black treatment sample gives higher correlation coefficients to work with, suggesting a more restricted set of drug/crime relationship types than among the active men. But unlike the white treatment sample, the black treatment sample gives coefficients that are nonetheless too small for ready interpretation without further analysis.

The historical variables may add more information with which to understand the black active/treatment differences. Table 9.2 indicates that these two samples are identical in regard to age at first crime (p = .999) and very similar in age at first continuous heroin use (p = .944); medians for these variables are close to 14 and 18 respectively in both samples. A possible difference is indicated, however, for age at first drug use, since the probability of no difference is .183. The frequency distributions indicate active/treatment medians of 14.3/15.4 (as opposed to 14.3/14.5 for the white samples), and the point of maximum difference in cumulative frequencies is at age 18: 98.5 percent of the active men, compared to 71.4 percent of the men in treatment, had used drugs by this age. A more definite difference appears for age at first alcohol high. Here, 61.9 percent of the 67 active men who had ever been high on alcohol reported that their first high occurred by age 13, compared to 10.5 percent of the 19 men in the treatment sample who had ever been high on alcohol; this point of maximum difference produces a probability figure of .001—a clear difference also indicated by 12.9 and 16.0 as the active/treatment medians. This recalls that with the white samples, in addition to the definitely earlier age for heroin, the treatment sample

TABLE 9.5

Age Variables	White Active	White Treatment	Black Active	Black Treatment
First alcohol high	13.6	15.3	12.9	16.0
First drug use	14.3	14.5	14.3	15.4
First heroin use	19.6	17.2	18.0	18.3
Begin continuous heroin use	20.5	17.2	18.5	18.3

had a possibly significantly later age for first alcohol high; the probability is only .213, but the medians are similar to those for the black samples: 13.6 for the active men, 15.3 for those in treatment. This all suggests that one general difference between the Miami active and treatment samples may be the phenomenon sometimes called "telescoping": a shortened time period between initial drug experimentation and problematic drug involvement. The difference can be summarized by considering the group medians for the age variables just discussed, listed in order of white active, white treatment, black active, and black treatment samples (see Table 9.5). For both blacks and whites, (1) for the active men, first alcohol high precedes first drug use, while for men in treatment the reverse is true; (2) for the active men, the transition from first drug use to continuous heroin use took 4 to 6 years, compared to under 3 years for the men in treatment; (3) for the active men, the transition from first alcohol high to continuous heroin use took 5.5 to 7 years, while for men in treatment it took about 2 years (1.9–2.3); so that (4) altogether, taking "first experimentation" as either first alcohol high or first drug use, whichever came first, the active men took 5.5 to 7 years from "first experimentation" to the start of continuous heroin use, while the men in treatment took less than 3 years. The black and white *treatment* samples differ in that a different end of the range accounts for the shortening effect in each (later start for blacks, earlier completion for whites), and the black and white *active* samples differ in that the whites took noticeably longer to complete the transition (and were the least likely to be using heroin daily by the time of the interview—43 percent were using less often, compared to 14–21 percent in the other three subsamples). Nonetheless, the overall result in both the black and white comparisons is a telescoped drug involvement history for the men now in treatment, compared to those still on the street.

For the black samples, a related phenomenon may be indicated by the active/treatment difference on the number of drug types tried, out of a list of twenty types (see note 2). The point of maximum difference in the cumulative frequencies is at eight: 33.8 percent of the active men had tried eight or fewer of the twenty drug types, compared to 76.2 percent of the men in treatment. The probability of no difference reported on Table 9.2 is .001, and the active/treatment medians of 10.1/7.2 also summarize the nature of this difference. This may indicate that the active men experimented with a wider range of substances before getting into continuous heroin use, while the men in treatment were more focused from the beginning. The groups are quite similar, it will be recalled, in terms of the number of these substance types they are currently using (p = .93; medians of 4.9 and 4.3 for active and treatment samples).

The two remaining variables pertain to the historical drugs/crime nexus. Table 9.2 indicates no difference in the age at which respondents had begun *both* drug use and crime; because of the later drug use of the men in treatment, they were also later on this variable (for example, medians of 15.2 and 16.3), but the cumulative frequency comparison gives .778 as the probability of no difference. A significant difference is indicated, however, for the sequence variable. The black and white distributions are close to identical, with the greater probability of difference for the black samples (.018, compared to .161 for the white samples) thus resulting only from the larger size of the black treatment sample. Specifically, the point of maximum difference is again at the −2 score: 57.1 percent of the men in treatment, but only 21.5 percent of the active men, had begun crime two or more years before drug use. Broken into three ranges, −5 to −2, −1 to +1, and +2 to +5, the active men are split 21.1/40.8/38.0 percent while the men in treatment are at 57.1/28.6/14.3 percent.

In summary, the primary differences between the black active and treatment samples appear to be in (1) the history of their entry into drug use and crime, and (2) their present criminality. The men in treatment most typically began crime before drug use; once they began drug use they escalated to continuous heroin use quite rapidly; and their present criminal activity involves only about a third as many theft-related offenses and drug sales as for men still active on the street. The latter more typically began crime at the same time or after initial drug use, had a longer period of developing from first substance experimentation to daily heroin use, and have rather intensive criminal activity averaging about 90 theft-related offenses and 150 drug sales in a twelve-month period. The current drug use of the two groups is highly similar, with the exception that frequent use of cocaine is more common in the treatment sample. It *may* be, then, that the treatment sample is composed of men whose subjective orientation (of which there are *no* measures in the present study) is primarily toward drug use, and that they commit only enough crime to support themselves and their drug habit in minimal fashion. The active sample, on the other hand, appears to have more men for whom some other concomitant or consequence of crime is at least as important as securing money for drug use. Again, the level of detail available in this data set and the primary focus of this chapter on differences rather than within-subsample analysis forbid much in the way of *explaining* the drugs/crime nexus among these men, particularly the active sample. But the point of direct importance to the discussion seems clear: For the black active and treatment samples in Miami, as for the corresponding white samples, there are significant differences in current and/or past drug use and in the relationship of this drug use to crime—*in spite of* the number of strong *similarities* that also exist between them. In addition, as was not the case for the white samples, there is also a difference in criminal activity between the black active and treatment samples, a difference that can be interpreted (although data are not available to explore the suggestion further) as a function of the greater importance of drug use per se in the lives of the men now in treatment.

THE SAN ANTONIO MEXICAN-AMERICAN SUBSAMPLES

Unlike the Miami tests, the San Antonio Mexican-American comparisons are done with an active and an *incarcerated* sample. The San Antonio samples are also large enough (76 active men, 37 in jail) that the test results appear to be fairly clear. Only one of the twenty probability figures in Table 9.2 for this comparison falls into the .26 to .74 range (rather than the ten to be expected by chance), and eight of the twenty indicate differences significant at the .05 level.

Again looking first at the current drug use variables, the San Antonio samples (unlike those in Miami) show no difference on use of either cocaine (p = .999) or heroin/illegal methadone (p = .930). The frequency distributions indicate that about two-thirds of the men in each sample were using heroin/illegal methadone daily, and just under 90 percent were using several times a week or more (roughly the same as in Miami); for cocaine, only 10–16 percent reported even sporadic use (compared to 49–85 percent in Miami). The other five current drug use variables, however, show a readily interpreted set of differences. Summarized in terms of the point of maximum difference in cumulative distributions, the active and jail sample percentages at these points (and the probabilities of no difference) are shown in Table 9.6. Obviously, the men still on the street reported much more drug use than did the incarcerated men: more frequent use of depressants other than heroin, more involvement with drugs other than depressants, and hence a higher number of drugs being used. The last difference can also be summarized by the active/jail medians of 5.0/3.5 drug types currently being used.

But while the active men are clearly more involved in drug use, differences in criminal activity are not large. For theft-related offenses, the point of greatest difference in cumulative frequencies is at 43: 21.3 percent of the

TABLE 9.6

| | Cumulative Percentages | | |
Points of Maximum Difference	Active Sample	Jail Sample	Probabilities
Depressants/analgesics			
several times a week or more	76.3%	21.6%	(p = .001)
Stimulants other than cocaine			
several times a week or more	38.2%	0.0%	(p = .001)
Hallucinogens/solvents-inhalants			
several times a month or more	38.2%	8.1%	(p = .022)
Alcohol at least once a week	94.7%	73.0%	(p = .189)
Using four or more drug types			
(of 20 listed; see note 2)	85.5%	48.6%	(p = .002)

active men, but 47.2 percent of the incarcerated men, had committed more than 43 such crimes during the last twelve months; Table 9.2 reports a .077 probability of no difference on this variable. The unimpressiveness of this significance level, given the sample sizes, is also reflected in the median number of theft-related offenses for each sample: 12.4 for the active men, and 34.5 for those in jail. While the latter is almost three times as large as the former, they are still quite close together in absolute terms, and they are also both noticeably lower than most of the subsample medians for the Miami offenders (about 60 for each of the white samples and 90 for the active black sample). The same kind of doubt can be raised concerning the difference for weapon uses. This test shows a difference significant at .006, with the frequency distributions indicating the largest difference to be at the lowest extreme: 56.8 percent of the incarcerated men, but only 22.4 percent of the active men, had used a weapon during the commission of a crime at least once. But in Miami, 22–37 percent of the men in each sample reported ten or more weapon uses during crimes, while this was true of only 11–12 percent of the San Antonio respondents. In fact, the San Antonio frequency distributions show that 35.1 percent of the incarcerated men reported using a weapon only once or twice. Hence, at the "twice or less" level, cumulative frequencies for the active and jail samples are quite close. How much emphasis can be placed on the some-versus-none use of weapons is therefore a matter of how much substantive difference one feels there is between no weapon uses and two weapon uses over a twelve-month period. As with theft-related offenses, then, weapon uses were more likely among the incarcerated men in San Antonio than among their peers on the street; but neither sample contained many men likely to be committing such an offense very often.

The comparison thus far has taken an interesting appearance. It would *not* be surprising to find that the men in jail were more criminally involved than those still on the street, but the evidence for this kind of difference is relatively weak. Instead, the differences between the samples in terms of *current drug use* are much stronger, just as in the case of the white Miami active-versus-treatment comparison (where a difference in drug use would be expected). The emphasis on more drug involvement among the active San Antonio men is supported by the data on drug sale offenses. Some 33–40 percent of each sample had committed at least 150 such offenses, so that the overall medians are about as large as those in Miami. But at the lower levels, there is some difference ($p = .137$). The maximum contrast occurs at the level of six sales: 67.6 percent of the incarcerated men, but 90.8 percent of the active men reported committing more than this number of drug sales. Further, the data on robberies, for which the probability of no difference is .230, also indicate that *if there is* a difference between the samples, it is in the direction of more robberies by the active men than by the men who had been incarcerated. Again, the maximum difference is at the zero-versus-any point: 42.1 percent of the active men compared to 23.0 percent of the incarcerated men had committed at least one robbery. Given this as the point of maximum difference and the .230 probability figure, there would seem to be little if any real difference. Finally, Table 9.2 reports that the samples are probably identical on assaults ($p = .999$); the frequency distributions show that assaults are rare for men in both samples, since only 6–8 percent of the respondents reported even two or more such offenses.

Taken altogether, then, the criminal patterns of the two San Antonio Mexican-American samples are not markedly different, especially in comparison to the size of the differences in their drug use patterns. The incarcerated men probably committed more theft-related offenses, and definitely were more likely to have used a weapon in one or two crimes. The active men, on the other hand, might be more involved in drug sales and even in robberies; it could be noted that more drug sales are consistent with more drug involvement, and that robbery is at least as likely to indicate criminal desperation—again consistent with more drug involvement—as it is to indicate "criminality" as such.

The discussion thus far implies that the more drug-involved active men would probably be devoting more of their criminal activity to the support of drug use than the incarcerated men. And this is apparently the case. Of the 71 active men giving estimates, 74.6 percent said that *all* of their crime was for the support of drug use, compared to 16.7 percent of the 36 incarcerated men giving estimates. The probability of no real difference is under .001 in this instance (and would remain there even if all the missing data went the opposite way, since there would still be a 70-versus-19-percent contrast).

The current drugs/crime relationships of these samples can also be examined by means of the correlations between frequency of use and number of offenses. Differences between the samples are not of the same type as those discussed for the Miami comparisons, since the San Antonio samples have about the same number of the same size correlation coefficients. These samples are also different in that use of cocaine (which is much more infrequent among these men than among the Miami offenders) is not significantly related to any of the five offense types for either sample, and the only relationship for heroin/illegal methadone is a positive one with drug sales for the active men (more use, more sales, at .39). Instead, the other stimulants and the hallucinogen/solvent-inhalant categories show much stronger relationships to crime than was the case in Miami. Two of these relationships are consistent in the two samples: robbery and depressants/analgesics (+.34 for the active men; +.38 for the incarcerated men), and robbery and hallucinogens/etc. (+.32 active, +.29 jail). But others appear to be different. For the active men, there is a positive relationship between robbery and stimulants of .49, while no relationship at all (rho = −.04) is indicated for the men in jail. Stimulant use and theft-related offenses are also positively related for the active men (.29), but not for the incarcerated men. On the other hand, stimulant use is related to drug sales (.36) and weapon uses (.30) for the inactive men, while no significant relationships appear for the active sample. Even more puzzling is a fairly large positive relationship (.55) between depressants/analgesics use and weapon uses for the incarcerated men, while for the active men there is a significant negative relationship (−.33). Altogether, eleven of the thirty computed correlations show differences of this type. Space limitations for this chapter again forbid satisfactory exploration of drugs/crime relationships within each of these samples. The analysis is instead compelled to stop at the point of examining the issue of central focus here: These samples are apparently *different* in regard to drug/crime *relationships* as well as drug involvement.

Finally, we turn to the drug/crime history variables. Neither Table 9.2 nor the frequency distributions indicate differences between the San Antonio Mexican-American samples on the age-at-first-use variables. A possible difference is indicated, however, for the number of drugs these men had at least tried, out of the list of twenty types. The maximum difference in cumulative distributions occurs at seven drug types: The percentage of incarcerated men who had at least tried more than this number (51.4 percent) is almost twice that of the active men (26.8 percent). As in the Miami black samples, the apparently more "drug-involved" sample had experimented with *fewer* drug types before starting continuous heroin use. But in the San

Antonio comparison, the difference is significant at only a .09 level, and the medians, accordingly, are not too different: 6.4 types for the active men, and 7.6 for those in jail. Again, this seems best classified as a "possible" difference.

There is no doubt, however, concerning the distributions on age at first crime. While 34.2 percent of the active men had committed a crime by age 15, this was true of 70.3 percent of the incarcerated men; the difference is significant at .003, and the median ages also show a contrast: 16.0 for the active men, 13.7 for those in jail. This difference *is* consistent with what one might expect of an active-versus-jail comparison, since it indicates that the men in jail had begun crime at a significantly earlier age.

On the historical nexus variables, no clear difference is shown for age at which respondents had engaged in *both* drug use and crime; the probability of difference is only .246, and the active and jail medians of 16.1 and 15.7 are rather close together. But the difference in the sequence variable is again quite strong (p = .001). For these samples, the point of maximum difference is at the 0 score: 67.7 percent of the incarcerated men had begun crime before or at the same age as drug use, compared to 27.8 percent of the active men. However, if frequencies are split into the three categories previously shown for the Miami samples (−5 to −2, −1 to +1, and +2 to +5), the active sample is distributed 10.5/51.2/38.2 percent, compared to 37.8/37.8/24.3 percent; this difference is still significant at the .05 level, with the point of maximum difference falling exactly where it did in the Miami samples (−2, crime two or more years earlier). Thus, the difference can be expressed in the same way as was done for the Miami cases. But in San Antonio, it seems more appropriate to the data to express the difference in the reverse way. That is: 72.4 percent of the active men, compared to 32.4 percent of the men in jail, *began drug use* at least one year before their first crime. Since the active men show more current involvement with drugs, this makes logical sense. Further, it is explained by the previously discussed difference in age comparisons. The San Antonio samples are not significantly different on age at first drug use, but the active men began crime at a significantly later age. Hence, their criminal activity followed their drug involvement, suggesting the possibility that it was primarily *because of* their drug involvement—financially, socially, or both.

CONCLUSIONS AND IMPLICATIONS

The empirical analysis presented in this paper supports several of the methodological arguments made at the outset. Most obviously, it illustrates the warning made long ago by statisticians: Captive drugs/crime samples cannot be used to generalize findings to all criminally involved drug users. Equally clearly, it testifies to the importance of using multiple controls for active/captive comparisons, since it shows that neither active samples nor captive samples can be considered all of a type, even for offenders of the same gender and age range. Further, this analysis also indicates the need for strict measurement comparability in an assessment of active/captive differences. This is implied in the fact that all six subsamples were interviewed with the same instrument in the same study, and yet there were *still* instances in which the same measure seemed to have different kinds of meanings in different drugs/crime contexts.

In addition, the separate analyses go beyond these general methodological arguments to the next step, that of suggesting the general dimensions along which active and captive samples are most likely to differ. It seems of particular significance in the context of this collection of studies that the most consistent area of difference is that of the drugs/crime nexus. Both past and current relationships between drug use and criminal behavior show differences in all three active/captive comparisons. Specifically, two of the nexus variables—historical drugs/crime sequence and current percentage of crime for the support of drug use—show differences in all three comparisons that are significant at the .16 level (6/6 or 100 percent, rather than the 16 percent to be expected by chance), and four of the six tests are significant at the .05 level. In addition to these tests, Spearman correlation coefficients were computed between six drug use frequency variables and five offense-type counts. The results in both cities are treated too briefly in this chapter to permit delineation of drug/crime relationships within each subsample, but they are consistent with the general conclusion from the variable tests in indicating apparent differences between active and captive samples in the nature of the drugs/crime relationship.

The source of these nexus differences may be located in the second major dimension along which active/captive differences were found in the three comparisons: drug use patterns. That is, one type or degree of drug involvement may well mean a kind of drug/crime relationship different from another type or degree of drug involvement. In any case, drug use patterns are also clearly different in the active and captive samples examined for this study. Altogether, eleven drug use variables were tested in each of the three subsample pairs, and 33.3 percent of these 33 tests showed differences significant at the .05 level. It should be specifically noted that while differences in drug use patterns might be expected for the active/*treatment* comparisons, the San Antonio active/*jail* analysis shows at least as many significant differences: 36.4 percent (4/11), compared to 36.4 percent and 27.3 percent in the white and black active/treatment Miami comparisons respectively. This implies that drug use patterns may be an important area of differences between active and captive samples, regardless of the particular type of captive sample in question.

Given the apparent difference between active and captive samples in how crime and drug use are related, the conclusion of an accompanying difference in drug use patterns stands in definite contrast to the conclusion regarding criminal activities. The separate analyses seem to indicate, on the whole, that criminal patterns do not show differences between active and captive samples of anywhere near the size and clarity of the differences for drug use. Only 16.7 percent of the 18 crime-variable tests show differences significant at the .05 level, and if the problematic San Antonio weapon uses test is not counted, the figure drops to 11.1 percent (2 of 18 tests)—in either case, clearly much less impressive than the number of differences found on either the drug use comparisons or the drugs/crime nexus variables. And again, differences in this set of variables do not seem to be a matter of the *type* of captive sample. The criminal patterns of the black Miami subsamples, although they are an active/*treatment* comparison, seem to differ more clearly than the active/*jail* contrast in San Antonio. Further, while one might expect men who have come to official attention to be more active criminals than their peers still on the street, the differences that actually appear in the Miami black subsample tests go in the opposite direction: more offenses by men in the active sample than those in the treatment sample.

These kinds of contrasts lead to another type of general conclusion. In all three substantive areas investigated, comparison of the separate analyses shows that the specific nature of the active/captive differences is not consistent from one active/captive pairing to the next. For example, current use of cocaine is significantly different in active and captive samples in the case of both black and white men in the Miami comparisons. But cocaine use is so minimal in both San Antonio samples that the active and incarcerated men are essentially identical on this particular variable. As another example, even though sequence differences appear in all three comparisons, in Miami the difference is that the more drug-involved samples began crime before drug use more often, while in San Antonio the more drug-involved sample began *drug use* first. These kinds of inconsistencies probably mean, as could be expected, that different variables are of different importance in different drugs/crime contexts. But their meaning for present purposes is that descriptions of *specific* differences between active and captive samples may be impossible. If this is true, then it is consequently also impossible to make the kinds of methodological—or at least interpretive—allowances for captive sample biases discussed as possibilities at the beginning of this chapter. *Areas* of difference may be identifiable on an overall basis, but not specific differences that will apply to any and all active/captive contrasts.

On the other hand, it must also be recalled that the present study was limited in both the number of variables examined and the degree to which analysis was pursued. Either additional data or further analysis might have permitted greater cross-comparison consistency. For instance, to continue the cocaine example, the data set from the total project includes information on age at first cocaine use, which can be used to look at how many respondents in each of the subsamples had at least tried cocaine. If this were done for the San Antonio comparison, it would show that 59.5 percent of the incarcerated men, compared to only 22.4 percent of the active men, had tried cocaine—a difference large enough to be statistically significant on any kind of test, and a difference that could be interpreted as further support for a suggestion that use of cocaine is a general difference between active and captive samples. Similarly, while the drugs-crime sequence differences were interpreted here in terms of degree of drug involvement, further analysis might encourage interpretation along another line (which is also suggested in the data): In both cities, greater drug involvement or not, it is the captive samples that are more likely to have begun crime before drug use. (For that matter, it is also the captive samples in all three comparisons that show more use, at some historical point or current level, of cocaine.)

This discussion implies that the present analysis must be considered only a preliminary study. As such, it gives empirical support to several methodological arguments and suggests the general dimensions along which active and captive offenders seem most likely to differ. But the next step, that of examining the particular nature of the drugs-crime relationship within specific active and captive subsamples, has not been taken here because of space limitations. It seems, however, to be a necessary type of analysis in order to determine how specifically and consistently active/captive differences can be described. This study has been too limited in focus to suggest an answer. The significance of this issue is, to repeat, that if such descriptions can be made, they would permit generalization from captive samples to at least *more* noncaptive offenders than is now possible. The consequent savings in research time and funds could be considerable, making further study of the question highly desirable.

NOTES

1. DHEW Grant 1-RO1-DA-0-1827-02, from NIDA's Division of Research. The Principal Investigator is James A. Inciardi; the author is presently Project Director and Co-Principal Investigator.

2. The twenty-category list on the interview schedule is: (1) heroin, (2) illegal methadone, (3) codeine cough syrup, (4) other narcotics, (5) barbiturates, (6) other sedatives, (7) minor tranquilizers, (8) major tranquilizers, (9) antidepressants, (10) cocaine, (11) methamphetamines, (12) amphetamines, (13) other stimulants, (14) other analgesics, (15) marijuana, (16) LSD, (17) other hallucinogens, (18) solvents/inhalants, (19) alcohol, (20) over-the-counter drugs of any type. The drug-type combinations used for the present study were drawn from this list: heroin/illegal methadone (1 and 2 above); alcohol (19); other depressants/analgesics (3, 4, 5, 6, 7, and 14); cocaine (10); other stimulants (11, 12, and 13); and hallucinogens/solvents-inhalants (16, 17, and 18). Hence, categories 8, 9, 15, and 20 were excluded, marijuana because of its ubiquity and the others because of their rarity. (Also see the text and note 3 regarding these drug-type combinations.)

3. The frequency categories are: (1) daily, (2) several times a week, (3) once a week, (4) every two weeks, (5) about once a month, (6) less often (but used during the last 90 days), and (7) no current use. For the drug-type combinations, computation was done by translating these codes into times-per-month (specifically, 30, 15, 4.25, 2, 1, 0.5, and 0 for the seven codes respectively), adding for the combinations as given in note 2, and then recoding back with these same numeric values defined as the *minimum* value needed in the value range for that particular recode (for example, 4.25 through 14.75 were all recoded back to "3" because the total had to be at least 15.0 to go up to "2"). In general, the resulting combination estimates were therefore slightly more conservative than logical argument might require.

4. Analysis was done by computer, using Version 7 SPSS (see Hull and Nie, 1979: 45–64). For further information on the Kolmogorov-Smirnov test, a standard text is Siegel (1956: 127–135).

5. Again, analysis was computer-assisted, using Version 7 SPSS; rho's were computed using the option of pairwise deletion of missing values. For any given variable, data were generally 100 percent complete for the smaller subsamples, and 96–100 percent complete for the larger ones.

6. For the total 133 active men, 3.0 percent gave no answer and another 5.3 percent had committed either no crime or no crime for money during the preceding twelve months. If the latter cases had been coded as "0 percent of crime for drug support," as would be possible, the difference between the samples would still be 21.8–64.3 percent, *even if all* the true missing data cases were actually in the "100 percent of crime for drug support" category. In short, the eleven active men not included in this test for difference could not significantly change the results of the test.

REFERENCES

CHAMBERS, C. D. (1974) "Narcotic addiction and crime: an empirical review," pp. 125–142 in J. A. Inciardi and C. D. Chambers (eds.) Drugs and the Criminal Justice System. Beverly Hills, CA: Sage.

ECKERMAN, W. C., J. V. RACHAL, R. L. HUBBARD, and W. K. POOLE (1976) "Methodological issues in identifying drug users," pp. 165–183 in Research Triangle Institute, Drug Use and Crime. Springfield, VA: National Technical Information Service.

ELINSON, J. and D. NURCO [eds.] (1975) Operational Definitions in Socio-Behavioral Drug Use Research 1975. Rockville, MD: National Institute on Drug Abuse.

GANDOSSY, R. P., J. R. WILLIAMS, J. COHEN, and H. J. HARWOOD (1980) Drugs and Crime: A Survey and Analysis of the Literature. Washington, DC: National Institute of Justice.

HULL, C. H. and N. NIE (1979) SPSS Update: New Procedures and Facilities for Releases 7 and 8. New York: McGraw-Hill.

INCIARDI, J. A. (1979) "Heroin use and street crime." Crime and Delinquency 25 (July): 335–346.

RITTENHOUSE, J. D. [ed.] (1978) Report of the Task Force in Comparability in Survey Research on Drugs. Rockville, MD: National Institute on Drug Abuse.

SIEGEL, S. (1956) Nonparametric Statistics for the Behavioral Sciences. New York: McGraw-Hill.

WINICK, C. (1962) "Maturing out of narcotic addiction." Bulletin on Narcotics 14: 1–7.

10

FROM VICTIMS TO CRIMINALS TO VICTIMS
A Review of the Issues

CHERYL R. TIEMAN

There was a time when there was little or no connection between crime and drugs. In the nineteenth century, drugs such as opium and morphine were commonly used throughout society, and addiction was viewed as a personal problem. Although pitied, addicts generally were not rejected by society. Late in the 1800s opium smoking was associated with the Chinese, and attempts to control this group as well as their behavior were to provide the justification for the first legislative controls.

Throughout much of this century a popular notion that also provided support for control measures was the belief that drug use and crime were linked. *How* drugs and crime were linked has been a controversial issue for decades. In the absence of empirical data, policy decisions often were based on the particular conception of the presumed linkage between drugs and crime that was popular at the time. There are four ways in which the relationship between drugs and crime has been characterized:

(1) Addicts ought to be the object of vigorous police activity, since the majority are members of a criminal element and drug addiction is simply one of the later phases in their criminal careers.

(2) Addicts prey upon legitimate society, and the effects of their drugs do indeed predispose them to serious criminal transgressions.

(3) Addicts are essentially law-abiding citizens who are forced to steal in order adequately to support their drug habits.

(4) Addicts are not necessarily criminals, but they are forced to associate with an underworld element which tends to maintain control over the distribution of illicit drugs (Inciardi, 1974a: 245).

Each of these characterizations has appeared as a recurrent theme in discussions of the drugs-crime relationship. None of these themes has ever had an era of prominence when it was carefully examined and, perhaps, laid to rest. Rather, the simultaneous popularity of two or more of these themes has usually been the case, which has only confused the issue further and justified society's reaction to drugs and the people who use them.

Although the history of drug control in this country has been analyzed in detail (for example, Musto, 1973; Duster, 1970), it is instructive to examine the popular characterizations of the drugs-crime connection in different time periods.

THE 1800s TO 1922

While a range of substances are currently abused, public concern was focused on opium and morphine in the nineteenth century. Little was known about addiction or the potential for abuse of these substances, although a tract by John Jones in 1700 had described withdrawal after prolonged use of opium. He also had warned of the possibility that death could result from withdrawal (Musto, 1973: 69). An article warning of the dangers of addiction appeared as early as 1856 (Inciardi, 1974a: 242), but physicians continued to prescribe morphine for a vast array of symptoms. Patent medicines containing opium or morphine were widely available for self-medication. Addiction was already widespread prior to the Civil War, but the sizable number of soldiers who became addicted during the war probably served to spread the popularity of these substances (Musto, 1973: 2). The majority of users were white, female, middle-aged, middle-class and continued to function in daily activities as long as they had a supply of morphine (Terry and Pellens, 1928; Duster, 1970). Apparently some people chose these substances because their use could be kept secret, while the individuals maintained an antialcohol stance before their temperance minded neighbors (Terry and Pellens, 1928).

Concern over the addictive potential of opiates and mounting criticism of physicians' eagerness to prescribe these substances began to build in the

1870s and 1880s (Marshall, 1878). As more was discovered about bacteria and the causes of diseases, less reliance was placed on opiates for the treatment of symptoms. However, physicians' prescriptions and the sales of patent medicines containing opiates did not peak until the 1890s (Musto, 1973: 3). By that time the patent medicine industry had received considerable criticism for its role in spreading addiction, and the industry responded by manufacturing medicines—usually laced with large quantities of opiates—to cure addiction (Eldridge, 1967). Opiates still had their advocates: In 1889, G. R. Black (in Lindesmith, 1968: 212) advocated for the alcoholic the substitution of opiates for alcohol, because they would produce less physical damage to the body and would result in a more peaceful, less violent person:

> The mayors and police courts would almost languish for lack of business; the criminal dockets, with their attendant legal functionaries, would have much less to do than they now have—to the profit and well-being of the community.

During this era there was little criticism of addicts. Physicians saw them as unfortunate victims of a disease and addiction or as patients dependent on their medication. A few people saw addiction as a vice and believed that it weakened the will and that drug use could be stopped if the addict desired to do so (Conrad and Schneider, 1980; Hartjen, 1977: 84). Indeed, some people were thought to be more susceptible to addiction than others because they were weak-willed. Addiction would, therefore, inevitably lead to further moral degeneracy (Musto, 1973: 72–73). Marshall (1878) concluded:

> The effects of the habit are degrading and demoralizing in the extreme. Those who have become its victims, sooner or later are impoverished and broken down in mind and body [in O'Donnell and Ball, 1966: 50].

This was apparently a minority view associated with a reform movement that was launched shortly after the Civil War, in which a return to Puritan values was advocated. At this time, public opinion was generally sympathetic toward the addict, not condemning.

In 1898 heroin was derived from morphine. It was hailed as the answer to morphine addiction because it was believed to be a nonaddictive substance. Within five years this error was recognized, but by this time its popularity had spread; hypodermic needles for its injection could even be ordered through the Sears catalogue (Conrad and Schneider, 1980: 121).

Eventually the medical community declared that heroin had no medicinal value. This had the effect of labeling heroin as a recreational substance and lent credence to the view that its users must be wicked, immoral, and weak.

There was growing interest in legal control of opiate use, even among physicians. The patent medicine industry continued to fight legal controls, including labeling of the contents of their wares, because they feared a decline in sales if the contents were known to include opiates (Musto, 1973: 4). With the passage of the Pure Food and Drug Act in 1906, they lost their battle.

During the latter part of the 1800s, the press had been reluctant to criticize either the drug companies or physicians for their role in the production of the growing number of addicts. Their caution was based on financial considerations, as they feared the loss of advertising dollars from the patent medicine industry (Conrad and Schneider, 1980: 120). However, powerless groups could be criticized without such caution.

The use of cocaine had, for example, been linked with blacks. Cocaine had been distributed to mine workers to increase productivity and had been used instead of alcohol in some dry states. It had also been used as a cure for opiate addiction. In the late 1800s, the use of cocaine by blacks had become a cause for concern among whites. Stories appeared that attributed increased sexual drives of blacks to the use of cocaine; this, supposedly, incited them to rape white women. Blacks' visual acuity was improved by cocaine, it was said, making them excellent marksmen. Presumably, cocaine also made them less vulnerable to .32 caliber bullets, so police departments switched to .38 caliber bullets (Musto, 1973: 7–8).

The public's response to the large population of Chinese in San Francisco was essentially racist, and the press carried stories concerning the opium smoking of Chinese laborers. This resulted in the 1875 ordinance that banned the smoking of opium in dens, and similar ordinances were passed elsewhere, "aimed at the 'un-American' drug habits of the 'yellow devils'" (Fuqua, 1978: 30). The federal response from 1883 to 1890 was to place a tariff on imported smoking opium, to prohibit its importation by Chinese, and finally to limit its manufacture to American citizens (Brecher et al., 1972: 42–44).

By this time, the smoking of opium had been adopted by some whites who had frequented the dens, which had been driven underground. They were an "elite underworld group which despised and generally avoided all contact with the hypodermic user or 'opium eater' of respectable society" (Lindesmith, 1968: 215). They were gamblers, thieves, and prostitutes who had not secured their drugs from physicians. Thus, they became the source of the idea that there was a direct link between drug use and crime.

Three concerns facing the country at the turn of the century would lead to the legal prohibition of all opiates; (1) a rising patriotism for a new world position, (2) an increasing fear of minorities, and (3) a growing dismay over the extent of addiction, then estimated at 250,000 (Musto, 1973: 5, 33). As a result of the Spanish-American War, the United States had emerged as a major world power and had acquired several territories. While this was a source of great pride for the country, it also presented some problems. In particular, one newly acquired territory, the Philippines, had a large number of addicts. Because the addiction problem was primarily among the Chinese, restrictions similar to those in the United States were quickly implemented (Platt and Labate, 1976: 5).

This immediately jeopardized the lucrative trade agreements under negotiation with China. Although China was becoming concerned about its own huge addict population, it resented the policies of the United States that it interpreted as racist and aimed specifically at the Chinese. The United States proclaimed itself a moral leader of the world in its fight against opiate addiction and persuaded China that addiction was its enemy, not the Chinese. This leadership role was played out in several international conferences on opiates, starting with the Shanghai Conference of 1909 (Platt and Labate, 1976: 6). Prior to this conference, the only federal law pertaining to opiates was one that prohibited the importation of smoking opium. This was a source of embarrassment for the leader in the fight against opiates (Duster, 1970: 14). It would be difficult to convince other nations that the United States viewed nonmedical drug use as immoral without strict laws here at home covering all of the opiates (Musto, 1973: 36).

The association—at least in the minds of the general public—of cocaine and nonmedical opiate use with blacks, Chinese, and criminals provided an easy justification for expanded controls. All were hated and dreaded groups and the prevailing stereotypes lent credence to the "dope fiend" myth: the "crazed" Negro who raped white women, the "yellow devils" who seduced white women to become their common-law wives, and the criminal who not only robbed but also enticed children to use drugs (Musto, 1973: 43; Reasons, 1974: 389–390). The dope fiend was not only someone who used drugs for pleasure, but also someone whose (criminal) behavior was thought to be the direct result of the biochemical action of a drug on the user—the "chemicalistic" fallacy. There was fear that the use of drugs for pleasure would spread beyond these marginal groups to the higher classes. The question was not whether to control these substances and their effects, but how to control them (Musto, 1973: 65).

Although addiction was not confined to these "undesirable" elements, a careful distinction was made between persons who used drugs for pleasure and individuals who were dependent on their medicine. However, addiction even from medical usage was now seen as a problem to be avoided, if at all possible. Physicians had lost much of their optimism regarding the opiates when heroin was found to be highly addictive. Now physicians wanted to prevent the creation of any new addicts through ill-advised prescription practices. Medicine and pharmacy were both emerging professions at this time, and physicians and pharmacists were in accord on the call for controls on opiates. The patent medicine industry became a target because it preyed on the misery of others (Bates and Crowther, 1977: 302; Musto, 1973: 22–23). Physicians and pharmacists lobbied for the Pure Food and Drug Act, in 1906, which required the labeling of contents of medicines and had two major effects. First, for a time, an addict was assured of the quality of the product he purchased (Brecher et al., 1972: 47). Second, it reduced the sales of patent medicines. The industry was forced to remove opiates from many preparations because customers would not buy them (Musto, 1973: 93).

By 1913, various states had passed laws to control the sale of opiates, but interstate controls were lacking and mail-order houses could send opiates anywhere (Reasons, 1974: 392). Physicians and pharmacists wanted protection for their own professions. They both had low status, "weak licensing laws, meager training requirements and a surplus of practitioners" (Musto, 1973: 13). They wanted to control the dispensing of drugs to enhance their status, to prevent new addicts, and to keep opiates away from the criminal classes. They called for a federal law to control opiates.

Thus, the three major concerns in 1900 converged in one solution, the Harrison Narcotics Act of 1914. It passed with no problem and little fanfare. It went through Congress in minutes and was not even mentioned in the New York Times' summary of the day's accomplishments in Congress (Bates and Crowther, 1977: 270). Some people worried that a control measure would create an underground, but the majority preferred this to overindulgence. It is interesting to note that the Prohibition Amendment did not get through Congress as easily. The Speaker of the House, Oscar W. Underwood, "who had shepherded the Harrison Act through the House the previous week, described the Prohibition Amendment as a 'tyrannous scheme to establish virtue and morality by law'" (Musto, 1973: 67).

Perhaps the Harrison Act passed so easily because it did not appear to be a law dictating morality. As written, it appeared simply to require a license (as well as a tax on opiates) of all individuals involved in the distribution of opiates—importers, manufacturers, distributors, physicians, and pharmacists—so that appropriate dispensing could be verified from import to patient (Reasons, 1974: 395). Records were to be kept of all such transactions and registration with the government was required of all people in this distribution chain. Dispensing of narcotics was restricted to pharmacists and physicians for legitimate medical purposes. There was no attempt by the framers of the act to deny addicts legal access to narcotics or to spell out "legitimate medical practice." It was assumed that physicians were in the best position to define this concept (Platt and Labate, 1976: 18). By implication, it was hoped that public opinion would be swayed against these substances:

> Symbolically, it represented a reaffirmation of the basic values of the dominant culture, e.g., rationality, self-control, nonhedonist, and the basic humanitarian spirit which aimed to help those who cannot help themselves [Reasons, 1974: 395].

The Harrison Act appeared to satisfy everyone. International commitments had been met. Patent medicines with one-eighth grain or less of narcotics were exempt from the act (Platt and Labate, 1976: 18). Criminal classes would find it difficult to acquire opiates without going through a physician, and this pleased the public. Physicians and pharmacists were given professional credibility as the legitimate controllers of opiate prescriptions. Addicts, who were not mentioned in the Act, had been reassured by the Surgeon General that they would not be cut off from their supply (Musto, 1973: 64). The public was satisfied that addicts were under doctors' care and would be "redeemed" and brought back to the mainstream of American life (Reasons, 1974: 396). And the Bureau of Internal Revenue had been charged with the task of eliminating the nonmedical use of opiates, or so it thought.

Physicians had a major role in the confusion that was to follow the passage of the Harrison Act. As a group, physicians did not have a consistent plan regarding their relationship with addicts. Some physicians were addicts themselves. Few physicians conceived of the "course of their professional practice" as including the dispensing of any amount of drugs an addict might want. The scientific community, as well as the public, largely believed the chemicalistic fallacy:

> Although some physicians continued to feel no discomfort in maintaining habits, medical experts as well as laymen commonly believed that addiction promoted criminal appetites and inclination, ruined the reproductive organs, and caused insanity [Musto, 1973: 64].

Although few physicians advocated maintenance, this seemed to some to be a reasonable course until a cure was found, for many doctors still believed that sudden withdrawal could prove to be fatal. Some physicians continued to prescribe opiates for their own addicted patients. "But when the physician became the only legal source of the drug supply, hundreds of thousands of law-abiding addicts suddenly materialized outside of doctors' offices"

(Duster, 1970: 15). They could not handle half a million new patients, and became dispensing stations rather than offering individualized treatment. A few physicians recognized the great profits to be earned by catering to the vast number of addicts; these "dope doctors" collected fees for writing thousands of prescriptions or dispensing opiates at their offices.

Another major source of confusion was the role of the Bureau of Internal Revenue, the agency charged with the tax collection and record-keeping tasks of the Harrison Act. Once these records were examined it became obvious that some physicians were writing a great many prescriptions. To the Bureau and to the public this seemed unwarranted and a violation of the practice of medicine in good faith. The public's growing fear of addicts was not diminished by the exposure of physicians who were maintaining their addict patients. The physicians became villains and the object of public animosity (Musto, 1973: 107). The Bureau, on the other hand, was moving in unchartered waters. Never before had federal agents been granted control over the states on matters of local or personal choice (King, 1974: 21; Musto, 1973: 63). Justification for interstate control rested on the international obligation to institute federal controls which, therefore, took precedence over states' rights (Platt and Labate, 1976: 19):

> In 1915 the Bureau issued guidelines for the enforcement of the act, that narcotics could only be obtained through a registered physician; record-keeping duties were maximal to monitor a physician's prescription philosophy; possession of narcotics obtained in any way other than by a doctor's prescription was considered a violation of the Act, and prescriptions for an addict would be considered valid only if they called for a "normal dose" of the drug.

A subsequent guideline indicated that the quantity prescribed must be reduced over time. Thus, maintenance was prohibited, and the only legal source for a supply of narcotics was to be gradually closed for each addict under treatment. Support for this tactic was provided by a 1915 Supreme Court decision (United States v. Jin Fuey Moy) in which the illegality of possession of narcotics by an unregistered person was upheld. By definition, addicts were criminals if they lacked a legitimate prescription for the drugs they possessed. This made the association of crime with addiction almost complete in the minds of the public.

World War I propaganda provided another reason to hate and fear addicts. The country was told that secret agents of the Germans were turning children into "fearsome heroin maniacs" (King, 1974: 21). Anything that sapped the energy needed for the war effort was feared; narcotics reduced productivity and were further condemned. In 1918 an amendment to the Harrison Act raised the tax and placed a stamp on narcotics: The tax was for the war effort; the stamp was to make it easier to identify illegal possession.

Passage of the Eighteenth Amendment in 1919, which prohibited the manufacturing and distribution of alcoholic beverages, added to the moral indignation and condemnation of any nonmedical use of drugs. A Narcotic Division of the Prohibition Unit in the Treasury Department was created to enforce the Harrison Act. Two Supreme Court decisions of that year (United States v. Doremus and Webb et al. v. United States) upheld the constitutionality of the Act and ruled that maintenance was not a legitimate medical practice (Musto, 1973: 132). The Division had carefully selected the Webb case. Webb not only had maintained his patients, but was peddling prescriptions at fifty cents apiece (Ploscowe, 1961: 71). Any physician with a large number of addict patients that could not be justified medically was now open to prosecution. "Scores of them were arrested, prosecuted, fined, imprisoned, and set forth as an example to others" (Duster, 1970: 16). Many physicians abandoned their contact with addicts. The only remaining source of opiates was the black market. Now addicts were people who necessarily consorted with criminals.

To make matters worse, a 1919 Treasury report estimated the number of addicts at one million. It further characterized addicts as persons with a disease who would commit crimes when denied drugs (Musto, 1973: 138). The report suggested treatment for addicts, but offered no cure. The thought of one million crazed addicts created panic. The Treasury Department subsequently provided temporary clinics in neighborhoods in which large numbers of "dope doctors" had been arrested. Both fear of crime by those whose supply had been terminated and fear of possible deaths from sudden withdrawal motivated this move (Musto, 1973: 134). The size of the doses dispensed at these clinics was rapidly reduced. When this did not result in death, the procedure was taken as evidence for the medical treatment of addiction (Platt and Labate, 1976: 21)

In 1919 the Public Health Service was asked to provide treatment for addicts, but it declined on the grounds that it did not know how to cure addicts. By this time the Treasury Department was no longer optimistic about its enforcement efforts to keep addicts away from drugs. It now looked to the medical profession for an answer (Musto, 1973: 146).

For a brief time a philosophy of tolerance of the addict as a victim of a dependency guided a reemergence of treatment attempts. Clinics were established around the country that provided ambulatory care of addicts. Some of the forty-four clinics were well organized and staffed; they provided low-cost doses of narcotics on a daily basis, and, in a few cases, gradually reduced the quantity supplied to secure withdrawal. Other clinics were so understaffed that long lines of addicts would wind around the streets for blocks—much to the chagrin of local residents (Duster, 1970: 18). A few clinics abused the ambulatory procedure by charging prices just slightly less than the black market price, but much more than necessary to provide their services. The result was huge profits. In New York City, the black market grew during the operation of the clinics; few addicts wished to submit to the required registration procedures, such as having a picture taken and providing their employer's name (Terry and Pellens, 1928).

The clinic era began optimistically. The clinics had expected a clientele of criminals and moral degenerates. S. D. Hubbard of the New York City Health Department reported in 1919 that their patients were not always what they had expected.

> There are drug addicts constitutionally inferior and superior; feeble-minded and strong-minded; physically below and above par; morally inferior and superior. No one class of society seems, in our experience, to enjoy a monopoly in this practice [in Ball and Chambers, 1970: 59].

Few patients died from withdrawal, which dispelled an old fear; hence only the aged and medically incurable patient could justifiably be maintained (Musto, 1973: 148). It appeared that withdrawal was an achievable goal, but it soon became apparent that most clinic patients returned to narcotics use soon after withdrawal. Coupled with the dismal success rates of the clinics was the growing criticism of clinic abuses. The courts had ruled out maintenance, and withdrawal alone was not a sufficient answer. A new idea emerged: addicts were willfully choosing addiction and, therefore, required corrective measures, not treatment. Clinics were not failures; the addicts were (Musto, 1973: 83; Duster, 1970: 11).

By 1920, the optimism surrounding the clinic approach had faded. The AMA called for the end of ambulatory treatment. Instead they favored hospitalization, or confinement in a drug-free environment in which withdrawal would be carried out. This coincided with the government's latest opinion that abstinence would be continued if the ex-addict could be returned to a community where no drugs were available, or where the price of black market drugs was prohibitively high and the risk of arrest was also high (Musto, 1973: 163). Between 1920 and 1922, all of the clinics were closed. Following the *Behrman* decision of 1922, no legal prescriptions for narcotics could be issued, either for relief of withdrawal symptoms or maintenance, except in institutional confinement (Platt and Labate, 1976: 22). Estimates of the size of the addict population began to decline, and the composition had shifted to slightly younger, mainly lower-class males (Duster, 1970: 11). As these addicts turned to the black market for their drugs, enforcement was intensified, and the number of arrests rose. The transformation was complete: Addicts were no longer a medical problem, but a criminal problem. They were disrespectful of the law: "The judgment had been made that addiction was essentially not a disease, but a willful indulgence meriting punishment rather than medical treatment" (Reasons, 1974: 398). This transformation had been accomplished by shifts in government policy and court decisions that permitted the circumvention of the lobbies of physicians and pharmacists that congressional action would have engendered (Reasons, 1974: 398).

1922 TO 1961

The primary characterization of addicts in this period was one of antisocial or even "psychopathic" persons who chose addiction. An expert during this period, Lawrence Kolb, contended that "normal" people would not choose addiction, nor would they derive pleasure from drugs. Only psychopaths would experience pleasure from drugs; similarly, they would derive pleasure from other criminal and antisocial activities (Musto, 1973: 84). Imprisonment for the violation of narcotics laws served to isolate this group and prevent their criminal activities (Kolb, 1925: 83). In addition Kolb laid a solid foundation for an emergent characterization of addicts as basically law-abiding people who might commit crimes in order to maintain a supply of drugs: "The narcotic laws have made a crime out of a weakness in order to protect persons from the consequence of this weakness, and as a result many of the weaklings have of necessity been sent to prison" (Kolb, 1925: 86). Although the argument had resurfaced in 1924 in hearings before Congress, Kolb also denied that narcotics precipitated or incited criminal behavior.

During the 1920s several antinarcotics groups, lodges, and civic clubs had launched massive propaganda campaigns against the evils of narcotics. These groups challenged the figures issued by the Narcotics Division as gross underestimates of the number of addicts. They also helped to associate crime, violence, drugs, and fear in the public mind and called for more government spending to handle the problem (Musto, 1973: 190). It is difficult to say whether misinformation was sent to these groups by the Narcotics Division as a calculated program to gain advocates for a larger agency budget (Dickson, 1975: 43; Hartjen, 1977: 86), or whether the Division simply benefited by the independent actions of these groups (Musto, 1973: 192).

It is, however, clear that the federal government was committed by this time to an enforcement approach. It was so committed, in fact, that it simply ignored a Supreme Court ruling in 1925 that contradicted its policies. In

Linder v. United States the Court stated that addiction was a disease and that doctors could prescribe small amounts of narcotics to a patient to relieve the symptoms of withdrawal even though "cure" was not sought (Platt and Labate, 1976: 23–24). This did not change earlier decisions that had ruled out maintenance, but it did establish the right of physicians to prescribe "in good faith and according to proper medical standards" (Ploscowe, 1961: 82). In any event, the necessary standards were never set forth. The government continued to arrest physicians, with little regard to the quantities they prescribed.

A similar problem arose in Britain in the early 1920s. A commission of medical experts was established to investigate the resulting controversy. The result was the "British system" of prescription of drugs to addicts under set guidelines (Lindesmith, 1959). No such commission was established in the United States; instead doctors were forced to abandon addicts out of fear of prosecution.

By 1928, one-third of federal prisoners in custody had been incarcerated for violations of the Harrison Act (Fuqua, 1978: 32). A 1929 law ordered the Public Health Service to open two narcotics "farms" to treat federal prisoner addicts in open-air, rural, drug-free settings (Platt and Labate, 1976: 24). Musto (1973: 85) argues that the main goal was not the establishment of treatment centers, but alternative prisons for these addicts. The Lexington and Fort Worth facilities opened in 1935 and 1938, respectively. It was hoped that a research unit at the Lexington farm would find a cure for addiction.

In 1930, the Federal Bureau of Narcotics (FBN) was created in the Treasury Department, and enforcement of the Eighteenth Amendment was shifted to the Justice Department. The new commissioner, Harry J. Anslinger, ordered agents to focus on street peddlers and smugglers. There is an indication, however, that some medical opponents of FBN regulations were harassed and prosecuted; the FBN only paid lip service to the principles of the Linder decision (Lindesmith, 1959). The number of physicians arrested increased in the next few years (Platt and Labate, 1976: 25). Kolb reported that from 1931 to 1935, 757 physicians were convicted for prescribing narcotics to addicts. From 1914 to 1938, some 25,000 physicians were arraigned, and 3,000 served prison sentences on narcotics charges (Chambers and Brill, 1973: 11).

Anslinger also wanted strong mandatory penalties for first convictions. Public opinion generally was in favor of this, as was Congress and President Roosevelt (Musto, 1973: 212). Anslinger quickly learned to play to these audiences for his purposes. He "allowed" certain prominent addicts to be treated privately rather than arrested, in return for appropriations and laws that he wanted (King, 1974: 24).

The failure of Prohibition and its repeal in 1933 taught Anslinger to avoid too much interference in the lives of ordinary citizens. For this reason he did not want to have control over barbiturates and amphetamines. Often he would let local police and courts handle cases so that the FBN could maintain a low profile. He also learned to use the WCTU and other antinarcotic and alcohol groups. Information on local hearings would be given to these groups, which then provided appropriate lobbying activities (Musto, 1973: 213–214).

Anslinger has probably been given more credit than he deserves for passage of the Marijuana Tax Act in 1937. As was true of narcotics, marijuana had been around for a long time, and it was thought to have some medicinal uses until the early part of the twentieth century. During Prohibition, marijuana was substituted for alcohol by some persons, and this contributed to the belief that it acted like alcohol to release inhibitions. But its use was not widespread (Ball et al., 1968), and there appears to have been only a modest move toward legal control of marijuana in the 1920s (Shroeder, 1975: 34; Musto, 1973: 220). The Treasury Department apparently was not too concerned about the drug when it issued a report in 1931 in which it minimized the spread and danger of marijuana (Schroeder, 1975: 35).

Immigration from Mexico increased in the 1920s and Mexican-Americans were linked with marijuana use. Prejudice against this group was exacerbated by competition for scarce jobs during the Depression (Musto, 1973: 219). The belief also was spreading that marijuana led to expressions of violence, homosexual desires, and "madness, murder, rape and pillage" (Schroeder, 1975: 35). In 1936 the movie *Reefer Madness* was released and added to the public's fears; by 1937 forty-six of the forty-eight states had passed laws controlling marijuana, often with the same severity of punishment as narcotics controls.

The FBN and Anslinger have been credited with orchestrating the antimarijuana campaign, either as moral entrepreneurs (Becker, 1963) or as a form of bureaucratic survival tactics to justify a larger budget and staff (Dickson, 1968). Millspaugh (1937) documented Anslinger's wish to have the states control marijuana and to keep the federal government out of this area. This appraisal of the FBN's efforts was supported by later research (Galliher and Walker, 1978).

Congressional hearings prior to passage of the Act offered a one-sided view of marijuana in which no scientific evidence or opposition was presented (Musto, 1973: 228; Galliher and Walker, 1977: 372). Anslinger supplied some of the horror stories that were presented, but "these stories fit the common sense opinion of the period and were quoted for this reason" (Galliher and Walker, 1977: 375). The belief that this drug incited criminal acts was common. The effect of the Marijuana Tax Act passed in 1937 was largely symbolic, to reassure the public that another menace was under control. In reality, Anslinger directed federal enforcement efforts toward smugglers rather than users. The FBN made some arrests, but also silenced some antimarijuana groups who contended that the problem was still out of hand (Musto, 1973: 228).

During this era, it appeared that most nonmedical drug users did not resort to crime to purchase their drugs. Black market supplies were relatively inexpensive, although many users were able to avoid this source. Until World War II, narcotics were available through quasi-legal prescriptions, diversion from medical inventories, pharmacists who juggled books, forged prescriptions, theft of medical stockpiles, or the use of uncontrolled codeine and paregoric (Glaser, 1978: 296). In New York City, addicts would turn to physicians' morphine when the street supply of heroin was low by presenting fake symptoms to the few physicians who would still prescribe (Agar, 1978). In Kentucky and other Southern states, some physicians apparently maintained addicts for years. Very few of these addicts had been involved in crime prior to addiction, and this pattern persisted until roughly the end of the 1940s (O'Donnell, 1969: 111).

World War II had an enormous effect on the addict subculture. Black market supplies were interrupted because of the disruption of shipping channels (Glaser, 1974: 46). Medical stockpiles were exhausted by the war effort. The price of black market narcotics soared, as did the growth of poppies, which had been outlawed in 1942 (Glaser, 1978: 296). The number of addicts declined to "practically an irreducible minimum" (Anslinger and Tompkins, 1953: 167).

By the end of the war, smuggling had increased, and there was more than enough heroin to go around. The number of addicts began to increase, with a noticeable shift in the addict population; now blacks and Puerto Ricans residing in inner-city slums became prominent:

> The concentration of both drug distribution and the new addicts in the minority-group urban ghettos suggests that when organized criminals smuggling heroin sought to expand their market, they did this close to their base by touting opiate use to youth who were already law violators [Glaser, 1978: 297].

No longer could the diversion of medical supplies meet the demand of an increasing number of addicts. Black market suppliers controlled the market, and the price of heroin would never again be low.

A country at peace with its world neighbors now concentrated on exposing the enemies within its own borders. The McCarthy era had dawned. Some authors suggest (Glaser, 1978: 299; Anslinger and Tompkins, 1953: 166; King, 1974: 26) that the growth of addiction among ghetto youth and hysteria over the menace of organized crime led to more repressive laws. Others (Musto, 1973: 231; Reasons, 1975: 23) claim that the general fear was of Communism; Red China was suspected of selling narcotics to dealers in the United States to subvert and corrupt the country. Regardless of the reasons, the effect was the most repressive drug law to date, the Boggs Amendment of 1951, which required two-year mandatory minimum sentences for first convictions, with no probation or suspended sentences on later convictions. In 1956 the Narcotics Control Act raised the minimum sentence to five years (Drug Abuse Council, Inc., 1973: 9). During this period, addiction per se was made a crime—for the first time a person was a criminal because of his status as an addict (Reasons, 1975: 23).

In 1952, Anslinger claimed that the increase in the number of addicts had been checked (Anslinger and Tompkins, 1953: 171). Mandatory minimum penalties provided law enforcement agencies with greater leverage to make suspects reveal connections, because the charge determined the sentence. However, the brunt of these tactics fell on street dealers and users, not the large suppliers whom no one could identify. Very quickly, there were fewer guilty pleas, as more and more defendants demanded jury trials to avoid convictions. The courts were clogged with the overload (Platt and Labate, 1976: 27).

An old portrayal of addicts reemerged: Addicts were basically antisocial individuals who willfully disrespected the law and, therefore, deserved to be controlled. Anslinger supported this view when he labeled addicts as "parasites":

> The person is generally a criminal or on the road to criminality before he becomes addicted. Once addicted he has the greatest reason in the world for continuing his life of crime [Anslinger and Tompkins, 1953: 170].

He argued that monetary reasons did not lead to criminal behavior after addiction, but rather that the effect of the drug "upon the moral fiber of the addict" resulted in the release of dormant criminal tendencies (Anslinger and Tompkins, 1953: 267).

Research on addicts during this period provided some evidence for Anslinger's portrayal of the drugs-crime connection. Previously, crime had generally followed addiction (Fort, 1954; O'Donnell, 1969). This pattern persisted, but the new addicts of the 1950s also had histories of crime before addiction. Indeed, the youngest addicts were most likely to have been involved in crime prior to addiction, which supported the belief that addiction was simply another aspect of an antisocial lifestyle (Greenberg and Adler, 1974: 224–226). Experts in the drug field at the time contended much the same thing. Which came first—crime or addiction—was not the main issue. Both were seen as probable outcomes for some individuals, either due to personality aberrations or the slum environment from which they came (Chein, 1956; Isbell, 1955; Finestone, 1957). Chein even raises the specter of whether elimination of the supply of narcotics might not unleash the addict to act out antisocial tendencies in less preferable ways as far as society is concerned.

The main disagreement among the experts was whether treatment or control was the best route to take. Was the addict psychologically disturbed or basically an evil, disreputable person? The New York Academy of Medicine (1955) had proposed a clinic system, with drugs to be sold at a reduced cost. Anyone failing to cooperate with the program would be committed to a hospital. Ausubel (1960) argued that ambulatory care could not work, because of the easy access to the black market; only isolation in a hospital would do. Finestone (1957) criticized hospitalization; he proposed that treatment in the addict's own milieu was the only way to prevent high relapse rates. Of course, the FBN still maintained that neither ambulatory care nor hospitalization were workable; only severe penalties could control addiction.

1961 TO THE PRESENT

The early 1960s marked another turning point in society's view of addiction. Prohibitive controls had become as much a cause for concern as the addicts they were to control. A transition period was beginning that would see the incorporation once again of medical intervention in addiction, but not the elimination of enforcement activities. Unlike the changes of the 1920s, when one view was replaced by another, an uneasy alliance of medical and legal personnel was created. The transformation of addicts from criminals to victims never was complete. They were to remain criminal victims and the center of a legal-medical controversy that has never been resolved.

By the early 1960s critics of repressive controls were becoming more vocal. Even the Federal Bureau of Prisons had come out against mandatory minimum sentences (Drug Abuse Council, Inc., 1973). Among the more respected critics was the Joint Committee of the ABA and AMA on Narcotic Drugs. Their report (1961) inspired controversy and change.

In their interim report, Ploscowe (1961) argued that drugs did not incite criminal behavior and that addicts would not have to resort to crime if they could be supplied drugs legally. He favored a clinic system, if only a drug were available that could be dispensed only once a day. But, he argued, addiction is a disease and punitive laws should be replaced by ones requiring treatment. Where that fails, the law should allow for a legal supply. The report also included a rather glowing review of the "British System" and other European countries' procedures for dealing with their addicts (King, 1961). The review concluded that very few countries found any relationship between drugs and crime; only in this country, in which repressive policies were operative, was there a drugs-crime connection.

The final report of the ABA-AMA Joint Committee (1961) encouraged greater participation by physicians in the treatment of addiction as well as research into the personality needs and social pressures of addicted individuals. Compulsory hospitalization or isolation was not considered necessary. They concluded (1961: 165) that, because of our laws, basically law-abiding individuals were forced to commit crimes in order to pay for their drugs; drugs do not cause crime: "In this connection the joint committee deplores the hysteria which sometimes dominates the approach to drug addiction problems by persons in positions of public trust."

Anslinger was critical of the report even before it was published, and labeled its authors "crackpots" (Musto, 1973: 234). He believed that clinics and physicians prescribing drugs would make enforcement much more expensive and difficult. His retirement in 1962 suspended his critics' activities for a time while they waited to see if someone more moderate would be named to replace him.

In 1962 the Supreme Court decision in Robinson v. California struck down addict status laws when it stated that addiction was a disease; punishment for such a condition was cruel and unusual punishment. However, the Court said that states could compel an addict to undergo treatment and provide sanctions for those who failed to comply (Platt and Labate, 1976: 28).

The movement had been launched to relabel addiction as a disease within the province of the medical community. This trend received another vote of support from the Presidential Commission on Narcotics and Drug Abuse

Report of 1963, in which it was recommended that mandatory minimum sentences be relaxed and that the medical profession be allowed to decide what was legitimate treatment practice for addiction (Platt and Labate, 1976: 28). It also recommended the dismantling of FBN and the shifting of its powers to the Department of Health, Education, and Welfare. Growing concern over other drugs was evidenced by the recommendation that these drugs (barbiturates, amphetamines, ether, airplane glue, LSD) also be included in control efforts.

The convergence of Court decisions, critical appraisals of control tactics, and a general rise of faith in medical personnel to solve the ills of society created an atmosphere of optimism in the mid-1960s. The number of addicts was increasing, use of a variety of other drugs was spreading to all classes and beyond minority-group boundaries, but, finally, it was hoped, the "right" people had been given the reins to solve the drug problem. "In general, people were beginning to consider drug use as an act by a private individual who was sick rather than as an act against society" (Bates and Crowther, 1977: 271).

In 1966, Congress passed the Narcotic Addict Rehabilitation Act, which implemented a program of civil commitment for federal prisoners who were addicts. The notion of civil commitment, or "incarceration for rehabilitation" (Fuqua, 1978: 277), was based on the same principle that permitted the confinement of persons for mental conditions that endangered either themselves or society. Addiction was viewed as a disease that justified the suspension of individual rights in favor of compulsory treatment:

> These programs, however, are based on the conviction that addicts will not be self-motivated toward rehabilitation and that any governmental program of institutionalization must be one based upon coercion [Eldridge, 1967: 147].

The Act provided for civil commitment of addicts in several categories. If a determination of addiction had been made, some addicts qualified for voluntary commitment in lieu of prosecution. Qualifications for the program restricted participation to those most likely to be rehabilitated: A person was not eligible if charged with a violent offense, or the sale or import of narcotics. Two or more prior felony convictions also disqualified a person from participation (Kittrie, 1971: 248). Confinement for treatment could be as long as three years, followed by outpatient aftercare. Anyone who failed to complete the treatment program, including aftercare, could be prosecuted under the original charge (Kittrie, 1971: 247).

In another category were those who had refused voluntary treatment. Following conviction, the Act allowed involuntary commitment for a maximum of ten years, but not in excess of the term of the criminal sentence. Another category permitted relatives of addicts and addicts who had not been charged with a criminal offense to apply for civil commitment: "An addict so committed cannot voluntarily withdraw from treatment during a forty-two month period and after release must remain under outpatient supervision for three additional years" (Kittrie, 1971: 247).

Originally, NARA participants were sent to Lexington or Fort Worth, or were "treated" in parts of prisons set aside for the program. Some politicians believed that the program was too lenient and allowed individuals to avoid prosecution. Ironically, law enforcement personnel seemed to like the program; it made it easier to confine some people for whom convictions might be difficult to obtain (Glaser, 1978: 304). Others criticized the prisonlike settings as not appropriate for treatment. In the latter part of the 1960s, the bars were removed from the Lexington and Fort Worth facilities (Musto, 1973: 235), but criticisms of the program went far beyond bars on windows.

Critics also contended that addiction did not constitute a serious enough threat to suspend civil rights (Eldridge, 1967; Lindesmith, 1968; Kittrie, 1971). Laws that set a specific period of time for treatment were criticized on two grounds: The optimum period of treatment was unknown, and the manner of treatment was not left to medical practitioners to decide on the basis of individual case needs (Eldridge, 1967: 115, 120). Indeed, an effective treatment was unknown.

Since the ABA-AMA Joint Committee report in 1961, more and more voices had called for legal access to drugs for addicts (Chein et al., 1964; Schur, 1965; Eldridge, 1967). If addiction could not be cured, and nothing thus far had been successful, perhaps the disease could be managed much as the diabetic's disease is managed by maintenance doses of insulin.

Others further argued that legal access would undercut the black market supplier. Packer (1964) described the "crime tariff" enforcement policies provided for those willing to take the risks of supplying illegal substances or services. The "tariff" eliminated competition in an area in which the demand was inelastic; regardless of the price charged, the demand would not be reduced. For the entrepreneur willing to take the risks, an increase in the penalties has the effect of raising the possible gains; and they can charge higher prices to cover the increased risks they face. Packer argued that removal of all controls would definitely cause the price to drop, although it was impossible to predict whether that would also lead to more or fewer users in the long run.

At this opportune moment in history, methadone maintenance was "discovered." Methadone had been used in detoxification of opiate addicts at the

Lexington facility for years, but maintenance had not been tried. At first, methadone was thought to act like an antibiotic to block the effects of heroin. Maintenance seemed to solve several problems: Addicts would be under physicians' care, they would be able to function "normally" on one dose per day (that is, they could get jobs and become productive), and because maintenance was inexpensive, they would not need to steal in order to purchase their drug supply.

In 1967, the Presidential Commission on Law Enforcement and Administration of Justice noted that use of marijuana and heroin had increased while the seizure of illicit supplies had been miniscule. The Commission recommended an increase in enforcement staff. It also criticized civil commitment as an infringement on individual rights (Musto, 1973: 240). In 1968, Nixon had made a political issue of crime in the streets and blamed much of the general increase in crime rates on the growing number of drug users. Researchers were talking about an epidemic in the late 1960s (Du-Pont, 1974) and were pointing out the large number of addicts with prior criminal histories (Ball, 1965; O'Donnell, 1966) and the disproportionate numbers of users among blacks and Puerto Ricans (Ball, 1967; Chambers and Moffett, 1970). Drugs, crime, and slums came to be strongly associated in the minds of the public during the unrest of the late 1960s (Lewis, 1976; Weiner, 1976). The Nixon administration capitalized on the disease connotation of drug abuse, and with phrases like "this rising sickness in our land" (King, 1974: 31), the "infectious disease" that was "a nightmare beyond belief with epidemic proportions" (Hartjen, 1977: 90) called for greater enforcement efforts.

In 1970 Congress passed the Comprehensive Drug Abuse Prevention and Control Act which superseded all previous federal drug legislation. This law eliminated taxation as the basis for legislative control and focused on the control of interstate commerce of all potentially abused drugs (Reasons, 1975). The Secretary of Health, Education, and Welfare would decide which drugs required controls and would establish schedules of drugs based on the potential for abuse with penalties scaled to each schedule. Mandatory minimum sentences were dropped, penalties were made harsher for frequent or large-scale dealers and were made more lenient for the "one-time" user. In addition, funds were appropriated for prevention, treatment, and rehabilitation (Platt and Labate, 1976: 29–30). Persons dependent on barbiturates, amphetamines, and tranquilizers were included in these efforts.

Methadone, still in favor with the administration, was to be handled by the medical profession in the treatment of addiction (Weiner, 1976: 350). This resolved a dispute that had plagued methadone maintenance since the first clinic opened in 1965. The Bureau of Narcotics and Dangerous Drugs (formerly FBN) contended that maintenance was forbidden by the Harrison Act and had prosecuted some physicians (King, 1974: 33). A guideline issued in 1971 further clarified the situation:

> The administrating or dispensing of narcotic drugs to narcotic drug dependent persons for the purpose of continuing their dependence upon such drugs in the course of conducting an authorized clinical investigation in the development of a narcotic rehabilitation program shall be deemed to fall within the meaning of the term "in the course of professional practice. . . ." [in Chambers and Brill, 1973: 39].

As an experimental modality, the spaces available for participants were limited to a few thousand, but by 1971 methadone was the main treatment modality for heroin addiction (Conrad and Schneider, 1980: 135). Within a few years, there were about 100,000 clients in methadone maintenance programs.

SAODAP (the Special Action Office for Drug Abuse Prevention) was created in 1972 to design strategy for treatment, education, rehabilitation, and research. It recommended the use of voluntary treatment, as opposed to civil commitment, and it funded numerous therapeutic communities, withdrawal and aftercare agencies, and clinics to provide methadone maintenance (Platt and Labate, 1976: 30–31). The strategy of SAODAP did not end the NARA program, but eventually it was expanded to include more federal prisoners with fewer restrictions on eligibility for participation. Persons convicted of violent crimes or trafficking, as well as individuals with two or more previous felony convictions, were declared eligible. Individuals on probation were also made eligible for participation. Treatment under NARA was expanded to include methadone maintenance (Weiner, 1976: 352).

In 1974, the Narcotic Addict Treatment Act specified that HEW was to set the medical standards for methadone maintenance and detoxification. Maintenance was defined as dispensing for more than twenty-one days; detoxification meant the gradual reduction in dosage over twenty-one days or less (Weiner, 1976: 353). The standards restricted methadone maintenance to approved government programs in hospitals or clinics; it was no longer left to the discretion of private physicians. The approved programs were to provide group therapy, family counseling, vocational training, and social services. Participants had to be at least sixteen years of age and had to have been a narcotic addict for a minimum of two years. Volunteers could choose detoxification (Schroeder, 1975: 140–141).

The shift to less punitive, voluntary treatment and to a broader definition of drugs of abuse had been precipitated by increased estimates of the number of drug users and the spread of abuse to whites in the middle class (Glaser, 1978: 335). By 1974, the number of clients in methadone maintenance was estimated at 80,000 (Conrad and Schneider, 1980: 139). Nevertheless, the presumed link between drugs and crime, although not always articulated, was a factor behind some or all of the administration's strategy. While the main focus of enforcement tactics was supposed to be big-time dealers, the street user was hardest hit (Drug Abuse Council, Inc., 1973). Operation Intercept, a major attempt to curtail marijuana smuggling, simply resulted in greater use of alternative drugs when marijuana was in short supply. The administration was convinced that drug users were not only an antisocial, criminal element by nature, but that their drug use was symbolic of their disrespect for authority and law and order; therefore, they posed a threat to all youth, whom they might contaminate with their values (Reasons, 1975: 26).

The administration also had become disillusioned with methadone maintenance. Initial beliefs that methadone blocked the euphoric effects of heroin were unfounded. The expected decline in the crime rate as addicts shifted to methadone never materialized (Conrad and Schneider, 1980: 140). Indeed, the only crimes that tended to decline, to any great extent, were drug-related ones such as possession (Vorenberg and Lukoff, 1973). At the individual level, there also appeared to be a slight drop in acquisitive crimes, if the patient stayed in maintenance treatment a number of years (Vorenberg and Lukoff, 1973; Alexander and McCaslin, 1974; Chambers, 1974). It has been suggested that this decline in acquisitive crime was not the result of less need for money, but that the diversion of methadone provided additional funds that precluded the need for other criminal acts (Greenberg and Adler, 1974: 255). By 1973, the easiest drug to buy in some areas was methadone (Conrad and Schneider, 1980: 139). As a result, the administration shifted funding priorities to drug-free treatment modalities.

Clinics continued to operate across the country and methadone did not disappear. Some programs are now experimenting with LAAM and other longer-lasting synthetic substances. A major concern is still diversion. Preble and Miller (1977) found that 15 percent of their sample of methadone patients were drug-free, except for methadone; they were socially productive and not involved in criminal activities. The remaining 85 percent diverted methadone. The money from this, plus welfare, meant that most were not heavily involved in other criminal activity or "hustles." There is, thus, a continuing tradeoff of one type of criminal activity for another: To reduce burglary, shoplifting, and con games among the participants in a methadone program does not necessarily mean the participants will be crime-free.

Other critics of methadone, particularly minority group spokespersons, feared maintenance as the ultimate attempt at racial control that would benefit whites more than blacks. There is a greater acceptance of methadone today by these leaders, although it is considered largely an ineffective treatment; unfortunately, the alternative is harsher penalties (Lewis, 1976: 31–32).

Another area of a growing medical-legal controversy concerns the commonly prescribed substances that were brought under federal control by legislation in 1972: barbiturates, tranquilizers, and amphetamines. For years a few people have criticized physicians for overprescribing these substances and paying little attention to the potential for abuse (see Lennard et al., 1971). Physicians had had little contact with street drug users and, like the lay public, could not perceive any potential for abuse among patients who had none of the characteristics of street users. Their patients were not minority group members from the lower classes with criminal involvement either before or after use of prescription drugs. However, by the mid-1970s a description of the group most likely to use and abuse these prescription drugs read very much like a description of morphine users in the 1800s: They were white, middle-class, mostly female, and, from those in their mid-thirties to the elderly, these patients frequently were prescribed these medications in the absence of a physical disease—simply for symptoms such as fatigue and nervousness (Lennard et al., 1971).

It was several years before the potential for abuse was recognized in these instances. Perhaps Betty Ford's case had more to do with generating public awareness on this issue than any critics of the medical profession. By 1979, hearings before a Senate health subcommittee were examining the legitimate uses of these substances and the extent of abuse (Clark and Hagar, 1979). The commonality between street users and middle-class prescription users was apparent: Use of these substances could lead to tolerance and dependence, regardless of the environment or ethnic group the user was from. This commonality could lead to a greater acceptance of a disease model of addiction, and less repressive policies.

A few months later, before another subcommittee, the Drug Enforcement Administration was seeking reauthorization for the agency. The new menace it faced was the diversion of these same substances to the illegal market. Since the 1960s, there has been evidence that street users are often multiple-drug users (Inciardi, 1974b). When the preferred drug was in short supply, users found substitutes. The DEA argued that its efforts had significantly raised the price of heroin and had caused a shift to other drugs. Further, it was suggested that enforcement efforts also must concentrate on the channels of diversion. The Administrator of DEA, Peter Bensinger, mentioned that they are considering seeking authorization to cancel the license of a practitioner (either a physician or a pharmacist) for violation of distribution regulations under the Controlled Substances Act (U.S. Congress, House of Representatives, 1980: 62–63). Whether this signals a continued era of prohibition tactics or a new arena for confrontation between enforcement and medical personnel is difficult to say at this time.

The DEA is obviously expanding prohibition tactics into another area. It has encouraged the states to pass laws regarding drug paraphernalia that would make illegal the possession, manufacture, delivery, and advertisement of any paraphernalia "when accompanied by an intent to use it with illicit drugs":

> Localities must decide whether they want to subject their young people to the enticement of drug paraphernalia stores which sell commodities with only one clear use—the abuse of substances we know to be harmful and unsafe for human consumption [U.S. Congress, House of Representatives, 1980: 89–90].

These laws would provide a further symbolic message that the use of drugs is still condemned. As far as actually preventing young people from using drugs, the laws probably will not be effective. Brotman and Suffet (1975) point out that prevention efforts have failed primarily because of false assumptions about the users of drugs. Others suggest that prohibition strategies themselves present an enticement for violation in the form of risk-taking (Jacobson and Zinberg, 1975; Feldman, 1977).

THE FUTURE

The extreme attempts at prohibition by enforcement personnel in the past and the disease model that is offered as an alternative ultimately must clash, because the attempts to intertwine them—methadone and civil commitment—have not been successful. As enforcement efforts move toward a broader range of controls over more substances and even the paraphernalia that go with their use, more and more people will be brought into contact with the criminal justice system. Total elimination of nonmedical drug usage is not a realistic goal, particularly when this society has begun to realize the potential hazards of the drugs it still chooses to use. The line between victim and criminal was thin when first drawn in 1914, but today there is only a gray area with no clearly drawn line. Heroin does not destroy the body of the addict as does alcohol, yet we permit alcohol under restrictive sale. Marijuana may or may not cause physical damage, but it does not lead to the physical dependence of barbiturates sold by prescription. Indeed, there are attempts today to have both heroin and marijuana reclassified so that patients may receive them by prescription for pain and for the nausea that accompanies chemotherapy.

The ultimate clash may occur over a definition of who constitutes the greatest victim of drug abuse. In 1965, Schur introduced the concept of crimes without victims to denote

> the willing exchange, among adults, of strongly demanded but legally proscribed goods and services. . . . Perhaps it is the *combination of an exchange transaction and lack of apparent harm* to others that constitutes the core of the victimless crime situation as here defined [Schur, 1965: 169–171].

Schur argued that laws pertaining to victimless crimes were largely unenforceable because there was no complainant; everyone was a willing participant. The criminalization of such acts as the purchase of drugs creates criminals and creates a subculture. Others who support this notion have argued that the worst thing about heroin addiction is the legal problems that go with it (Chein et al., 1964; Hills, 1980). Undoubtedly, there are some "law-abiding" individuals who have resorted to criminal activities in order to finance their drug supply. Without quality controls, addicts die of overdoses, adulterants, and through use of dirty hypodermic needles. In these instances drug users have become their own victims or the victims of laws passed to protect them:

> Thus, most of the crime, disease, and death commonly associated with heroin use [is] not particularly a result of the pharmacological properties of heroin but the social conditions—the illegality—under which the addict must secure the drug. In such ways do repressive legal policies help artificially *create* some of the very features of drug use that dominant groups in society find most repugnant [Hills, 1980: 48].

There are other "victims" of prohibition strategies, if the concept is used in a broader sense to include all of those people who must bear the costs of drug abuse (Koch and Grupp, 1971; Phares, 1975; McGlothlin and Tabbush, 1974). Enforcement of these laws requires a great deal of money and time with little noticeable effectiveness. There is corruption within the system and a reduction of justice through illegal procedures that lead to a loss of respect for the system. The expense of incarceration as well as the risk of introduction to other drugs while in prison are other costs to be considered (Mushkin, 1975; Glaser, 1974). Also, society has to bear the additional costs of the loss of productivity of some of its members, the disruption of families, and the loss of property through theft (Phares, 1975).

There are obvious costs to both the drug user and society associated with our present policies. To change our policies requires a very accurate accounting of all costs, including those of less restrictive alternatives. For example, less enforcement may actually mean less crime, because the drop in the price of drugs might reduce the acquisitive crime connected with drug use, but it might also result in a greater drop in productivity as more people use drugs (Weissman, 1979). Therefore, it becomes crucial to appraise accurately the drugs-crime connection to assess the cost of present and alternate strategies.

We are finally making advances in accurately assessing the drugs-crime connection, whether it is that addicts are criminals first, become criminals in order to support their habits, are criminals by participating in the illicit supply network, or are incited to commit criminal acts by the drugs they use. If the history of drug abuse policies in this country indicates anything, it is that issues left unresolved will simply reemerge. None of the portrayals of the drugs-crime connection ever had an era of prominence when it was raised, examined, and put to rest. Each has been a recurring theme, sometimes with little or no supporting evidence to justify its persistence.

Finally, some attempts to examine these issues have been made. Evidence that links violence and paranoia to heavy amphetamine use and not to other substances, except perhaps alcohol, can only serve to clarify one characterization of drugs and crime to the benefit of public understanding and policy decisions (Asnis and Smith, 1978). With careful research, the other portrayals of the drugs-crime connection may be similarly specified (see McBride and McCoy, forthcoming, for a discussion of methodological issues associated with this task). Without such research, an informed assessment of the costs and benefits of various approaches cannot be undertaken. It may be that the best solution is a more tolerant approach—for example, one in which some substances are controlled as alcohol is now, while others are controlled by prescription. Ultimately, this may be less costly for the drug user and society than the prohibitive policies we now have or the solution sociologists have noted for years: elimination of the environments and social conditions that produce both drug use and crime.

REFERENCES

AGAR, M. (1978) "When the junk disappeared." Journal of Psychedelic Drugs 10 (July–September): 255–261.

ALEXANDER, M. and C. McCASLIN (1974) "Criminality in heroin addicts before, during, and after methadone treatment." American Journal of Public Health 64 (December supplement): 51–56.

ANSLINGER, H. J. and W. F. TOMPKINS (1953) The Traffic in Narcotics. New York: Funk & Wagnalls.

ASNIS, S. F. and R. C. SMITH (1978) "Amphetamine abuse and violence." Journal of Psychedelic Drugs 10 (October–December): 371–377.

AUSUBEL, D. P. (1960) "Controversial issues in the management of drug addiction." Mental Hygiene 44 (October): 535–544.

BALL, J. C. (1967) "Onset of marijuana and heroin use among Puerto Rican addicts." Presented at the annual meeting of the Committee on Problems of Drug Dependence, National Academy of Sciences—National Research Council, Lexington, Kentucky.

————— (1965) "Two patterns of opiate addiction." Journal of Criminal Law, Criminology and Police Science 56 (June): 203–211.

————— and C. D. CHAMBERS [eds.] (1970) The Epidemiology of Opiate Addiction in the United States. Springfield, IL: Charles C Thomas.

————— C. D. CHAMBERS, and M. J. BALL (1968) "The association of marijuana smoking with opiate addiction." Journal of Criminal Law, Criminology and Police Science 59 (June): 171–182.

BATES, W. and B. CROWTHER (1977) "Drug abuse," pp. 259–317 in E. Sagarin and F. Montanino (eds.) Deviants: Voluntary Actors in a Hostile World. Morristown, NJ: General Learning Press.

BECKER, H. S. (1963) Outsiders. New York: Free Press.

BRECHER, E. M. and the editors of *Consumer Reports* (1972) Licit and Illicit Drugs. Mount Vernon, NY: Consumers Union.

BROTMAN, R. and F. SUFFET (1975) "The concept of prevention and its limitations." Annals of the American Academy of Political and Social Science 417 (January): 53–65.

CHAMBERS, C. D. (1974) "Narcotic addiction and crime," pp. 125–142 in J. A. Inciardi and C. D. Chambers (eds.) Drugs and the Criminal Justice System. Beverly Hills, CA: Sage.

————— and L. BRILL [eds.] (1973) Methadone: Experiences and Issues. New York: Behavioral Publications.

————— and A. D. MOFFETT (1970) "Negro opiate addiction," pp. 178–201 in J. C. Ball and C. D. Chambers (eds.) The Epidemiology of Opiate Addiction in the United States. Springfield, IL: Charles C Thomas.

CHEIN, I. (1956) "Narcotics use among juveniles." Social Work 1 (April): 50–60.

————— D. L. GERARD, R. S. LEE, and E. ROSENFELD (1964) The Road to H. New York: Basic Books.

CLARK, M. and M. HAGER (1979) "Valium abuse." Newsweek (September 24): 66.

CONRAD, P. and J. W. SCHNEIDER. (1980) Deviance and Medicalization. St. Louis: C. V. Mosby.

DICKSON, D. T. (1975) "Narcotics and marijuana laws," pp. 35–49 in R. L. Rachin and E. H. Czajkoski (eds.) Drug Abuse Control. Lexington, MA: D. C. Heath.

————— (1968) "Bureaucracy and morality." Social Problems 16 (Fall): 143–156.

Drug Abuse Council, Inc. (1973) A Perspective on "Get Tough" Drug Laws. Washington, DC: Author.

DuPONT, R. L. (1974) "The rise and fall of heroin addiction." Natural History 83 (June/July): 66–71.

DUSTER T. (1970) The Legislation of Morality. New York: Free Press.

266   THE DRUGS-CRIME CONNECTION

ELDRIDGE, W. B. (1967) Narcotics and the Law. Chicago: University of Chicago Press.
FELDMAN, H. W. (1977) "A neighborhood history of drug switching," pp. 249–278 in R. S. Weppner (ed.) Street Ethnography. Beverly Hills, CA: Sage.
FINESTONE, H. (1957) "Narcotics and criminality." Law and Contemporary Problems 22 (Winter): 69–85.
FORT, J. P. (1954) "Heroin addiction among young men." Psychiatry 17 (August): 251–259.
FUQUA, P. (1978) Drug Abuse: Investigation and Control. New York: McGraw-Hill.
GALLIHER, J. F. and A. WALKER (1978) "The politics of systematic research error." Crime and Social Justice 10 (Fall/Winter): 29–33.
———— (1977) "The puzzle of the social origins of the Marijuana Tax Act of 1937." Social Problems 24 (February): 367–376.
GLASER, D. (1978) Crime in our Changing Society. New York: Holt, Rinehart & Winston.
———— (1974) "Interlocking dualities in drug use, drug control, and crime," pp. 39–56 in J. A. Inciardi and C. D. Chambers (eds.) Drugs and the Criminal Justice System. Beverly Hills, CA: Sage.
GREENBERG, S. W. and F. ADLER (1974) "Crime and addiction." Contemporary Drug Problems 3, 2: 221–270.
HARTJEN, C. A. (1977) Possible Trouble. New York: Praeger.
HILLS, S. L. (1980) Demystifying Social Deviance. New York: McGraw-Hill.
INCIARDI, J. A. (1974a) "The villification of euphoria." Addictive Diseases 1, 3: 241–267.
———— (1974b) "Drugs, drug-taking and drug-seeking," pp. 203–220 in J. A. Inciardi and C. D. Chambers (eds.) Drugs and the Criminal Justice System. Beverly Hills, CA: Sage.
ISBELL, H. (1955) "Medical aspects of opiate addiction." Bulletin of the New York Academy of Medicine 31 (December): 886–901.
JACOBSON, R. and N. E. ZINBERG (1975) The Social Basis of Drug Abuse Prevention. Washington, DC: Drug Abuse Council, Inc.
Joint Committee of the American Bar Association and the American Medical Association on Narcotic Drugs (1961) Drug Addiction: Crime or Disease? Interim and Final Reports. Bloomington: Indiana University Press.
KING, R. (1974) "'The American system': legal sanctions to repress drug abuse," pp. 17–37 in J. A. Inciardi and C. D. Chambers (eds.) Drugs and the Criminal Justice System. Beverly Hills, CA: Sage.
———— (1961) "An appraisal of international, British and selected European narcotic drug laws, regulations and policies," pp. 121–155 in Joint Committee of the American Bar Association and the American Medical Association on Narcotic Drugs, Drug Addiction: Crime or Disease? Interim and Final Reports. Bloomington: Indiana University Press.
KITTRIE, N. N. (1971) The Right to be Different. New York: Penguin.
KOCH, J. V. and S. E. GRUPP (1971) "The economics of drug control policies." International Journal of the Addictions 6 (December): 571–584.
KOLB, L. (1925) "Drug addiction in its relation to crime." Mental Hygiene 9 (January): 74–89.
LENNARD, H. L., L. J. EPSTEIN, A. BERNSTEIN, and D. C. RANSOM (1971) Mystification and Drug Misuse. San Francisco: Jossey-Bass.
LEWIS, D. L. (1976) "Color it black." Journal of Social Policy 6 (March/April): 26–32.
LINDESMITH, A. R. (1968) Addiction and Opiates. Chicago: AVC.
———— (1959) "Federal law and drug addiction." Social Problems 7 (Summer): 48–57.
MARSHALL, O. (1878) "The opium habit in Michigan," pp. 63–73 in Michigan State Board of Health, Annual Report.
McBRIDE, D. and C. McCOY (forthcoming) "Crime and drugs." Journal of Drug Issues.
McGLOTHLIN, W. H. and V. C. TABBUSH (1974) "Costs, benefits, and potential for alternative approaches to opiate addiction control," pp. 77–124 in J. A. Inciardi and C. D. Chambers (eds.) Drugs and the Criminal Justice System. Beverly Hills, CA: Sage.

MILLSPAUGH, A. (1937) Federal Crime Control. Washington, DC: Brookings.

MUSHKIN, S. (1975) "Politics and economics of government response to drug abuse." Annals of the American Academy of Political and Social Science 417 (January): 27–40.

MUSTO, D. F. (1973) The American Disease. New Haven, CT: Yale University Press.

New York Academy of Medicine (1955) "Report on drug addiction." Bulletin of the New York Academy of Medicine 31 (August): 592–607.

O'DONNELL, J. A. (1969) Narcotic Addicts in Kentucky. U.S. Public Health Service Publication 1881. Washington, DC: Government Printing Office.

_____ (1966) "Narcotic addiction and crime." Social Problems 13 (Spring): 374–385.

_____ and J. C. BALL [eds.] (1966) Narcotic Addiction. New York: Harper & Row.

PACKER, H. L. (1964) "The crime tariff." American Scholar 33 (Autumn): 551–557.

PHARES, D. (1975) "Heroin and society: an economist's perspective on public policy," pp. 147–169 in R. L. Rachin and E. H. Czajkoski (eds.) Drug Abuse Control. Lexington, MA: D. C. Heath.

PLATT, J. J. and C. LABATE (1976) Heroin Addiction: Theory, Research and Treatment. New York: John Wiley.

PLOSCOWE, M. (1961) "Some basic problems in drug addiction and suggestions for research," pp. 15–120 in Joint Committee of the American Bar Association and the American Medical Association on Narcotic Drugs, Drug Addiction: Crime or Disease? Interim and Final Reports. Bloomington: Indiana University Press.

PREBLE, E. and T. MILLER (1977) "Methadone, wine, and welfare," pp. 229–248 in R. S. Weppner (ed.) Street Ethnography. Beverly Hills, CA: Sage.

REASONS, C. E. (1975) "The addict as a criminal." Crime and Delinquency 21 (January): 19–27.

_____ (1974) "The politics of drugs." Sociological Quarterly 15 (Summer): 381–404.

SCHROEDER, R. C. (1975) The Politics of Drugs: Marijuana to Mainlining. Washington, DC: Congressional Quarterly Inc.

SCHUR, E. M. (1965) Crimes Without Victims. Englewood Cliffs, NJ: Prentice-Hall.

TERRY, C. E. and M. PELLENS (1928) The Opium Problem. New York: Bureau of Social Hygiene.

U.S. Congress, House of Representatives (1980) "Drug Enforcement Administration reauthorization." Hearing before a Subcommittee of the Committee on Interstate and Foreign Commerce. 96th Congress, 2nd Session on H.R. 6700 (March 10). Washington, DC: Government Printing Office.

VORENBERG, J. and I. F. LUKOFF (1973) "Addiction, crime, and the criminal justice system." Federal Probation 37 (December): 3–7.

WEINER, R. J. (1976) "Shifting perspectives in drug-abuse policy." Crime and Delinquency 22 (July): 347–358.

WEISSMAN, J. C. (1979) "Drug control principles." Journal of Psychedelic Drugs 11 (July–September): 203–210.

ABOUT THE AUTHORS

JOHN C. BALL is a sociologist at Temple University's School of Medicine in Philadelphia. He received his doctorate in sociology from Vanderbilt University in 1955. He is a widely recognized authority on the social epidemiology of drug abuse. During the past two decades he and his colleagues have pioneered a whole series of basic sociological studies pertaining to the behavior of opiate addicts in the United States. These studies have delineated and analyzed the history and etiology of drug abuse, its regional changes and metropolitan concentration, the incidence and prevalence of abuse by particular drugs, and particularly, the association of criminal behavior with illicit drug use. From 1962 to 1968, Dr. Ball conducted research pertaining to drug abuse at the Addiction Research Center in Lexington, Kentucky. Since 1968 he has been at Temple University, where he has a joint appointment in the Departments of Psychiatry and Sociology. While at Temple University, he was invited to serve in the Executive Office of the President in Washington, D.C., as Director of Research and Evaluation at the Special Action Office for Drug Abuse Prevention. During the past several years, he has undertaken a series of international studies pertaining to drug abuse. The most recent of these studies involved the collection and analysis of data from 25 nations.

CARL D. CHAMBERS is a medical sociologist with extensive publications in the field of substance abuse. He is currently the director of the Health Services Administration Program at Ohio University. Prior to joining Ohio University, he was the director of the Consortium for Health Education in Appalachia, Ohio. He has also held positions with the Personal Development Institute in Florida; the NIMH Clinical Research Center in Lexington, Kentucky; the West Philadelphia Mental Health Consortium drug rehabilitation program; the New York State Narcotic Addiction Control Commission; and the University of Miami School of Medicine Division of Addiction Sciences.

RICHARD R. CLAYTON has been in the department of sociology at the University of Kentucky since the fall of 1970. From 1973 to the present he has been involved in a nationwide study of drug use (see O'Donnell et al.,

Young Men and Drugs: A Nationwide Survey, 1976) and in a study of young men who grew up in areas of Manhattan known to be high in drug use. From June 1977 through June 1978 he was a Visiting Scientist at the National Institute on Drug Abuse, responsible for the crime-drugs area. Currently, he and Harwin Voss of the University of Kentucky are engaged in a follow-up study of 450 men from the national sample, focusing on the effects of chronic marijuana use.

SUSAN K. DATESMAN is currently an Assistant Professor in the Center of Criminal Justice at Arizona State University. She received her Ph.D. in sociology from the University of Delaware in 1979. She has written articles, chapters, and professional papers in the areas of female criminality and drug abuse, juvenile delinquency, and juvenile justice, and is coeditor of *Women, Crime, and Justice* and *Drugs and the Youth Culture*.

SARA W. DEAN is a public health educator and research scientist. She is currently the coordinator for professional health education for the Consortium for Health Education in Appalachia, Ohio. Prior to joining CHEAO, she was program director at the Athens Mental Health and Retardation Center in Athens, Ohio.

CHARLES E. FAUPEL is a research associate in the Division of Criminal Justice, University of Delaware, and is a candidate for the Ph.D. degree at the University of Delaware. His current research is in the area of drug abuse, with particular focus on the relationship between heroin use and street crime. Prior to his current activity in drug research, he researched and published in the area of disaster and disaster response.

JOHN A. FLUECK is a Professor of Statistics and Director of the Data Analysis Laboratory at Temple University. He received his Ph.D. from the University of Chicago in 1967. He has authored over 50 publications on topics in theoretical statistics, meteorology, economics, health care, and survey sampling. He is presently serving as the Chairman and Executive Secretary, Committee of Presidents of Statistical Societies.

FRED GOLDMAN is an Assistant Professor in the School of Public Health, Columbia University. He holds a doctorate in economics and specializes in the field of health economics, defining the term *health* broadly. He has conducted several research projects in the areas of drug abuse and crime. These include NIDA-sponsored studies of an econometric analysis of drug expenditures and income-generating activities, and the medical care costs of drug abuse. During the 1981–1982 academic year he will be on leave as a Postdoctoral Fellow at the Hastings Center.

PAUL J. GOLDSTEIN received the B.A. from New York University and the M.A. and Ph.D. from Case Western Reserve University. He has been employed by the New York State Office of Crime Control Planning and the New York State Office of Drug Abuse Services. He is presently employed by Narcotics and Drug Research, Inc., and has taught sociology at Case Western Reserve University and at Adelphi University. He is presently project director of a federally funded study of the economic behavior of street-level opiate users.

JAMES A. INCIARDI is Professor and Director, Division of Criminal Justice, University of Delaware. He has extensive teaching, research, field, and clinical experiences in the areas of substance abuse and criminal justice. Dr. Inciardi has been the director of the National Center for the Study of Acute Drug Reactions at the University of Miami School of Medicine, Vice President of Resource Planning Corporation, and Associate Director of Research at the New York State Narcotic Addiction Control Commission. He is currently editor of *Criminology: An Interdisciplinary Journal* and has published more than seventy books and articles in the areas of substance abuse, medicine, criminology, and criminal justice.

DUANE C. McBRIDE received his Ph.D. in sociology from the University of Kentucky in 1976. He is currently an Associate Professor in the Department of Psychiatry at the University of Miami School of Medicine and serves as the Associate Director of the department's Division of Addiction Sciences. He has had extensive research experience in the study of the relationship between crime and drug using behavior and has published a variety of articles in that area of study.

DAVID N. NURCO is Chief of the Social Research Unit at Friends Medical Research Center in Baltimore, Maryland. He has a D.S.W. degree, and has had extensive experience in conducting studies pertaining to drug abuse, alcoholism, and criminal behavior. His published works include local, state-wide, and national studies of drug abuse epidemiology and research methodology. In this latter regard, he has completed a number of studies based on follow-up interviews with active street addicts.

MICHAEL F. PLETCHER is a public health educator and research scientist. He is currently the coordinator for manpower and training for the Consortium for Health Education in Appalachia Ohio. He is also actively involved as a counselor in substance abuse programs.

ANNE E. POTTIEGER is director of a research project on crime and drug use sponsored by the National Institute on Drug Abuse at the University of Delaware, Division of Criminal Justice. She is Managing Editor of *Criminology: An Interdisciplinary Journal* and has published in the areas of drug and alcohol abuse, suicide, and criminological theory.

LAWRENCE ROSEN is an Associate Professor of Sociology at Temple University, and a former faculty member at Smith College. He has published widely in the area of crime and delinquency and has coauthored a book on research methods. He has been a member of the editorial board of *Criminology* and has served as consultant to the Family Court of Philadelphia, Pennsylvania Governor's Justice Commission and the Federal DAWN and TASC programs.

CHERYL R. TIEMAN received her Ph.D. in sociology in 1976 from the University of Kentucky, where she was a National Institute of Mental Health trainee and a Law Enforcement Assistance Administration Dissertation Year Fellow. For the past five years, she has been Assistant Professor in the Department of Sociology at Auburn University in Montgomery, Alabama, where she teaches courses in deviant behavior, criminology, and juvenile delinquency.